a
YEAR
of
PAGAN
PRAYER

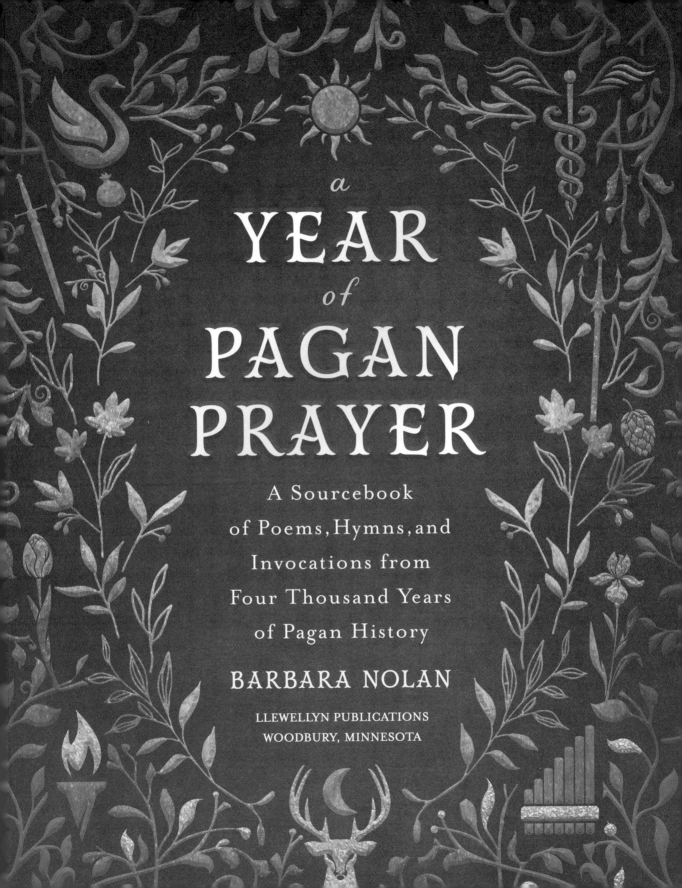

a

YEAR

of

PAGAN

PRAYER

A Sourcebook
of Poems, Hymns, and
Invocations from
Four Thousand Years
of Pagan History

BARBARA NOLAN

LLEWELLYN PUBLICATIONS
WOODBURY, MINNESOTA

FIRST EDITION
Second Printing, 2022

Book design by Donna Burch-Brown
Cover design by Shira Atakpu

For a full list of copyright information please see page 411

Llewellyn Publications is a registered trademark of Llewellyn Worldwide Ltd.

Library of Congress Cataloging-in-Publication Data
Names: Nolan, Barbara, author.
Title: A year of pagan prayer : a sourcebook of poems, hymns, and
  invocations from four thousand years of pagan history / Barbara Nolan.
Description: First edition. | Woodbury, Minnesota : Llewellyn Publications,
  [2021] | Includes bibliographical references and index. | Summary: "A
  big book of Pagan prayers, organized month by month for various Pagan
  festivals, plus extra chapters for lunar events, weddings, funerals, and
  so on"— Provided by publisher.
Identifiers: LCCN 2021026290 (print) | LCCN 2021026291 (ebook) | ISBN
  9780738768151 (paperback) | ISBN 9780738768335 (ebook)
Subjects: LCSH: Neopaganism—Prayers and devotions. | Paganism—Prayers and
  devotions. | Devotional calendars.
Classification: LCC BP605.N46 N65 2021 (print) | LCC BP605.N46 (ebook) |
  DDC 299/.94—dc23
LC record available at https://lccn.loc.gov/2021026290
LC ebook record available at https://lccn.loc.gov/2021026291

Llewellyn Publications
A Division of Llewellyn Worldwide Ltd.
2143 Woodside Drive
Woodbury, MN 55125-2989
www.llewellyn.com

Printed in the United States of America

For my mother

CONTENTS

INTRODUCTION

Welcome to *A Year of Pagan Prayer*, a collection of poems, hymns, prose, and prayers from four thousand years of Pagan history. The pieces gathered together here are drawn from many different times, places, and traditions. They include works by English Renaissance poets, ancient Sumerian priestesses, twentieth-century Californian Pagans, French Romantics, ancient Greek playwrights, *fin-de-siècle* British occultists, Imperial Roman poets, ancient Egyptian hymnists, and Baroque Italian librettists—in short, by hundreds of women and men, known and unknown, who have contributed to a long tradition of poetry and prose celebrating Pagan deities and the turning of the year. The selections have been arranged in a month-by-month format with separate sections for lunar holidays, weddings, and funerals, but this layout is only meant as a suggestion and an organizational guide. Readers should feel free to mix and match pieces to go with their personal calendar and practices.

The holidays chosen for inclusion here are mostly a synthesis of selected Greek and Roman festivals, as well as the quarter and cross-quarter days observed in the Celtic traditions. These traditions are emphasized because they are the most well-known, because more historical material is available for them than for most others (Greek and Roman material is especially abundant), and because despite the historical animosity that sometimes existed between these peoples, their traditions are fairly closely linked within the larger Indo-European tradition. Nonetheless, an effort has been made to include works from other, related traditions when possible, including the Norse and Germanic traditions and those Near Eastern and North African traditions (Sumerian/Mesopotamian and Egyptian) which were already syncretized with classical beliefs in antiquity.

I hope that the large body of literature collected here will make it clear to the reader that our past has always been at least partly Pagan, whatever prevailing historical narratives may say. Although Christianity dramatically altered the relationships that Western cultures had with their traditional gods and goddesses, it never dissolved those relationships completely. For more than fifteen hundred years after the Christianization of Europe until well into the twentieth century, all educated Europeans and Americans had at least a passing acquaintance with classical Paganism, and many rural communities in Europe still marked seasonal holidays with celebrations drawn from the Pagan past. As a result, European and, later, North American and Australian writers often chose to express themselves within a Pagan framework, regardless of their official church affiliation. In every generation they wrote hymns to honor various deities, asked them for favors in verse, and retold and reimagined their stories. Whether or not the authors in question were conscious of it, this was a form of devotion, one that allowed the old gods to survive in the popular imagination long after official homage had ceased. These works form crucial links in the chain that stretches between the Pagan past and the present day, when the worship of the old gods has come out into the open again.

This volume, then, is a tribute to the resiliency of Pagan thought, and the beauty of Paganisms past and present. May it serve as a companion to the Pagan future!

CAVEAT LECTOR

A few pieces presented here, such as Robert Herrick's carol and two Scottish prayers from the *Carmina Gadelica*, make some reference to Christian entities. My feeling is that given the amount of borrowing that Christianity did from various Pagan traditions in the early days of Christianity, there can be no complaining if Pagans decide to do some borrowing back. For example, English poet Robert Herrick's Yuletide carol mentions the birth of an unnamed king, which is usually taken to be a reference to Jesus. But since Herrick is not specific and the Northern Sun king is always born at the winter solstice, there is no reason why we necessarily have to regard the king in the lyrics as Christ. After all, an important part of Paganism is its ability to see through the veneer of the present and glimpse the lineaments of the past. Likewise, the "Three" in the Scottish fire-prayer for Imbolc doubtless referred to the Christian Trinity when the prayer was written down in the nineteenth century, but it can just as easily refer to a Triple Goddess if the reader wants it to—and may originally have done so. Those who feel uncomfortable with these occasional repurposings will find that they're few and far between, and easily avoided.

In addition, I have taken for granted that any archaic language now seen as outdated—such as the use of "men" or "mankind" for the human race—can and will be modified as needed by the reader. The pieces included here are offered as inspiration, as material that can and should be adapted to modern practices.

A note on translations: In order to make as wide a variety of material available as possible, I've provided a number of translations and versions myself. However, I've only attempted to capture the sense of the pieces; I have not made any effort to keep the structure of the originals, particularly in the case of poetry—a matter best left to more competent translators. My only aim has been to provide reasonably close and reasonably mellifluous English versions of pieces that might otherwise remain inaccessible.

JANUARY

January is the month when everything changes. The reign of darkness, broken at the Solstice, begins to visibly diminish as the days lengthen. New calendars are opened and dates are changed; in many countries around the world, politicians take up their elected offices, following the ancient practice of the Roman consuls. The journey through the new year has just begun, and, for a moment at least, it seems as if anything might be possible.

But if change brings opportunity, it also brings the potential for danger. To counter this possibility, our Pagan ancestors honored guardian gods and goddesses during this month and celebrated a series of festivals designed to confer protection and health on both the individual and society.

JANUARY 1: NEW YEAR'S DAY

Although contemporary Pagans often think of November 1 (the traditional New Year's day for insular Celts) as the beginning of the Pagan year, our secular New Year's Day is itself a Pagan holiday. We inherit it from the ancient Romans, who began their new year by honoring the god Janus—the two-headed god of time, travel, doors, and transitions—with offerings of spelt cakes and salt. Other celebrations on January 1 commemorated the day the Greek god of healing, Asclepius, was brought with his daughter Hygieia (Health) into Rome.

These New Year deities are everywhere in the modern world: *January* is named for Janus, Asclepius's serpent-twined rod is an international symbol of medicine, and Hygieia has given us our modern word *hygiene*. Although they aren't nearly as well-known as many other Pagan deities, the powers they embody (time, transitions, health) still resonate with our New Year's activities today, from the New Year's Eve countdown to the common practice of forming New Year's resolutions. Here, then, is a collection of prayers and poems in their honor, to bring health, protection, and happiness to the coming year.

ROMAN MEDLEY

Horace, Martial, and Ovid (ca. late first BCE–early first CE), translated by B. Nolan

This little prayer combines lines about Janus from some of the most famous Roman poets—Horace, Martial, and Ovid—into one work honoring the lord of beginnings.

Father Morning (or Janus, if you prefer that name), since the gods have decreed that you will be the beginning of life and of labor, be also the start of my song. Sower of the years, of the glittering, most beautiful world, to whom people first offer vows and prayer. ... Two-headed Janus, father of the gently opening year, you who alone can see your own back, come favorable to the leaders whose work brings peace to the fertile earth, peace to the sea; come favorable to the Senate and to the people. ... A prosperous day dawns, full of pleasant speech and thoughts. On this good day let good words be spoken!

A PRAYER FOR THE FIRST OF JANUARY

Decimius Magnus Ausonius (ca. 310–395 CE),
translated by Hugh G. Evelyn-White; modernized by B. Nolan

Ausonius was a Romanized Gaul—nowadays we would say Celt—from Bordeaux, who was a tutor of the Emperor Gratian.

Oh year, you who are the father of all things that roll onward from the month of two-faced Janus to wintry December's icy close, come, gracious New Year, and on the heels of the Old Year bring in merry January. Drive through your gates the twelve months that are to follow. Move on along the accustomed ways. ... While thirteen times the horned moon shall return newborn, your hand will bring round in succession dawn and evening, still keeping the sun to his destined course amid the signs of heaven.

OFFERING TO JANUS

Cato the Elder (ca. 234–149 BC), from *De agri cultura,* translated by B. Nolan

Cato the Elder was an arch-conservative who constantly complained that the Rome of his day was going to hell in a decadent Greek handbasket. He isn't a very sympathetic character, but he did make note of many little everyday ceremonies and prayers that took place inside the Roman household— religious practices we wouldn't know about if he hadn't written them down.

The cakes mentioned here may have been made of spelt, which was traditional at the New Year celebration, or they may have been the common Roman libum, *a sort of little cheesecake that Romans offered at other times of the year. Nowadays, however, any sort of cake will work.*

As you offer cakes to Janus, say these words: "Father Janus, as I offer these cakes, I ask most humbly that you will be kind and merciful to my children and myself, to my household and my home."

HYMN TO HECATE AND JANUS

Proclus Lycaeus (410–485 CE), translated by B. Nolan

Proclus was one of the last great Pagan philosophers of the classical world. He was born in Constantinople but lived for much of his life in Athens, the home of his patron goddess Athena. In this hymn he equates Janus with the Greek Zeus, and also honors two goddesses: the Mother of the Gods and Hecate, goddess of thresholds.

Hail to you, many-named Mother of the Gods, mother of beautiful children! Hail, Hecate of the Doorway, great of strength! Hail to you as well, Ancestor Janus, Zeus Everlasting, hail to you, highest Zeus.

Brighten the path of my life with your light, strengthen my life with goodness, force evil diseases from my body, and recapture my soul, raging about in the material world, through the purification of your enlightening rites. I beg you, give me your hand and reveal to me, a desperate soul, the paths of the gods, so I may see the holy light through which we are able to escape the pain of our dark origins. Oh, give me your hand, please, and with your breezes drive me, exhausted, into the harbor of piety.

Hail to you, many-named Mother of the Gods, mother of beautiful children! Hail, Hecate of the Doorway, great of strength! Hail to you as well, Ancestor Janus, Zeus Everlasting, hail to you, highest Zeus.

COME JANUS, COME NEW YEAR

Decimius Magnus Ausonius (ca. 310–395 CE),
translated by Hugh G. Evelyn-White, modernized by B. Nolan

Pomona is the Roman goddess of fruit, while "the Crab" is the constellation Cancer. March is "the father of the old-style year" because at one time, the Romans celebrated their new year then.

Come Janus, come New Year; come, Sun, with strength renewed!

Year, that begins with good augury, give us in healthful Spring winds of sunny breath; when the Crab shows at the solstice give us dews, and allay the hours of September with a cool north wind. Let shrewdly-biting frosts lead in Autumn and let Summer wane and yield her place by slow degrees. Let the south winds moisten the seed corn, and Winter reign with all her snows until March, the father of the old-style year, comes back anew.

Come Janus, come New Year; come, Sun, with strength renewed!

Let May come back with new grace and fragrant breath of flowers, let July ripen crops and give the sea respite from eastern winds, let Sirius' flames not swell the heart of Leo's rage, let party-hued Pomona bring on array of luscious fruit, let Autumn mellow what Summer has matured, and let jolly Winter enjoy his portion due. Let the world live at peace, and no stars of trouble hold sway.

Come Janus, come New Year; come, Sun, with strength renewed!

HOMERIC HYMN TO ASCLEPIUS

Anonymous (ca. 700–500 BCE), translated by Hugh G. Evelyn-White

The so-called "Homeric" hymns weren't really written by a man named Homer—indeed, "Homer" is now often considered to be the name given to centuries of oral tradition rather than an individual writer—but they're among the oldest extant Pagan prayers, although the dates of their composition seem to vary. Thirty-three hymns of varying lengths have survived. This one, to Asclepius, is among the shortest.

The "Dotian plain" is in Thessaly, an ancient region of Greece. Coronis, mother of Asclepius, was a Thessalian princess beloved of Apollo.

I begin to sing of Asclepius, son of Apollo and healer of sicknesses. In the Dotian plain fair Coronis, daughter of King Phlegyas, bore him, a great joy to men, a soother of cruel pangs. And so hail to you, lord: in my song I make my prayer to thee!

ORPHIC HYMN TO ASCLEPIUS

Anonymous (ca. 2 CE?), translated by Thomas Taylor

The Orphic Hymns were written by devotees of Orphism, an ancient mystery religion said to have been founded by Orpheus that emphasized the worship of those who had gone into the underworld and returned. Followers especially honored Persephone and Dionysus but worshipped many other gods and goddesses as well, and their hymns are a treasure trove of ancient Pagan prayers.

Thomas Taylor (1758–1835) was an English Neoplatonist, whose "frank avowal of philosophic polytheism created a strong feeling against him," as the Dictionary of National Biography, 1885–1900, *put it. (In other words, he was an eighteenth-century Pagan.)*

Great Asclepius, skilled to heal mankind,
All-ruling Paean, and physician kind;
Whose arts medicinal can alone assuage
Diseases dire, and stop their dreadful rage:
Strong lenient God, regard my suppliant prayer,
Bring gentle Health, adorned with lovely hair;
Convey the means of mitigating pain,
And raging, deadly pestilence restrain.
O power all-flourishing, abundant, bright,
Apollo's honored offspring, God of light;
Husband of blameless Health, the constant foe
Of dread Disease the minister of woe:
Come, blessed savior, and my health defend,
And to my life afford a prosperous end.

FROM "ERYTHRAEAN PAEAN TO ASCLEPIUS"

Isyllus of Epidaurus (ca. 380–360 BCE), translated by Emma and Ludwig Edelstein

This hymn was found inscribed on the walls of an ancient temple to Asclepius in Epidaurus, a town near the coast of the Aegean Sea. "Paean" is a title of both Asclepius and his father Apollo, and in English is also a name given to a poem of thanks or exultation. The "golden-haired son of Leto" and "son of Zeus" is Apollo; the goddess Lachesis is one of the Fates. Malus was the great-grandfather of Asclepius.

O people, praise the god to whom "Hail, Paean" is sung. … [A] child was begotten, and she was named Aigle; this was her name, but because of her beauty she was also called Coronis. Then Phoebus of the golden bow, beholding her in the palace of Malus, ended her maidenhood. You went into her lovely bed, O golden-haired son of Leto. I revere you. Then in the perfumed temple Aigle bore a child, and the son of Zeus, together with the Fates and Lachesis, the noble midwife, eased her birth pains. Apollo named him Asclepius from his mother's name, Aigle the reliever of illness, the granter of health, great boon to mankind. Hail Paean, hail Paean. Asclepius … send bright health to our hearts and bodies, hail Paean, hail Paean.

PRAYER TO HYGEIA

Ariphron of Sicyon (ca. 400 BCE), translated by B. Nolan

Hygeia or Hygieia, goddess of health and cleanliness, was often worshipped alongside her father Asclepius, since the ancients understood that healing and hygiene were closely linked.

Hygeia, goddess most beloved of all humankind, may I live with you for the rest of my life, may you be my kindly companion. Any happiness we have, whether wealth or children, or that royal power which makes humans feel like gods, or those desires that we chase with the secret snares of Aphrodite, or any other joy or leisure that the gods have given to humankind—it is only with you, blessed Hygeia, that it grows and gleams in the keeping of the Graces. Without you no one is happy.

FROM "ODE TO HYGEIA"

Susanna Centlivre (ca. 1670–1723)

Susanna Centlivre was a famous playwright and actress of the eighteenth-century English stage.

Best of all our earthly wealth,
Everlasting charmer, Health,
Blooming Goddess far more gay
Than the flow'ry meads in May.
When the airy warblers meet
Than thy voice their songs less sweet,
When thou dost thy sight refuse
Gold and gems their value lose,
Take thy downy joys away
And no other joy will stay.
Wanting thee what monarch knows
Taste of power, or sweet repose,
To enjoy Thee is to live,
Thou dost all our blessings give.

ORPHIC HYMN TO HYGEIA

Anonymous (ca. 2 CE?), translated by B. Nolan

O desirable, sweet-natured Queen of all, wealth-giving Universal Mother, hear me, blessed Lady Hygeia. You drive away from us the diseases that destroy us; when you are with us our homes are happy. All the universe worships you; only Death himself excoriates you. O eternal queen, your abundant blessings sustain the souls of mortals; there is no work that can be performed without your assistance. Who lives without you is miserable—without you, wealth is worthless and life itself cut short. O goddess, ruler of all things, come with kindness to this mystic rite, and drive off the terrible pains of sickness.

FROM "TO HYGEIA"

Anonymous (London, 1822)

From The Gentleman's Magazine *comes this nineteenth-century plea to the goddess, in which the writer asks for mental as well as physical health. Zephyrs are soft breezes.*

Come, Maiden of the mountain wild,
    And strew your roses o'er my brow;
Come, fan with zephyrs sweetly mild,
    And let me Health's pure blessing know.

O, chase away the fiend Despair,
    And shed a gleam of heavenly ray;
Above—O! place my every care,
    And Hope shall point the happy way.

EARLY JANUARY: COMPITALIA

The Lares were the little gods of every Roman household, who seem to have been regarded as a combination of brownies, guardian angels, and ancestral spirits. They were prayed to daily in many Roman households, but once a year in late December or early January, the Lares of the city were worshipped publicly at a crossroads during the Compitalia, a festival that supposedly pre-dated the founding of Rome itself. Though our cities no longer gather together to honor their guardians, now would be a good time to remember the little spirits that live beside us with a few prayers and offerings at the crossroads or at a home altar. They don't need anything fancy (in the words of French poet Leconte de Lisle, "better than the richest gifts, the Gods love barley and salt"), but they do like to feel welcome in our lives.

FROM "A HYMN, TO THE LARES"

Robert Herrick (1591–1674)

Few ancient prayers to the Lares have survived—they were so well-known that no one bothered to describe their worship in detail. But a thousand years after the fall of Rome, English poet Robert Herrick wrote this short hymn to his Lares, which would go well with the small offerings of food and drink that they love (which could indeed include parsley and chives).

It was, and still my care is,
To worship ye, the Lares,
With crowns of greenest parsley,
And garlic chives not scarcely;
For favors here to warm me.
And not by fire to harm me;
For gladding so my hearth here
With inoffensive mirth here. …

FROM ELEGY 1.10

Albius Tibullus (ca. 55 BCE–19 BCE), translated by B. Nolan

From an ancient poem, an ancient prayer.

Guard me, Lares of my house! You nourished me when, as a child, I ran before your feet. … O Lares, turn aside from me weapons of metal [bronze].

A SHORT HYMN, TO THE LARES

Robert Herrick (1591–1674)

It is not clear if the poet is offering poppy flowers or poppy seeds to the Lares here, but either would be a perfectly acceptable offering.

Though I cannot give thee fires
Glit'ring to my free desires:
These accept, and I'll be free,
Offering poppy unto thee.

FROM "TO THE LARES"

John James Piatt (1835–1917)

Dear Household Deities, worshipped best, we deem,
    With gentle sacrifice of Love alone!
Guardians of Home, who make the hearthstone seem
    Altar and shrine, O make our hearth your own. …

LATE JANUARY (MOVEABLE): ÞORRABLÓT

Thor, the red-haired lord of thunder, is probably the best known of all Norse gods. He is honored during the thirteenth week of winter, in a moveable feast, Thorrablot or Þorrablót, devised to honor him during the nineteenth century. Unfortunately, little in the way of hymns or prayers has survived from Norse antiquity, but the fierce, glittering god has managed to capture the devotion of a number of more recent writers. Here, then, are a few later poems in his honor.

FROM *THE GODS OF THE NORTH*
Adam Oehlenschläger (1779–1850), translated by William Edward Frye

Asa is one of the many epithets of Thor; it means something like "of the Æsir," the Æsir being the primary Norse gods. Mjölnir *or* Miölner *is the short-handled hammer of Thor, which is the source of thunder and earthquakes as well as a devastating weapon. A scald or skald is a Scandinavian court-poet. Adam Oehlenschläger was a well-known Danish Romantic poet.*

> Thus sang in days of yore a Scald,
> And I from him repeat the song:
> A land there is, Trudvanger call'd,
> Where frowns a castle huge and strong:
> This building boasts its massive walls,
> And many a spacious colonnade;
> Its forty and five hundred halls
> With silver or with gold inlaid.
>
> How many forests, lakes and fields
> On every side this pile surround!
> The roof is tiled with copper shields,
> Which shed a dazzling luster round.
> Therein the mighty Asa dwells,
> Whom mortals term the god of war;
> Odin excepted, he excels
> All other gods: his name is Thor.
>
> Around his waist a belt he wears,
> And gloves of steel his hands protect;
> Miölner, a hammer vast, he bears,
> When in the fight he stands erect.

That belt a tenfold power doth give,
When round his loins he girds it tight;
Nor doth the foe remain alive,
On whom his hammer haps to light.

FROM "THE CHALLENGE OF THOR"

Henry Wadsworth Longfellow (1807–1882)

Today American poet Longfellow is best remembered for his epic Song of Hiawatha, *but he wrote on Norse subjects as well. Megingjörð, the girdle or belt of Thor, doubles the god's divine strength, while his iron gauntlets allow him to safely handle his hammer.*

I am the God Thor,
I am the War God,
I am the Thunderer!
Here in my Northland,
My fastness and fortress,
Reign I forever!
Here amid icebergs
Rule I the nations;
This is my hammer,
Miölner the mighty;
Giants and sorcerers
Cannot withstand it!
These are the gauntlets
Wherewith I wield it,
And hurl it afar off;
This is my girdle;
Whenever I brace it,
Strength is redoubled!
The light thou beholdest
Stream through the heavens,
In flashes of crimson,
Is but my red beard
Blown by the night-wind,
Affrighting the nations!
Jove is my brother;
Mine eyes are the lightning;

The wheels of my chariot
Roll in the thunder,
The blows of my hammer
Ring in the earthquake!

FROM *BONDUCA*

John Fletcher (1579–1625)

This excerpt from Renaissance playwright John Fletcher's play Bonduca *(an unusual variant of the name of the British queen now better known as Boudica) is a great rarity: an English Renaissance paean to Taranis (here called Tiranes), an ancient, apparently pan-Celtic god of thunder—and cognate of Thor. Here Taranis is specifically invoked to avenge the wrongs of his female followers.*

Thou great Tiranes, whom our sacred Priests,
Armed with dreadful thunder, placed on high
Above the rest of the immortal gods,
Send thy consuming fires, and deadly bolts,
And shoot 'em home. . . .
O thou god,
Thou feared god, if ever to thy justice
Insulting wrongs, and ravishments of women,
Women derived from thee, their shames, the sufferings
Of those that daily filled thy Sacrifice
With virgin incense, have access, now hear me,
Now snatch thy thunder up. . . .

FROM "TO THE GODS"

Adam Oehlenschläger (1779–1850), translated by Rune Bjørnsen

A jotun *or* jötunn *is a supernatural being in Scandinavian mythology; they are often equated with giants but do not have to be supernaturally large. Midgard or "Middle-earth" is our world, while the* Jörmungandr *or Midgard serpent is an enormous snake that encircles the world in Norse mythology.*

Give me strength Asa-Thor!
Strengthen my hammer of war;
Teach me on this wild Earth.

To fight the jotuns of darkness.
Teach me from my own spirit
The Midgard serpent's devious pain,
That smothers my heart,
To cast away with my hand.

HAMMERSONG

Lavrans Reimer-Møller (1941–2016)

A modern prayer to channel anger to a sacred outlet.

I have made an oath most mighty   Sworn upon that sacred Hammer
Pledged on the most holy Troth   Hallowed by that mighty Hammer
I will give my rage to Thor

I have not gained the Warrior's strength   To bear the power of my anger
Flailing wildly all about me   Harming those I would protect
I will give my rage to Thor

With this bindrune on this hammer   I have made my sacrifice
Giving up that gift of power   To the One who thrives upon it
I will pledge my rage to Thor

Seek the inner calm and courage   Calm the anger in my heart
Earn the right to wear the Bear-shirt   Learn the Warrior's inner secret
Sacrifice my rage to Thor

White hot steel, forged by my anger   Tempered in my blood thus given
Fashioned by Thor's mighty Hammer   Honed and polished, sharpened fine
Sanctify my rage to Thor

I will be worthy of the power   Flowing mighty through this Hammer
Strengthened by the flow of anger   Save it for the worthy foe
Giving all my rage to Thor

Power flow from thee through me	Shaped and fashioned by my oath
Power flow through me to Thee	Hallowed by my sacrifice

Gladly give my rage to Thor

Joyously Thor wields the Hammer	Crushing all my enemies
He rejoices in the power	Of the gift of rage I give him

Give my holy rage to Thor

FROM *THE DESCENT OF FREA*

Frank Sayers (1763–1817)

Thor has the power to calm storms as well as create them.

God of the wandering air,
Whose forked flashes tear
The pine high-towering on the mountain-side;
Who joys o'er shaking rocks to guide
The thunder's fiery course;
Who bids thy dark clouds pour
The vast and whelming mower
And swell the torrent's force.
God of storms, when levelling hail,
When hollow-roaring whirlwinds fail,
Sweeping o'er the valley's pride,
Rolling high the weltering tide,
Thou speak'st—thy potent voice disarms
The tempest's rage—thy genial calms,
Thy sultry gales, and fostering dew
Clothe the wasted earth anew.

JANUARY 27: THE FEAST OF THE DIVINE TWINS

At the end of January comes the feast day of Castor and Pollux (or Kastor and Polydeuces/ Polydeukes), the Divine Twins whose images are seen in the constellation Gemini. The horse-riding Twins were widely worshipped in antiquity and can be found under various names from Wales (Nissyen and Evnissyen) to India (Nastaya and Dasra). In Greek and

Roman mythology they're demigods who live half the year in the underworld and half the year in Elysium. Although they are the children of Zeus, they inherited the mortal nature of their mother Leda, a princess who was courted by Zeus in the form of a swan (their sister was Helen of Troy). But despite being born human, Castor and Pollux achieved immortality through their valor and, above all, their brotherly devotion: when Zeus offered immortality only to Pollux, he refused to abandon his beloved twin and rejected the offer of paradise. As a compromise, Zeus halved the divinity of Pollux and gave the other half to Castor, allowing them both to spend half the year in Elysium.

Perhaps because of their dogged devotion to one another even in the face of death, the brothers became known as the gods of last resort, rather as Catholics regard St. Jude today. And because of the assistance they once gave to Jason and the Argonauts, they also gained a reputation as the patron gods of sailors. During storms they occasionally manifest themselves as the phenomenon now called St. Elmo's fire, and their appearance in the form of those flashes of light is regarded as the certain salvation of a distressed ship.

They are gods to pray to during any crisis, but it is traditional to honor them during the first month of the year, as we embark on the course of the future.

FRAGMENT OF A HYMN TO THE DIOSCURI

Alcaeus of Mytilene (ca. sixth century BCE), translated by David A. Campbell

The "island of Pelops" is the Peloponnese region of Greece, traditional birthplace of the Twins. This hymn calls upon the gods to manifest as St. Elmo's fire; it is as those flashes of light that they will "run up the fore-stays," the rigging that keeps the mast in place on a ship. "Dioscuri" means "Zeus' sons."

Come hither, leaving the island of Pelops, strong sons of Zeus and Leda; appear with kindly heart, Kastor and Polydeukes, who go on swift horses over the broad earth and all the sea, and easily rescue men from chilling death, leaping on the peaks of their well-benched ships, brilliant from afar as you run up the fore-stays, bringing light to the black ship in the night of trouble.

FROM "BOATMAN'S SONG TO THE DIOSCURI"

Johann Mayrhofer (1787–1836), translated by B. Nolan

This German Romantic poem was set to music by Franz Schubert (Op. 65 No. 1, D. 360) in 1816. It's a lovely song but challenging to sing. Fortunately, the poem is beautiful on its own.

The ship referred to here, as in other hymns to the Twins, could easily be interpreted as the course of the individual's life—or, for that matter, the Ship of State.

Divine twins, double stars,
Who shine upon my ship,
Ever gentle, ever watchful,
You soothe me on the seas.

Those strong ones stoutly righteous
Who meet the storm undaunted,
Always in your bright light live
Doubly brave and blessed.

FROM THE HOMERIC HYMN TO CASTOR AND POLLUX
Anonymous (ca. 700–500 BCE), translated by Hugh G. Evelyn-White

Here the Twins are called the Tyndaridae *after their mortal foster-father Tyndareos, husband of Leda. The "Son of Cronos" is, of course, Zeus. The Taygetus is a mountain in the Peloponnese.*

Bright-eyed Muses, tell of the Tyndaridae, the Sons of Zeus, glorious children of neat-ankled Leda, Castor the tamer of horses, and blameless Polydeuces. When Leda had lain with the dark-clouded Son of Cronos, she bore them beneath the peak of the great hill Taygetus—children who are deliverers of men on earth and of swift-going ships when stormy gales rage over the ruthless sea. Then the shipmen call upon the sons of great Zeus with vows ... but the strong wind and the waves of the sea lay the ship underwater, until suddenly these two are seen darting through the air on tawny wings. Forthwith they allay the blasts of the cruel winds and still the waves upon the surface of the white sea: fair signs are they and deliverance from toil. And when the shipmen see them they are glad and have rest from their pain and labor.

Hail, Tyndaridae, riders upon swift horses!

CASTOR AND POLLUX

George Croly (1780–1860)

George Croly was an Irish Anglican priest who did not let his official calling stop him from writing this pretty paean to the Twins. The Cyclades are a group of Greek islands.

When winter dips his pinion in the seas,
And mariners shudder, as the chilling gale
Makes its wild music through the Cyclades;
What eyes are fixed upon the cloudy veil,
Twin Warriors! to behold your sapphire mail,
Shooting its splendors through the rifted sky!
What joyous hymns your stars of beauty hail!
For then the tempests to their caverns fly,
And on the pebbled shore the yellow surges die.

FROM "IDYLL XXII"

Theocritus (ca. 300–260 BCE), translated by B. Nolan

Theocritus was an important ancient poet, a Sicilian who wrote in Greek and is credited with being the father of pastoral poetry. The brothers are "Lacedemonian" because they were born in the Laconian region of the Peloponnese. The Aegis is a goatskin covering or shield with the head of Medusa on it; it gives us our modern expression "under the aegis."

We sing the two sons of Leda, and of Zeus who bears the Aegis: Castor and his brother Polydeukes, that boxer with whom it is impossible to contend. … Two and three times we sing the sons of Leda … the two Lacedemonian brothers, the saviors of mortals who stand on the edge of the abyss; of horses mad with fear during war; and of those ships which, ignoring the rising and setting stars, have sailed into storms that raise huge waves around the stern, at the prow, everywhere, throwing masses of water into the holds, shattering the bulwarks, while the sails hang limp and torn, and torrents of rain fall from the sky as darkness falls, and the endless ocean resounds, beaten by the wind and the never-ending hail.

But you can draw ships and their sailors, who had believed themselves lost, from the deeps; suddenly the winds die, the seas are calmed, and the clouds open … O saviors of mortals! O beloved twins, riders and harpers, athletes and musicians!

FROM "HOMER'S HYMN TO CASTOR AND POLLUX"

Translated by Percy Bysshe Shelley (1792–1822)

Nineteenth-century poet Percy Shelley was the prototype of the 1960s radical: a vegetarian pacifist democrat and believer in free love who embraced Eastern mysticism and was thrown out of Oxford for denouncing Christian doctrine. But like many poets of his day, he also had a keen interest in the classics, and he translated many of the Homeric hymns into English verse. His poetic rendition of the Twins' hymn is so different from the prose translation above as to almost be a different prayer altogether.

    Zeus is here given his Roman name, Jove, while his father Cronos has become the Roman Saturn.

Ye wild-eyed Muses, sing the Twins of Jove,
Whom the fair-ankled Leda, mixed in love
With mighty Saturn's Heaven-obscuring Child,
On Taygetus, that lofty mountain wild,
Brought forth in joy: mild Pollux, void of blame,
And steed-subduing Castor, heirs of fame.
These are the Powers who earth-born mortals save
And ships, whose flight is swift along the wave.
When wintry tempests o'er the savage sea
Are raging, and the sailors tremblingly
Call on the Twins of Jove with prayer and vow,
Gathered in fear upon the lofty prow. …
    they suddenly appear,
On yellow wings rushing athwart the sky,
And lull the blasts in mute tranquillity,
And strew the waves on the white Ocean's bed,
Fair omen of the voyage; from toil and dread
The sailors rest, rejoicing in the sight,
And plough the quiet sea in safe delight.

FRAGMENT 2

Alcman (seventh century BCE), translated by David Campbell

Most worthy of reverence from all gods and men, they dwell in a god-built home beneath the earth always alive, Castor—tamers of swift steeds, skilled horsemen—and glorious Polydeuces.

FEBRUARY

February's lengthening days are ushered in by the Celtic festival of Imbolc, one of the four great agricultural festivals of northwestern Europe. Centered around the worship of the pan-Celtic goddess Brigit or Brigid, Imbolc is a celebration of the very first stirrings of spring. Fast on the heels of Imbolc comes the Roman festival of Concordia, goddess of peace; later in the month, a Roman festival called the city *Faunalia,* in honor of Faunus or Pan, combines the themes of fertility and peace in a joyous pastoral celebration.

FEBRUARY 1: IMBOLC

The origins of Imbolc, the Pagan ancestor of the later holiday Candlemas, are still shrouded in mystery. Its name may be a reference to the fact that ewes are often pregnant at this time of year (the Irish phrase *i mbolg,* "in the belly," is sometimes cited as the likely etymology of the name), while surviving folk traditions strongly connect it to Brigid or Brigit ("the High One"), the pan-Celtic goddess of poetry, fire and smiths, prophecy, and healing. Regardless of its origin, it represents the year's first tentative steps toward the fertility of summer.

Unfortunately, there are no surviving written texts (apart from a few inscriptions) about the goddess Brigid, and there's little folk material about her that hasn't been entirely Christianized. This makes it a challenge to find historical material for this holiday. Thankfully, new works are being written to honor Brigid in her divine (rather than saintly) incarnation, a trend that began with the Celtic Revival in the nineteenth century. But since historical prayers in honor of Brigid are hard to come by, I've included some works in this section from other traditions, works which honor goddesses who share some of her traits. Because Brigid is the patroness of poets, I've added a selection of poems honoring the Muses; and because Brigid is associated with prophecy, a hymn to Themis as giver of oracles is also included. A prayer to the Norse fertility-goddess Freya rounds out the selection, as Freya presides over the awakening earth. Although they belong to disparate traditions, together these goddesses embody the idea of Imbolc: a brightening light amid the darkness.

BRIGIT OF THE JUDGEMENTS
Nora Chesson (1871–1906)

Nora Chesson was part of the nineteenth-century Celtic Revival, a renewal of interest in the Celtic heritage of Europe by artists and writers from historically Celtic-speaking regions and the Celtic diaspora. This extraordinary poem, published in 1906, extols Brigit as the goddess of all living things. The "Lianan-sidhe" or leannán sí *referred to in the poem is the harsh faery mistress of nineteenth-century lore, who vampirizes and destroys her mortal lovers—the opposite of Brigit.*

I am Brigit—Wisdom, Light: yea, I am Bride.
I loosen all the knots that wrong has tied;
I knot all threads that should be woven in one.
I am the giver of laws; all evil done
Is on my heart until I may unravel
Its web with heavy tears and bitter travail.
My hair is colored like the heather honey;
My brows are cloudy and my eyes are sunny.
Judgment I hold in one hand, in the other Pity;
I am both maiden and a mother.

I am the judgment-giver; but I give
Compassion to all burdened things that live,
Struggle, and prey, and so are preyed upon.
Because the work-girl's hollow cheeks are wan,
Mine are so pale. Because the red ant dies
Under a careless foot my deathless eyes
Are dark with dole. Because the red fox went
Snarling to death, the lilies have no scent
That are amid my breast-knots tied, to show
I am the mother of all that fade and grow.

One man may call me Wisdom who has heard
Some darkling midnight stabbed through with my word.
One man will call me Light who, ere he dies,
Grasps at my hand and looks me in the eyes.
I am no Lianan-sidhe; I will not follow
The soul that seeks me even in the hollow
Lands where the moon is not or any sun,
No travail ended and no quest begun.
I slay the man who called me Law and strove
To slay me, but one name of mine is Love.

SMOORING THE FIRE

Traditional Scottish, translated by Alexander Carmichael

Since Brigid is strongly associated with fire and is often portrayed as a Triple Goddess, this little blessing charm seems worth including with her prayers. It was collected in Scotland in the late nineteenth century, after having been passed down through many generations. To smoor *a fire in Scotland is to dampen it, a process which would be done every night before the household went to bed. The fire, which would not go out entirely, would then be built up again in the morning. This charm would traditionally have been said during this process, but it also works as a general protection prayer.*

The sacred Three
To save,
To shield,
To surround
The hearth,
The house,
The household,
This eve,
This night,
Oh! this eve,
This night,
And every night,
Each single night.

IMBOLC CHANT

Annie Finch (2009)

Annie Finch is a modern American poet, feminist, playwright, and teacher. She lives in Maine.

From the east she has gathered like wishes.
She has woven a night into dawn.
We are quickening ivy. We grow
where her warmth melts out over the ice.

Now spiral south bends into flame
to push the morning over doors.
The light swings wide, green with the pulse
of seasons, and we let her in

We are quickening ivy. We grow

The light swings wide, green with the pulse

till the west is rocked by darkness
pulled from where the fire rises.
Shortened time's reflecting water
rakes her through the thickened cold.

Hands cover north smooth with emptiness,
stinging the mill of night's hours.
Wait with me. See, she comes circling
over the listening snow to us.

Shortened time's reflecting water

Wait with me. See, she comes circling

FROM *WHERE THE FOREST MURMURS*

William Sharp (1855–1905)

William Sharp, a Scottish writer whose works frequently appeared under the pen name Fiona MacLeod, was a member of the Hermetic Order of the Golden Dawn. The Fémor or Fomorians seem to have been chthonic deities, usually interpreted as the Gaelic equivalent of the Titans. Angus Óg is a youthful Irish god of love, while Oisín was a famous poet, the son of legendary hero Finn Mac Cumhaill. Midir is the son of the Dagda, the Good God.

[Those who speak of Brighid] refer to one whom the Druids held in honor as a torch-bearer of the eternal light, a Daughter of the Morning, who held sunrise in one hand as a little yellow flame, and in the other held the red flower of fire without which men would be as the beasts who live in caves and holes, or as the dark Fémor who have their habitations in cloud and wind and the wilderness. They refer to one whom the bards and singers revered as mistress of their craft, she whose breath was a flame, and that flame song: she whose secret name was fire and whose inmost soul was radiant air, she therefore who was the divine impersonation of the divine thing she stood for, Poetry. … [S]he, that ancient goddess, whom our ancestors saw lighting the torches of sunrise on the brows of hills, or thrusting the quenchless flame above the horizons of the sea: whom the Druids hailed with hymns at the turn of the year, when, in the season we call February, the first-comers of the advancing Spring are to be seen on the grey land or on the grey wave or by the grey shores: whom every poet, from the humblest wandering singer to Oisin of the Songs, from Oisin of the Songs to Angus Óg on the rainbow or to Midir of the Under-world, blessed, because of the flame she put in the heart of poets as well as the red life she put in the flame that springs from wood and peat. None forgot that she was the daughter of the ancient God of the Earth, but greater than he, because in him there was but earth and water, whereas in her veins ran the elements of air and fire.

ORPHIC HYMN TO THE MUSES

Anonymous (ca. 200 CE), translated by B. Nolan

Sometimes the Muses are nine and sometimes they are all subsumed into one Muse who governs all inspirational endeavors, but in this hymn there is a rare surprise: a tenth name listed with the nine Muses. Hagne was originally a goddess of springs and later a form of the goddess Persephone— which is probably how she is intended to be viewed in this Orphic hymn. Mnemosyne, the titaness whose name means "memory," is the mother of the Muses, who are "Pierian" because the Pierian Spring in Macedonia was sacred to them.

Daughters of Mnemosyne and thundering Zeus, glorious, renowned Pierian Muses, greatly-loved, many-formed, source of pure virtue in learning, you feed the soul and guide the mind, setting it on the right path. Queens and mistresses of souls, Kleio, Euterpe, Thalia, Melpomene, Terpsichore, Erato, Polymnia, Urania, Calliope, and great goddess Hagne: you revealed the sacred rituals to humankind. Now come, goddesses, to your worshippers, come bringing glory and love that will be sung in numberless hymns.

FROM "A HYMN TO THE MUSES"

Robert Herrick (1591–1674)

English Renaissance poet Herrick here calls upon the Muses to bless him, and promises them his eternal worship in return.

O you the virgins nine!
That do our souls incline
To noble discipline!
Nod to this vow of mine. ...
Then I'll your altars strew
With roses sweet and new;
And ever live a true
Acknowledger of you.

TO THE MUSES

Proclus Lycaeus (ca. 412–485 CE),
translated by R. M. van den Berg and Robbert Berg

Here Proclus asks the Muses to set him apart from the rest of humankind not by bestowing upon him literary gifts—the usual request made to these goddesses—but by giving his intellect the strength to resist the temptations of materialism. Here the goddesses are not just associated with the arts, as they usually are today, but also with philosophy. Noeric is very roughly equivalent to intellectual.

We hymn, we hymn the light that raises man aloft,
On the nine daughters of great Zeus with splendid voices
Who have rescued from the agony of this world, so hard to bear,
The souls who were wandering in the depth of life
Through immaculate rites from intellect-waking books,
And have taught them to strive eagerly to follow the track leading
Beyond the deep gulf of forgetfulness, and to go pure to their kindred star
From which they strayed away, when once they fell
Into the headland of birth, mad about material lots.

But goddesses, put an end of my much-agitated desire too
And throw me into ecstasy through the noeric words of the wise.
That the race of men without fear for the gods may not lead me
Astray from the most divine and brilliant path with its splendid fruit;
Always draw my all-roving soul toward the holy light,
Away from the hubbub of the much-wandering race
Heavy-laden from your intellect-strengthening beehives,
And everlasting glory from its mind-charming eloquence.

HYMN TO THE MUSE

Mesomedes of Crete (second century CE), translated by B. Nolan

Mesomedes, a slave of the Emperor Hadrian who eventually won his freedom, worked at the Musaeum, the artistic and scholarly complex in Alexandria, Egypt (which included the famous Library). Several of his hymns are still extant, along with musical notation to which they can be sung. This, to the Muse, is his shortest.

Sing to me, dear Muse,
At the beginning of my song.
Let the breezes from your groves
Blow through my mind.

FROM "A HYMN TO THE MUSES"

Robert Herrick (1591–1674)

The "well of wit" is a reference to the Pierian spring.

Honor to you who sit
Near to the well of wit,
And drink your fill of it.

Glory and worship be
To you, sweet maids (thrice three)
Who still inspire me.

ORPHIC HYMN TO THEMIS

Anonymous (ca. 200 CE?), translated by B. Nolan

Themis is primarily known as the goddess of justice (and in this form she can be seen with her sword and her scales in many public buildings throughout America), but she is also the goddess who gives the gift of prophecy to the gods and mortals alike. This hymn credits her with starting the famous Oracle at Delphi, where the Pythia, the high priestess of Phoebus Apollo, would prophesy with the words of the god. (The title of the priestess recalls Python, the huge serpent whom Apollo slew at the site before it became an oracle.) Themis is also credited with creating the foundations of religion itself.

I call on sacred Themis, maiden daughter of majestic parents, child of the Sky, born of Earth, bright-faced maiden, you who first revealed the holy prophecies of the gods to mortals, and the Oracle at Delphi, on the field where King Python reigned. You taught Lord Phoebus the power of prophecy. Greatly honored, greatly revered, you shine in the darkness, bringing holy worship to humankind, and the Bacchic nights of revelry. You teach the honors of the blessed gods, and their mysteries. O holy maiden, come with blessings to those who celebrate your mysteries.

FROM "FOR THE VANADÍS"
Gudrun of Mimirsbrunnr (twenty-first century)

This beautiful invocation of the Norse fertility goddess Freya, the Vanadís, asks her to help us renew ourselves as the year itself is renewed. Óðr or Odr is the frequently absent husband of Freya; he seems to have been originally a form of Odin, her father.

Hail to Odr's widow
on Imbolc morning
searching for her lost husband,
whipped by salt-sea wind,
waiting in the winter harbor for her father's return.
O Freya weeping tears of amber
help me to wake to the dawn of rebirth
for I am dull and beaten with years of mourning
and I have forgotten the mystery of the melting frost.

O Vanadís, may I be open to all you have to teach
in spite of all I have become
and because of all I yet could be.

FEBRUARY 5: CONCORDIA

Concordia is the Roman goddess of peace, both the sort which exists between nations and that which exists between individuals. Although she had several annual festivals in antiquity, she is now a rather overlooked deity—but it is she who makes our lives worth living, along with her Greek sister-goddesses Harmonia, goddess of divine and human harmony; Eunomia, goddess of good governance; and Dike, goddess of public order.

"HYMN TO PEACE" FROM *THE FASTI*

Ovid (43 BCE–17/18 CE), translated by B. Nolan

Come to us, Peace, with your beautiful locks crowned with laurels, and let your gentle spirit live throughout the whole world. Without enemies, there will be no cause for triumphs; may you be to our leaders a glory greater than war. May soldiers only wield their weapons for defense, and may the blaring trumpet only be played on ceremonial occasions.

PRAYER TO CONCORDIA FROM *PHARSALIA*

Lucan (ca. 39–65 CE), translated by B. Nolan

Be here now, you who hold all things in an everlasting bond, O Concordia, savior of the world and of all things, sacred love of the world.

FROM "PYTHIAN ODE 8"

Pindar (ca. 518–438 BCE), translated by Diane Arnson Svarlien

Porphyrion was the King of the Giants. When he attempted to rape the goddess Hera, he was killed by an arrow from the bow of Herakles.

Kindly Peace, daughter of Justice, you who make cities great, holding the supreme keys of counsels and of wars … you know both how to give and how to receive gentleness, with precise timing. And yet, whenever anyone drives pitiless anger into his heart, you meet the strength of your enemies roughly, sinking Arrogance in the flood. Porphyrion did not know your power, when he provoked you beyond all measure. Gain is most welcome, when one takes it from the home of a willing giver. Violence trips up even a man of great pride, in time.

CHORUS FROM *PEACE*

Aristophanes (ca. 446–ca. 386 BCE),
translator unknown (nineteenth century), modernized by B. Nolan

Aristophanes is the Father of Comedy, one of the great comedic playwrights of ancient Greece, or indeed of the world. This excerpt from his anti-war play Peace *is a hymn to the Greek goddess of peace, Eirene, written in the midst of Athens's war with Sparta.*

Hail, hail, beloved divinity! your return overwhelms us with joy. When far from you, my ardent wish to see my fields again made me pine with regret. From you came all blessings. O much desired Peace! You are the sole support of those who spend their lives tilling the earth. Under your rule we had a thousand delicious enjoyments at our beck; you were the husbandman's wheaten cake and his safeguard. So that our vineyards, our young fig-tree woods and all our farms hail you with delight and smile at your coming.

FROM "A HYMN TO HARMONY"

William Congreve (1670–1729)

William Congreve was an English Restoration playwright. Here he invokes the ancient idea of the "music of the spheres," the idea that the precise movements of the planets create a sort of universal music.

O Harmony, to thee we sing,
To thee the grateful tribute bring
Of sacred verse, and sweet resounding lays;
Thy aid invoking while thy power we praise.
All hail to thee
All-pow'rful Harmony!
Wise Nature owns thy undisputed sway,
Her wond'rous works resigning to thy care;
The planetary orbs thy rule obey,
And tuneful roll, unerring in their way,
Thy voice informing each melodious sphere.

PRAYER TO EUNOMIA

Solon (ca. 630–560 BCE), translated by B. Nolan

Solon was an ancient Athenian politician who made a major contribution to the development of democracy. Unsurprisingly, then, we find him here condemning Dysnomia (lawlessness) and extolling the virtues of Eunomia (good governance).

My spirit moves me to tell Athens this:
Lawlessness brings endless evil to the city, but Eunomia
Brings order and makes all things right. She

Shackles the wicked in chains, smooths what has been rough,

Puts an end to greed, checks arrogance,

Stops anger and warfare, causes the flowers

Of ruin to wither on the stalk, and

Corrects flawed judgments.

She throws down pridefulness, and

Restrains anger and fighting.

Under her rule all things are done right,

And wisdom guides the affairs of humankind.

FEBRUARY 13: THE CITY FAUNALIA

In ancient Rome, the Horned God known to the Romans as Faunus and to the Greeks as Pan was celebrated twice a year: once in mid-February (the urban festival, which took place on Tiber Island in Rome) and then again in December. That Pan should have two holidays isn't surprising, for the goat-foot god, whose name is the Greek word for "all," has proven to be enormously popular down through the ages. From Sophocles to Oscar Wilde, the Great God Pan has been a source of inspiration for generation after generation of writers. Sometimes he's the kindly god of shepherds who plays on his rustic pipe, and sometimes he's the mysterious force behind the expanding universe, but he's always, as the English poet Ben Jonson had it, "our all."

"OF PAN WE SING" FROM *PAN'S ANNIVERSARY*

Ben Jonson (1572–1637)

Ben Jonson, a friend of William Shakespeare, was a playwright of the English Renaissance. In these lines from one of his more popular plays, a group of shepherds explain their complete reliance on the Great God Pan.

Pan is our All, by him we breath, we live,

We move, we are; 'Tis he our lambs doth rear,

Our flocks doth bless, and from the store doth give

The warm and finer fleeces that we wear.

He keeps away all heats, and colds,

Drives all diseases from our folds:

Makes everywhere the spring to dwell,

The ewes to feed, their udders swell;
But if he frown, the sheep (alas)
The shepherds wither, and the grass.
Strive, strive, to please him then by still increasing thus
The rites are due him, who doth all right for us.

AN INVOCATION TO PAN

Hilary Llewellyn-Williams (2002)

In this beautiful invocation, modern Welsh poet Hilary Llewellyn-Williams celebrates a cognate of Pan: Cernunnos, the stag-antlered god of the Celts.

Come, eye of the forest
come, beast-footed
stag-crowned
man-membered; come, tree-sinewed
soil-rubbed, leaf-garlanded;
come, goat-nimble
come, bird-joyful
come, fox-cunning;
out of the boles and burrows
out of the humps and hollows
out of the heaps of leaves;
out of mist and darkness
out of sunshafts, gold motes,
flowers, insects humming:
brown lying down in summer by the river
your flute notes cool
and black striding up from the woods in winter
wreathed in fogs, your voice belling;
come, old one, come, green one,
tree-protector, beast-befriender
good shepherd, wise steward:
come, earth-brother
long long lost

long long lost
let us find you
call you
call you up, out, back, forth –
be here now!
O musk of fur sour
in the wind, your branched head
through the thickets
coming, coming
in your power, your power, your power.

STROPHE FROM *AJAX*

Sophocles (ca. 497/6–406/5 BCE),
adapted from the translation by R. C. Trevelyan

Io! is an ancient Greek cry of triumph or ecstasy, the equivalent of the English oh! (and you can say it that way if you want to). Cyllene or Kyllini is one of the higher mountains in Greece and is strongly associated with Pan's father, Hermes. Nysa is the mythical land where Dionysus was raised, and Cnossus is Knossos, the ancient city of Crete.

I thrill with rapture, flutter on wings of ecstasy.
Io, Io, Pan, Pan!
O Pan, Pan! from the stony ridge,
Snow-bestrewn, of Cyllene's height,
Appear roving across the waters
O dance-ordering king of gods,
That you may join me in flinging free
Fancy measures of Nysa and of Cnossus.
Yes, for the dance I now am eager.

FROM "SUN AND FLESH (CREDO IN UNAM)"

Arthur Rimbaud (1854–1891), translated by B. Nolan

Syrinx was a nymph whom Pan loved; she did not return his affection, and chose to become a reed rather than the god's lover. From this reed Pan made the first pipe.

I wish the times would return when the sap of the world,
The water of the chattering river, the blood of green trees
Put an entire universe in Pan's veins!
When all that is born lived under his long goatish feet;
When, gently kissing the naive Syrinx, his lip
Murmured the great hymn of love under the heavens;
When, standing in the fields, he heard all around him
Living Nature respond to his call;
When the quiet trees, sheltering the singing bird,
Earth sheltering man, and the long blue river,
And all the animals loved at the feet of a God!

A NOTE FROM THE PIPES

Leonora Speyer (1872–1956)

Leonora Speyer was a German-American violinist and poet who won the Pulitzer Prize for Poetry in 1927.

Pan, blow your pipes and I will be
Your fern, your pool, your dream, your tree!

I heard you play, caught your swift eye,
"A pretty melody!" called I,
"Hail, Pan!" And sought to pass you by.

Now blow your pipes and I will sing
To your sure lips' accompanying!

Wild God, who lifted me from earth,
Who taught me freedom, wisdom, mirth,
Immortalized my body's worth,—

Blow, blow your pipes! And from afar
I'll come—I'll be your bird, your star,
Your wood, your nymph, your kiss, your rhyme,
And all your godlike summer-time!

PROLOGUE OF THE UNBORN

Aleister Crowley (1875–1947)

Aleister Crowley surely needs no introduction to modern Pagans. His "Hymn to Pan" is well-known, but far superior is this piece from his Holy Books of Thelema *in which he describes an absolute surrender to the god.*

1. Into my loneliness comes—
2. The sound of a flute in dim groves that haunt the uttermost hills.
3. Even from the brave river they reach to the edge of the wilderness.
4. And I behold Pan.
5. The snows are eternal above, above—
6. And their perfume smokes upward into the nostrils of the stars.
7. But what have I to do with these?
8. To me only the distant flute, the abiding vision of Pan.
9. On all sides Pan to the eye, to the ear;
10. The perfume of Pan pervading, the taste of him utterly filling my mouth, so that the tongue breaks forth into a weird and monstrous speech.
11. The embrace of him intense on every centre of pain and pleasure.
12. The sixth interior sense aflame with the inmost self of Him,
13. Myself flung down the precipice of being
14. Even to the abyss, annihilation.
15. An end to loneliness, as to all.
16. Pan! Pan! Io Pan! Io Pan!

"BELOVED PAN" FROM *PHAEDRUS*

Socrates (ca. 470–399 BCE), translated by Harold N. Fowler

Socrates is, of course, one of the earliest Western philosophers, and the foundation upon which all philosophers who followed after him have built. He was famously forced to commit suicide by drinking hemlock after a politically motivated show trial; one of the charges against him was "impiety." There is, however, no trace of impiety in this beautiful prayer to Pan.

O beloved Pan and all ye other gods of this place, grant to me that I be made beautiful in my soul within, and that all external possessions be in harmony with my inner man. May I consider the wise man rich; and may I have such wealth as only the self-restrained man can bear or endure.

FROM "VILLANELLE OF THE LIVING PAN"

Walter Adolphe Roberts (1886–1962)

Walter Adolphe Roberts was a Jamaican poet and journalist. In this poem he refers to the famous episode in Plutarch in which a sailor named Thamus, at about the time of Jesus's execution, suddenly heard an unknown voice calling him by name and declaring, "Great Pan is dead!" Although the sailor in question almost certainly heard and misunderstood the ritual cries for the annual "death" of the god Tammuz (Thamus Panmegas tethneke, the All-great Tammuz is dead), this incident has inspired a great deal of monotheistic jubilation down through the centuries. Roberts, however, isn't having any of it: like many poets, he knows that Pan may sleep but cannot die.

Pan is not dead, but sleeping in the brake,
    Hard by the blue of some Aegean shore.
Ah, flute to him, Beloved, he will wake.

Vine leaves have drifted o'er him, flake by flake,
    And with dry laurel he is covered o'er,
Pan is not dead, but sleeping in the brake.

Dreaming of one that for the goat god's sake
    Shall pipe old tunes and worship as of yore.
Ah, flute to him, Beloved, he will wake.

So once again the Attic shore shall shake
　　With a cry greater than it heard before.
"Pan is not dead, but sleeping in the brake!"
Ah, flute to him, Beloved, he will wake.

FROM "NYMPHS"

Ivan Turgenev (1818–1883), translator unknown (1883)

Turgenev was a Russian novelist, best known in the West for Fathers and Sons.

… I called out with all my might:—"He has risen; great Pan has risen!"

And suddenly, a miracle! There echoed immediately as if in answer to my call, along the whole broad crescent of the green mountains, a universal laugh and murmur and joyous prattling. "He has risen; Pan has risen!" cried youthful voices. All around me broke out gay rejoicing, brighter than the sun overhead, gayer than the brooks running under the grass. …

FROM THE HOMERIC HYMN TO PAN

Anonymous (ca. 700–500 BCE), translated by Hugh G. Evelyn-White

Pan *means "all" in Greek, and this hymn offers an explanation of the name.*

Muse, tell me about Pan, the dear son of Hermes, with his goat's feet and two horns—a lover of merry noise. Through wooded glades he wanders with dancing nymphs who foot it on some sheer cliff's edge, calling upon Pan, the shepherd-god, long-haired, unkempt. He has every snowy crest and the mountain peaks and rocky crests for his domain; hither and thither he goes through the close thickets, now lured by soft streams, and now he presses on amongst towering crags and climbs up to the highest peak that overlooks the flocks. Often he courses through the glistening high mountains, and often on the shouldered hills he speeds along slaying wild beasts, this keen-eyed god. Only at evening, as he returns from the chase, he sounds his note, playing sweet and low on his pipes of reed: not even she could excel him in melody—that bird who in flower-laden spring pouring forth her lament utters honey-voiced song amid the leaves. At that hour the clear-voiced nymphs are with him and move with nimble feet, singing by some spring of dark water, while Echo wails about the mountain-top, and the god on this side or on that of the choirs, or at times sidling into the midst, plies it nimbly with his feet. On his back he wears a spotted lynx-pelt, and he delights in high-pitched songs in a soft meadow where crocuses and sweet-smelling hyacinths bloom at random in the grass.

They sing of the blessed gods and high Olympus and choose to tell of such an one as luck-bringing Hermes above the rest, how he is the swift messenger of all the gods, and how he came to Arcadia, the land of many springs and mother of flocks, there where his sacred place is as god of Cyllene. For there, though a god, he used to tend curly-fleeced sheep in the service of a mortal man, because there fell on him and waxed strong melting desire to wed the rich-tressed daughter of Dryops, and there he brought about the merry marriage. And in the house she bare Hermes a dear son who from his birth was marvellous to look upon, with goat's feet and two horns—a noisy, merry-laughing child. But when the nurse saw his uncouth face and full beard, she was afraid and sprang up and fled and left the child. Then luck-bringing Hermes received him and took him in his arms: very glad in his heart was the god. And he went quickly to the abodes of the deathless gods, carrying his son wrapped in warm skins of mountain hares, and set him down beside Zeus and showed him to the rest of the gods. Then all the immortals were glad in heart and Bacchic Dionysus in especial; and they called the boy Pan because he delighted all their hearts.

And so hail to you, lord! I seek your favor with a song. . . .

PAN

Francis Ledwidge (1887–1917)

Francis Ledwidge was an Irishman whose poverty forced him out of school at age thirteen but who nonetheless became a noted poet before his death during World War I, at the Battle of Passchendaele.

He knows the safe ways and unsafe
And he will lead the lambs to fold,
Gathering them with his merry pipe,
The gentle and the overbold.

He counts them over one by one,
And leads them back by cliff and steep,
To grassy hills where dawn is wide,
And they may run and skip and leap.

And just because he loves the lambs
He settles them for rest at noon,
And plays them on his oaten pipe
The very wonder of a tune.

FROM "THE ETERNAL PAN"

Ralph Waldo Emerson (1803–1882)

Emerson is perhaps the most famous of all the nineteenth-century American Transcendentalists (Transcendentalism is a philosophical movement closely allied to Unitarianism). A religious and political radical who believed that all things were connected to the Divine and that God could be known through communion with nature, he was also an ardent abolitionist and a supporter of women's rights. He wrote a number of works in which he identified his conception of divinity with the god Pan.

As the bee through the garden ranges,
From world to world the godhead changes;
As the sheep go feeding in the waste,
From form to form He maketh haste;
This vault which glows immense with light
Is the inn where he lodges for a night. . . .
Alike to him the better, the worse,—
The glowing angel, the outcast coarse.
Thou meetest him by centuries,
And lo! he passes like the breeze;
Thou seek'st in glade and galaxy,
He hides in pure transparency;
Thou askest in fountains and in fires,
He is the essence that inquires.
He is the axis of the star;
He is the sparkle of the spar;
He is the heart of every creature;
He is the meaning of each feature;
And his mind is the sky,
Than all it holds more deep, more high.

WE WORSHIP PAN

Anonymous, from the *Palatine Anthology,* (before 980 CE), translated by W. R. Paton

The fountain mentioned here could be a physical spring, or it could be interpreted as the metaphorical fountain of knowledge.

We do worship the horned Pan, the walker on the crags, the leader of the nymphs, who dwells in this house of rock, praying him to look with favor on all us who came to this constant fountain and quenched our thirst.

FROM "APOLLO"

Eugene Lee-Hamilton (1845–1907)

Oh strong rough Pan,
God of lone spots where sudden awe o'erwhelms
Weak souls, but never mine—I love thy realms!
    I love the wan
Half-leafless glens, which Autumn's plaint repeat
From tree to tree; I love the shy fawn's bleat;
    The cry of lynx and wood-cat safe from man;
The fox's short sharp bark from sure retreat.

EPIDAURIAN HYMN

Anonymous (ca. 400 CE) translated by B. Nolan

This hymn was found written on an ancient stone in Epidaurus, a little town in Greece often considered to be the birthplace of the god Asclepius; nowadays it is best known for its well-preserved amphitheater.

I sing to Pan, the leader of the nymphs, beloved of the water-nymphs, famous in glittering dances, prince of the people's music.

From his resounding pipes seductive, enthralling music spills out, and he dances lightly to the tune. He leaps through shadowed caves, showing off his shape-shifting body, a graceful dancer with a handsome face and a beard of pure spun gold. His music echoes to starry Olympus, where the gods luxuriate in the immortal melodies.

All the earth and all the sea join in your joy; you are the uplifter of all. O hail Pan! Pan!

FROM "HOLY SATYR"

HD (1886–1961)

Hilda Doolittle (HD) was an American poet whose haunting verse reflects her deep interest in classical Paganism.

Most holy Satyr,
like a goat,
hear this our song,
accept our leaves,
love-offering,
return our hymn;
like echo fling
a sweet song,
answering note for note.

FROM "NYMPHOLEPT"

Algernon Charles Swinburne (1837–1909)

Victorian poet Swinburne wrote frequently about Pagan deities. His poem "Nympholept" (a nympholept is one possessed by a nymph) is not the easiest of his works to decipher, but it well repays the extra effort.

Thee, thee the supreme dim godhead, approved afar,
    Perceived of the soul and conceived of the sense of man
We scarce dare love, and we dare not fear: the star
    We call the sun, that lit us when life began
    To brood on the world that is thine by his grace for a span,
Conceals and reveals in the semblance of things that are
    Thine immanent presence, the pulse of thy heart's life, Pan.

The fierce mid noon that wakens and warms the snake
    Conceals thy mercy, reveals thy wrath: and again
The dew-bright hour that assuages the twilight brake
    Conceals thy wrath and reveals thy mercy: then
    Thou art fearful only for evil souls of men
That feel with nightfall the serpent within them wake,
    And hate the holy darkness on glade and glen.

Yea, then we know not and dream not if ill things be,
    Or if aught of the work of the wrong of the world be thine.
We hear not the footfall of terror that treads the sea,
    We hear not the moan of winds that assail the pine:
    We see not if shipwreck reign in the storm's dim shrine;
If death do service and doom bear witness to thee
    We see not,—know not if blood for thy lips be wine.

But in all things evil and fearful that fear may scan,
    As in all things good, as in all things fair that fall,
We know thee present and latent, the lord of man;
    In the murmuring of doves, in the clamouring of winds that call
    And wolves that howl for their prey; in the mid-night's pall,
In the naked and nymph-like feet of the dawn, O Pan,
    And in each life living, O thou the God who art all.

A HYMN TO PAN

John Fletcher (1579–1625)

John Fletcher took over the position of playwright for the King's Men, a theater troupe, after the death of the previous incumbent, William Shakespeare.

All ye woods and trees and bowers,
All ye virtues and ye powers
That inhabit in the lakes,
In the pleasant springs or breaks,
Move your feet to our sound,
Whilst we greet all this ground
With his honor and his name
That defends our flock from blame.

He is great and he is just;
He is ever good and must
Thus be honor'd. Daffodillies,
Roses, pinks, and lovèd lilies,
Let us fling, whilst we sing.
Ever holy, ever holy,
Ever honor'd, ever young!
Thus great Pan is ever sung!

MARCH

Balanced midway between darkness and light, cold and warmth, death and growth, March is the stormy month of opposites. It opens with the birthday of the hypermasculine god Mars and continues with the very female-oriented Lesser Eleusinian Mysteries, a celebration of the return of the goddess Persephone to her mother Demeter, which occurred at roughly the time of the vernal equinox. Just before we move into gentler April, however, comes the City Dionysia, which honors the god Dionysus, lord of the vine and the grape, and of ecstatic revelation—and a god in whom both male and female are harmoniously combined.

MARCH 1: THE BIRTHDAY OF MARS

Happy birthday to Mars! Today marks the ceremonial birthday of Mars, god of war, who gives the month its name. Originally this day was also the Roman New Year, but that honor was switched to Janus's feast day at some point in the second century BCE. Still, the first of March remains a celebration of the fiercest of gods.

It may seem strange that the Romans once started the New Year off with a war god, but Mars wasn't just a god of war in antiquity. He was also the father of Rome's founders, Romulus and Remus, as well as a deity of protection and fertility. Indeed, the ancient Roman prayer known as the "Carmen Arvale" calls upon Mars to make the seeds sprout. As time passed, Mars's fecund functions seem to have been forgotten, and he was equated more and more with Ares, the ferocious Greek war god who lacks the gentler side of the Roman deity. The following prayers, however, celebrate Mars (and Ares) as protector, or urges him to put away the weapons of war.

CARMEN ARVALE (SONG OF THE ARVALS)

Anonymous, (before 400 BCE), translated by B. Nolan (after the Fitzhugh interpretation)

The Arval Brothers were a very ancient Roman priesthood, supposedly founded by the demigod Romulus himself. For thousands of years they offered annual sacrifices to the city Lares, the Good Goddess, and other deities to ensure good harvests and the safety of Rome. In this prayer, written down around 218 CE in archaic Latin and believed to be a millennium older, they call upon the Lares and Marmar (an ancient name for Mars) to do both.

Help us, O Lares!
Help us, O Lares!
Help us, O Lares!

O Marmar, protect the people from disease and destruction!
O Marmar, protect the people from disease and destruction!
O Marmar, protect the people from disease and destruction!

Rage, fierce Marmar, leap the boundary, but hold back your spear!
Rage, fierce Marmar, leap the boundary, but hold back your spear!
Rage, fierce Marmar, leap the boundary, but hold back your spear!

In turn invoke the spirits of the seeds!
In turn invoke the spirits of the seeds!
In turn invoke the spirits of the seeds!

Help us, O Marmar!
Help us, O Marmar!
Help us, O Marmar!

Triumph!
Triumph!
Triumph!
Triumph!
Triumph!

ORPHIC HYMN TO ARES

Anonymous (ca. 200 CE), translated by B. Nolan

O Ares, great-souled, undefeated, strong and terrible spirit, unstoppable man-killer who rejoices in battle, whose strength shakes walls loose from their foundations; Lord Ares, terrifying death-lover, blood-spattered and delighting in the din of battle, you love the sight of blood-stained swords and spears and the insane destruction of war. But hold your hand, pull back vengeance and fury, those things which break the hearts and lives of humans; open yourself to Dionysus, and to seductive Aphrodite; let your swords become Demeter's ploughshares. Allow Peace to reign, Peace who nurtures youth and grants riches.

"FATHER MARS" FROM *DE AGRI CULTURA*

Cato the Elder (234–149 BCE), translated by B. Nolan

Father Mars, I pray and beg that you be kind and merciful to me, my house and my household, that you keep away, ward off, and take away sickness both visible and invisible, barrenness and bane, destruction and unseasonable influences; let my harvests, my grain, my vines, and my farms grow and flourish … and grant health and strength to me, my house, and my family.

HYMN TO MARS

Henry James Pye (1744–1813)

Henry Pye, one of Britain's Poets Laureate, adapted many of the Homeric hymns to what was, at the time, modern English verse. This is really the "Homeric Hymn to Ares," but Pye used the interpretatio Romana, *the Roman habit of equating foreign gods with their nearest Roman equivalent, to dedicate his version to Mars.*

   Car, *here, is a chariot.*

Mars! god of armies! 'mid the ranks of war
Known by thy golden helm, and rushing car,
Before whose lance with sound terrific fall
The massy fortress and the embattled wall;
Father of victory! whose mighty powers
And brazen spears protect Olympus' towers;
By whom the brave to high renown are led,

Whom justice honors and whom tyrants dread;
Who mid the seven revolving orbs above,
O'er heaven's blue arch thy fiery coursers drove.
Hail, friend to man! whose cares to youth impart
The arm unwearied, and the undaunted heart.
O, be thy favoring ear to me inclined,
Breathe martial vigor through thy votary's mind;
So shall my breast the bold attack oppose,
Or mock the vengeance of insidious foes:
Yet while my bosom glows with martial fire,
Still with the love of peace my soul inspire.
Be concord's sacred laws my first delight;
Far from the dangers and the toils of fight.

FROM THE ORPHIC HYMN TO THE KOURETES

Anonymous (ca. 200 CE?), translated by B. Nolan

This section closes with a hymn not to Mars/Ares himself, but to a group of similar deities, the Kouretes or Corybantes, who are also both warlike and fertile. They were the first to wear metal armor, and, like Mars, they can be both fierce and protective; they are said to have protected the infant Zeus from his murderous father, Cronos. They are also guardians of shepherds and beekeepers.

Samothrace is an island off the coast of Greece.

Kouretes, bronze-clashing, dressed in the armaments of Ares, gods who dwell in the air, the earth, and the sea, and so are three times blessed; you give the breath of life, you great saviors of the universe, dwelling in the holy land of Samothrace, and you stave off danger from sailors wandering the seas. … Imperishable Kouretes, with the arms of Ares you rule the oceans, the seas, and the forests, while the earth resounds with your stamping footsteps and your shining armor glitters, and all wild animals flee before your approach. Your shouts and din climb to the heavens, and the dust from your marching feet reaches up to the clouds. Then every flower bursts forth in bloom. Indestructible deities, you grant life and also destroy. When humankind angers you, you destroy wealth, livelihoods, and life itself. The wide, deep-churning sea moans, great trees are shaken to the roots and fall, and the rush of shaking leaves echoes through the sky. Kouretes, Korybantes, mighty masters, lords of Samothrace, true sons of the god, ever-blowing winds, nourishers of the soul … who exhale sweet breaths, gentle, kindly guardians, bringing calm weather, nurturing the seasons and the harvest. Inspire us, O lords!

LATE MARCH: THE VERNAL EQUINOX AND THE LESSER ELEUSINIAN MYSTERIES

The birth of spring is a time to pay homage to the goddess Persephone (also known as Proserpine or Kore), who, along with her mother Demeter (Ceres), brings about the changing of the seasons and the growth of plants. Their sacred story—of the abduction of young Persephone by Hades, Lord of the underworld; of Demeter's desperate efforts to locate her missing daughter and her refusal to allow plants to grow during their separation; and of Persephone's eventual return to her mother for part of the year—has served as both an explanation for and a celebration of the cycle of the seasons from time immemorial.

The Two Goddesses, as they were known, were worshipped during the fabled Eleusinian Mysteries, a two-part festival held annually in Eleusis, Greece. The first part, the so-called Lesser Mysteries, were held in early spring, at the approximate time of the vernal equinox, while the second part, the Greater Mysteries, occurred in the fall. For about two thousand years, men and women came to Eleusis from all over the world in order to gain initiation into the mysteries, until the Christian Emperor Theodosius closed the sanctuary in 392 CE. While the rites themselves were secret and remain a source of much speculation—initiates took strict vows of secrecy, and no one is known to have violated them—they seem to have revealed to their initiates the immortality of the soul through the story of the changing seasons. But while the specifics of their rites have been lost to us in the mists of time, the Two Goddesses have given birth to a vast body of Western literature. What follows are some examples drawn from this literary tradition, along with other pieces celebrating the return of spring.

FROM THE HOMERIC HYMN TO DEMETER

Anonymous, (ca. 700–500 BCE), translated by Hugh G. Evelyn-White

This is a small piece of the longest of all the Homeric hymns. Although Persephone's return from the underworld occurs during the spring, she was also abducted in the spring, as she reached to grasp a daffodil that Hades had planted to tempt her. It seems fitting, therefore, to begin the season with a reminder of how winter came to be.

Here, car *means* chariot. *Oceanus is the god of fresh waters as well as the oceans; Hades is called Aidoneus, the Host of Many, and the Ruler of Many (the Many are, of course, the souls of the dead). Rhea is a Titaness, the wife of Cronos and the mother of Demeter, Hades, and Zeus; Helios is the Sun.* Son of Cronos *refers here to both Hades and Zeus, who are brothers. And, of course, Demeter is* awful *in the oldest sense of the word: one who inspires awe.*

I begin to sing of rich-haired Demeter, awful goddess—of her and her trim-ankled daughter whom Aidoneus rapt away, given to him by all-seeing Zeus the loud-thunderer.

Apart from Demeter, lady of the golden sword and glorious fruits, Persephone was playing with the deep-bosomed daughters of Oceanus and gathering flowers over a soft meadow, roses and crocuses and beautiful violets, irises also and hyacinths and the narcissus, which Earth made to grow at the will of Zeus and to please the Host of Many, to be a snare for the bloom-like girl—a marvellous, radiant flower. It was a thing of awe whether for deathless gods or mortal men to see: from its root grew a hundred blooms and it smelled most sweetly, so that all wide heaven above and the whole earth and the sea's salt swell laughed for joy. And the girl was amazed and reached out with both hands to take the lovely toy; but the wide-pathed earth yawned … and the lord, Host of Many, with his immortal horses sprang out upon her—the Son of Cronos, He who has many names.

He caught her up reluctant on his golden car and bore her away lamenting. Then she cried out shrilly with her voice, calling upon her father, the Son of Cronos, who is most high and excellent. But no one, either of the deathless gods or of mortal men, heard her voice, nor yet the olive-trees bearing rich fruit: only tender-hearted Hecate, bright-coiffed … heard the girl from her cave, and the lord Helios, Hyperion's bright son, as she cried to her father, the Son of Cronos. But he was sitting aloof, apart from the gods, in his temple where many pray, and receiving sweet offerings from mortal men. So he … of many names, who is Ruler of Many and Host of Many, was bearing her away by leave of Zeus on his immortal chariot—his own brother's child and all unwilling.

FROM "PROSERPINE GATHERING VIOLETS"

Jean Moréas (1856–1910), translated by B. Nolan

Jean Moréas was a Greek poet who wrote mostly in French, and was a member of the French Symbolist movement. Cyane is a nymph who attempted to stop Proserpine's abduction. Camarine or Kamarina was an ancient Sicilian city; Proserpine was widely believed to have been abducted in Sicily.

In this little laughing valley, while you pluck
The sweet violet with delicate leaves,
O daughter of Ceres, alas! You don't know
That dark Pluto pursues you everywhere.

He can no longer stand to be named sterile.

For Venus has suddenly wounded him with the same shafts

As those she strikes, deep in the ancient forests,

Into the race of birds and the beautiful agile deer.

Hear the cries of the god! under his terrifying arm

His rearing horses that fear the brightness,

Break under their hooves the reed that bows

Over the sluggish marsh that feeds the Camarine.

In her grottoes moans Henna, mother of flowers,

And Cyane makes her waters grow with her tears.

Among the pale dead soon you will be queen,

O daughter of Ceres, and subterranean Juno. . . .

FROM "THE RETURN OF PERSEPHONE"

A. D. Hope (1907–2000)

After the abduction of Persephone, Demeter, goddess of fertility and agriculture, refused to allow anything to grow, and humankind starved. So too did the gods, who no longer received offerings from malnourished humans. As a result of Demeter's strike, Zeus, who had consented to the abduction, relented and allowed Persephone to be returned to her mother for nine months out of the year.

The "Traveller God" in this poem by Australian poet A.D. Hope is Hermes, who descends to the underworld to guide Persephone back to earth.

The summer flowers scattering, the shout,

The black manes plunging down to the black pit—

Memory or dream? She stood awhile in doubt,

Then touched the Traveller God's brown arm and met

His cool, bright glance and heard his words ring out:

"Queen of the Dead and Mistress of the Year!"

—His voice was the ripe ripple of the corn;

The touch of dew, the rush of morning air—

"Remember now the world where you were born;

The month of your return at last is here."

FROM THE HOMERIC HYMN TO DEMETER

Anonymous (ca. 700–500 BCE), translated by Hugh G. Evelyn-White

In this selection from her hymn Demeter, after an appeal by her mother the Titaness Rhea, allows spring to return to earth in exchange for the return of her daughter.

The Rharus is a field near Eleusis.

And [Demeter] did not disobey the message of Zeus; swiftly she rushed down from the peaks of Olympus and came to the plain of Rharus, rich, fertile corn-land once, but then in nowise fruitful, for it lay idle and utterly leafless, because the white grain was hidden by design of trim-ankled Demeter. But afterwards, as spring-time waxed, it was soon to be waving with long ears of corn, and its rich furrows to be loaded with grain upon the ground, while others would already be bound in sheaves. There first she landed from the fruitless upper air: and glad were the goddesses to see each other and cheered in heart. Then bright-coiffed Rhea said to Demeter:

"Come, my daughter; for far-seeing Zeus the loud-thunderer calls you to join the families of the gods, and has promised to give you what rights you please among the deathless gods, and has agreed that for a third part of the circling year your daughter shall go down to darkness and gloom, but for the two parts shall be with you and the other deathless gods: so has he declared it shall be and has bowed his head in token. But come, my child, obey, and be not too angry unrelentingly with the dark-clouded Son of Cronos; but rather increase forthwith for men the fruit that gives them life."

So spake Rhea. And rich-crowned Demeter did not refuse but straightway made fruit to spring up from the rich lands, so that the whole wide earth was laden with leaves and flowers.

FROM "THE ROAD MENDER"

Margaret Fairless Barber (1869–1901)

Margaret Fairless Barber was a famous Christian writer of the late nineteenth century, but she did not feel that her Christianity was a bar to a love of and appreciation for the Pagan past. "We can never be too Pagan if we are truly Christian," she wrote, "and the old myths are eternal truths held fast in the Church's net." Her personal synthesis of the two faiths led to some beautiful writings on the Eleusinian Mysteries.

Once Demeter in the black anguish of her desolation searched for lost Persephone by the light of Hecate's torch; and searching all in vain, spurned beneath her empty feet an earth barren of her smile; froze with set brows the merry brooks and streams; and smote forest, and plain, and fruitful field, with the breath of her last despair, until even Iambe's laughing jest was still. And then when the desolation was complete, across the wasted valley where the starveling cattle scarcely longed to browse, came the dreadful chariot—and Persephone. The day of the prisoner of Hades had dawned; and as the sun flamed slowly up to light her thwarted eyes the world sprang into blossom at her feet.

AT ELEUSIS

Ella Wheeler Wilcox (1850–1919)

Ella Wheeler Wilcox was a nineteenth-century American poet and Spiritualist.

I, at Eleusis, saw the finest sight,
    When early morning's banners were unfurled.
    From high Olympus, gazing on the world,
The ancient gods once saw it with delight.
Sad Demeter had in a single night
    Removed her sombre garments! and mine eyes
    Beheld a 'broidered mantle in pale dyes
Thrown o'er her throbbing bosom. Sweet and clear
There fell the sound of music on mine ear.
    And from the South came Hermes, he whose lyre
    One time appeased the great Apollo's ire.
The rescued maid, Persephone, by the hand,
    He led to waiting Demeter, and cheer
And light and beauty once more blessed the land.

FROM "SPRING"

Margaret Fairless Barber (1869–1901)

The gentle wind from out the west
Toys with the lilac pretty maids;
Ruffles the meadow's verdant-vest,
And rings the bluebells in the glades;

The ash-buds change their sombre suit,
The orchards blossom white and red—
Promise of Autumn's riper fruit,
When Spring's voluptuousness has fled.
Awake! awake, O throstle sweet!
And haste with all your choir to greet
This Queen who comes with wakening feet.

Persephone with grateful eyes
Salutes the Sun—'tis Paradise:
Then hastens down the dewy meads,
Past where the herd contented feeds,
Past where the furrows hide the grain,
For harvesting of sun and rain;
To where Demeter patient stands
With longing lips and outstretched hands,
Until the dawning of one face
Across the void of time and space
Shall bring again her day of grace.
Rejoice, O Earth! Rejoice and sing!
This is the promise of the Spring,
And this the world's remembering.

SONG OF PROSERPINA

Percy Bysshe Shelley (1792–1822)

Percy Shelley wrote these verses for his wife's play Proserpine.

Sacred Goddess, Mother Earth,
Thou from whose immortal bosom
Gods and men and beasts have birth,
Leaf and blade, and bud and blossom,
Breathe thine influence most divine
On thine own child, Proserpine.

If with mists of evening dew
Thou dost nourish these young flowers
Till they grow in scent and hue
Fairest children of the Hours,
Breathe thine influence most divine
On thine own child, Proserpine.

From "The Story of Eleusis"

Louis V. Ledoux (1880–1948)

A spring prayer for a good fall harvest.

…Mother of the beasts and birds and flowers.
Gracious bringer of the barley and the grain,
Earth awakened feels thy sunlight and thy showers;
Great Demeter! Let us call thee not in vain;
Lead us safely from the seed-time to the threshing,
Past the harvest and the vineyard's purple stain;
Let us see thy corn-pale hair the sunlight, meshing,
When the sounding flails of autumn swing again.

Greek Fragments

Bacchylides and Anonymous (sixth–fifth century BCE), translated by B. Nolan

In these fragments Persephone is called Kore, *or* Maiden.

I sing of Demeter, Queen of Sicily, rich in corn, and of Kore with her chain of violets; I sing of the mother of Wealth, Demeter Olympia, in the season of garlands, and of Persephone daughter of Zeus. Hail to you both! Take good care of our city!

ORPHIC HYMN TO PERSEPHONE

Anonymous (ca. 200 CE?), translated by Frederick C. Grant

Here Persephone is identified with Praxidike, the goddess of just vengeance, and is also named as the mother of Dionysus; this unusual attribution may reflect the fact that she was the first to go into the land of death and be reborn—which Dionysus did, in a different way, when he was born again from his father's thigh after his mother's death.

The Eumenides are goddesses of vengeance; Eubuleus is a god associated with the Eleusinian Mysteries. Pluto is another name for Hades.

O Persephone, daughter of great Zeus,
Come, only-begotten goddess, and receive the offering piously dedicated unto thee—
To thee, Pluto's honored bride,
The kindly, the lifegiver;
Thou who rulest the gates of Hades in the clefts of the earth,
Executrix of punishments, the lovely-tressed, pure daughter of Zeus;
Mother of the Eumenides, Queen of the nether world,
Whom Zeus by a secret union begat as his daughter;
Mother of the noisy, the many-formed Eubuleus,
Leader of the dance of the Hours, Light-bringer, beautiful in form,
Exalted, all-ruling Kore, bounteous in fruits,
Clear-shining one, horned, the one and only desired of all mortals:
The bringer of springtime, when thou art pleased with the sweet-smelling meadows,
When thou dost let thy heavenly form be seen
In the green, fruit-bearing growth of the field,
And art set free for the gathering of the mighty harvest sheaves;
Thou who alone art life and death to mortals, greatly plagued, Persephoneia!
For thou ever bringest forth all things
And slayest all!
Hear, O blessed goddess!
Let the fruits of the earth spring forth
And grant us peace alway, sound health, and a prosperous life;
Then at last, after a hale old age,
Lead us down to thy realm, O Queen,
And to Pluto, the Lord of all.

ORPHIC HYMN TO THE HORAI

Anonymous (ca. 200 CE?), translated by B. Nolan

The Horai are the Greek goddesses of the seasons and companions of Persephone. They are not personifications of the seasons themselves, but rather the goddesses who keep the year in good working order, making sure that things happen at the appointed time. They have other functions, as well—Dike is the goddess of justice, Eunomia of moral order, and Eirene of peace—but here they are asked to bring fertility to the earth.

Horai, daughters of Themis and Father Zeus, O Eunomia, Dike, and Eirene of the many blessings, holy spirits of the flowering meadow, beautiful, many-colored, many-scented, sweet-breathed, always flourishing, draped all in dew-studded dresses, you dance hand-in-hand in a ring. Rejoicing in flowers, you are the companions of blessed Persephone when she is at play, when the Fates and the Graces lead her in a spiralling dance toward the light, to the delight of Zeus and Mother Demter who makes the fruit grow. Come to the new initiates at our pious rites, and bring with you flawless seasons full of good fruit.

ORPHIC HYMN TO THE NYMPHS

Anonymous (ca. 200 CE?), translated by B. Nolan

Demeter and Persephone were the essential givers of plant and animal life to the ancient Greeks, but they were not the only givers. Here the nymphs are also celebrated for their ability to nourish plants and animals.

They are called "Nysian" because they were believed to spend time on Mount Nysa.

Nymphs, daughters of great-souled Ocean, in the watery caverns of the earth you make your homes. By hidden pathways, merry earthly nurses of Bacchus, pure ones, you grow fruit in meadows and move along hidden paths. You love caves and visit springs, flying, airy, pouring out dew. Sometimes seen, sometimes unseen, you haunt the valleys, crowned with flowers, dancing with Pan upon mountains, harmonious, skipping down the rocks. Leaf-clad, perfumed maidens of the fields and the forests and the streams, dressed in white, sweet-breathed friends of shepherds, rich in fruit and pastures; the animals adore you. Tender you may be, but you love the frost; you make all things grow and you feed the multitudes. Hamadryad maidens, playful, walking the watery paths, Nysian, frenzied by the companionship of Bacchus and Demeter, you bring grace to humankind. Come to this sacred rite with happiness, and pour a stream of life-giving rain down upon us during the fertile seasons.

From "For the Vanadís"

Gudrun of Mimirsbrunnr (twenty-first century)

Here Freya, the Norse goddess of love and fertility, is called upon to renew human life even as she awakens the earth.

Hail to the Spring Maiden
on the Equinox morning
as she rises and walks the fields;
flowers bloom in her footsteps
and the earth wakes anew.
O Freya snowdrop-bedecked,
wake my life anew and teach me wonder,
for I am dull and grey with years of burdens
and I have forgotten the mystery of the rising seed.

On Lady Day

Gwydion Pendderwen (1946–1982)

Around the time of the equinox, Catholics celebrate Lady Day, a feast day of the Blessed Mother. This may well be a remnant of Pagan practices, and some modern Pagans have decided to incorporate the day back into Paganism. This is a lovely example of reclamation, written by Gwydion Pendderwen (Thomas deLong), who is probably best known as the author and performer of the songs on the 1970s LP Songs for the Old Religion. *He was a student of Victor Anderson and a member of the Church of All Worlds.*

When the silent barren winter
Casts its frozen pall
Over trees and grassy hilltops,
Rivers large and small,
Suddenly, the snow stops falling,
And from out of the cold
Comes the form of a fairy maiden
As the legends foretold.

Lady Day, on quiet Lady Day,
With blossoms in her hair
Comes the form of a fairy maiden
Leaving green everywhere.

Lo, the mighty fairy maiden
Rises from the earth.
Dismal winter, gently thawing,
Heralds her rebirth.
Softly now, the budding branches
Offer new life for old,
And in splendor the holy maiden
Lets her mantle unfold.

Lady Day, on quiet Lady Day
The world is poised for spring
And in splendor the holy maiden
Lifts her silvery wing.

Treading softly through the valley
Across the snowy field,
She has brought the tufts of grass
Which every step revealed.
Quietly, she bares her bosom
Where the fountain once played
And in answer the waters come forth
To the will of the Maid.

Lady day, on quiet lady day,
Her smile has thawed the spring
And in answer the waters come forth
To feed the winter-born King.

ORPHIC HYMN TO ADONIS

Anonymous (ca. 200 CE), translated by B. Nolan

Adonis was originally a Lebanese vegetation god who was adopted by the Greeks; he is the equivalent of the Sumerian Tammuz, consort of the goddess Inanna. In the Greek tradition he was raised by the goddess Persephone after his mother was turned into a myrrh tree, and when he grew up he became the lover of Aphrodite. He angered the goddess Artemis, however, by his hubris, so she sent a boar to gore him to death. He died in Aphrodite's arms, and his blood became the anemone, or wind-flower. As a god of plants, he is called on here to bring fertility.

The meaning of Eubouleus *is unclear here, but, since the Greek means "sage advice," it is probably meant as an epithet of Adonis. In other hymns, Eubouleus seems to refer to Iacchos or Dionysus, and he may once have been a separate god.*

Hear my prayer, many-named Lord, great one, crowned with beautiful locks, solitary, and celebrated in song: Eubouleus, many-formed, virgin, youthful, always flourishing. O Adonis, you die, and then burst forth again as the year turns to spring. Two-horned, most-loved, most-mourned, beautiful one, happy hunter, thick-haired god, dear flower, seed of love, beloved of Aphrodite, born in the bed of Persephone of the charming locks. You have dwelt in the depths of Tartarus; lift your flowering head toward Olympus. Come to us, blessed one, bringing the earth's bounty to your initiates.

LATE MARCH/EARLY APRIL: THE CITY DIONYSIA

Dionysus (known to the Romans as Bacchus), the god of ecstasy, madness, wine, and fertility, is a singular god, one in whom all contradictions meet. The ancient Greeks perceived him as a foreign deity, but he was worshipped throughout Greece. In his honor, Greek women, many of whom lived in purdah under the complete control of their male relatives, took to the hills for days to celebrate his rites alone without male chaperonage; he was born from both his mother and his father and has both male and female qualities; he is described as a beardless youth, barely more than a child, but is capable of spectacular and violent retribution when attacked. Then, too, he is the only Pagan god who demands worship (see *The Bacchae* of Euripides), though of course he does not demand exclusive homage. Perhaps it would be appropriate to think of him as the personification of the life-force itself: universal, intoxicating, occasionally terrible, and utterly unstoppable.

The ancients held two large festivals in honor of Dionysus: the City Dionysia and the Country Dionysia. The City Dionysia was a movable feast heralding the beginning of spring. Since Dionysus is also the god of the theater, part of the celebrations included competitive performances of those plays which have come down to us as the foundations of Western literature: *Oedipus Rex, Antigone, The Trojan Women,* and so on. Sometimes Dionysus himself is a character in these plays and sometimes not, but all were performed in his honor. Selections from many of these plays are included here, for nothing could be more fitting for worship of the god. And even outside the theater, classical literature is full of paeans to him and his attributes—particularly as the god of ecstasy and freedom—have inspired poets throughout the ages, resulting in a rich body of literature.

Dionysus is also a god with a multitude of epithets: Bromios (Roarer), Thyoneus (Inspired), Eleuthereus (Liberator), Lyaeus (Deliverer), Lenaeus (of the Wine-Press), Nysaeus (of Nysa), Taurus (Bull), and many others—which regularly appear in his paeans.

DIONYSUS, THE GIVER OF THE GRAPE

Meleager of Gadara (first century BCE), translated by W. R. Paton

Meleager was a poet who lived in what is now Jordan. Euvoi! is a Greek cry of ecstasy. The reference to bees coming from a bull's carcass reflects the ancient belief in spontaneous generation. Zephyr is the god of the gentle west wind.

Windy winter has left the skies, and the purple season of flowery spring smiles. The dark earth garlands herself in green herbage, and the plants bursting into leaf wave their newborn tresses. The meadows, drinking the nourishing dew of dawn, laugh as the roses open. The shepherd on the hills delights to play shrilly on the pipes, and the goatherd joys in his white kids. Already the mariners sail over the broad billows, their sails bellied by the kindly Zephyr. Already, crowning their heads with the bloom of berried ivy, men cry *Euvoi!* to Dionysus the giver of the grape. The bees that the bull's carcass generates take thought of their artful labours, and seated on the hive they build the fresh white loveliness of their many-celled comb. The races of birds sing loud everywhere: the kingfishers by the waves, the swallows round the house, the swan by the river's brink, the nightingale in the grove. If the foliage of plants rejoices, and the earth flourishes, and the shepherd pipes, and the fleecy flocks disport themselves, and sailors sail, and Dionysus dances, and the birds sing, and the bees bring forth, how should a singer too not sing beautifully in the spring?

FROM "THE PRAISE OF DIONYSUS"

Sir Edmund William Gosse (1849–1928)

Dionysus was often depicted riding on the back of a panther (perhaps as a nod to his magnificent and occasionally dangerous nature) and he can sometimes be seen playing the lyre in ancient art.

But oh! within the heart of this great flight,
Whose ivory arms hold up the golden lyre?
What form is this of more than mortal height?
What matchless beauty, what inspired ire!
The brindled panthers know the prize they bear,
And harmonise their steps with stately care;
Bent to the morning, like a living rose,
The immortal splendor of his face he shows,
And where he glances, leaf and flower and wing
Tremble with rapture, stirred in their repose,
And deathless praises to the vine-god sing.

Prince of the flute and ivy, all thy foes
Record the bounty that thy grace bestows,
But we, thy servants, to thy glory cling,
And with no frigid lips our songs compose,
And deathless praises to the vine-god sing.

"O YOU OF MANY NAMES" FROM *ANTIGONE*

Sophocles (ca. 497–406 BCE), translated by R. C. Jebb

Antigone *is one of the great tragedies of the world, the enduring story of a woman who chose to defy a king and die for the sake of her principles. In this excerpt, the "Cadmeian bride" is Semele, mother of Dionysus; "Eleusinian Deo" is Demeter, and the Bacchants and Thyiads are female followers of Dionysus. The nymphs are "Corycian" because the Corycian Cave on Mount Parnassus is sacred to them.*

Thebes (the Greek one, not the Egyptian one) was the birthplace of Dionysus or Iacchus. The city is supposed to have been founded by the legendary king Cadmus, who killed a dragon and under instructions from Athena, sowed its teeth in the ground. From these teeth the Theban people were said to have sprung.

O you of many names, glory of the Cadmeian bride, offspring of loud-thundering Zeus! you who watch over famed Italia, and reign, where all guests are welcomed, in the sheltered plain of Eleusinian Deo! O Bacchus, dweller in Thebes, metropolis of Bacchants, by the softly-gliding stream of Ismenus, on the soil where the fierce dragon's teeth were sown!

You have been seen where torch-flames glare through smoke, above the crests of the twin peaks, where move the Corycian nymphs, your votaries, hard by Castalia's stream.

You come from the ivy-mantled slopes of Nysa's hills, and from the shore green with many-clustered vines, while your name is lifted up on strains of more than mortal power....

O you with whom the stars rejoice as they move, the stars whose breath is fire; O master of the voices of the night; son begotten of Zeus; appear, O king, with thine attendant Thyiads, who in night-long frenzy dance before you, the giver of good gifts, Iacchus!

FROM *THE BRIDE OF DIONYSUS*

R. C. Trevelyan (1872–1951)

Dithyrambos is a name for a hymn in honor of Dionysus; it is also an epithet of the god, along with Thyoneus. *Tartarus is the Underworld.*

Our Thyoneus, the hope and the delight
Of deities and mortals, yea, our Evius, the Lord
Of the Vine of Life, whose roots,
Deep as Tartarus entwined,
From the strong heart of the Earth draw their might:
And abroad o'er all the world to the starry Heavens above
Are its leaves and tendrils curled, and from its fruits
He presseth forth his wine into the bowl
Of rapture and remembrance, that the soul of all mankind
From sorrow and from death setteth loose.
Dithyrambos, son of Zeus!

"NOW CALL THE GOD" FROM *THE FROGS*

Aristophanes (ca. 446–ca. 386),
translated by Gilbert Murray, modernized by B. Nolan

Iacchus was originally a separate, minor god associated with the Eleusinian Mysteries, but he was identified with Dionysus/Baccus by the fifth century BCE. Here he is seen welcoming the poorest of his followers to his worship. "The Maiden" is a title of Persephone.

Now call the God of blooming mien;
Raise the mystic chorus:
Our comrade he and guide unseen,
With us and before us.

Iacchus high in glory, you whose day
Of all is merriest, hither, help our play;
Show, as we throne you at your Maiden's side,
How light to you are our long leagues of way.
Iacchus, happy dancer, be our guide.

Yourself, that poorest men your joy should share,
Did rend your robe, your royal sandal tear,
That feet unshod might dance, and robes rent wide
Wave in your revel with no after care.
Iacchus, happy dancer, be our guide

ORPHIC HYMN TO DIONYSUS LICNITUS

Anonymous (ca. 200 CE), translated by Thomas Taylor

Liknitan seems to mean something like "of the winnowing basket." Dionysus's mortal mother, Semele, gave birth to him prematurely when she was consumed by lightning after gazing on the face of her divine lover; Zeus saved the incomplete infant and nurtured him until the term of his development was complete. After his second birth from the thigh of his father, Dionysus was put in a winnowing basket and taken away to be reared by nymphs.

Liknitan Bacchus, bearer of the vine,
You I invoke to bless these rites divine:
Florid and gay, of nymphs the blossom bright,
And of fair Venus, Goddess of delight,
'Tis your mad footsteps with mad nymphs to beat,

Dancing through groves with lightly leaping feet:
From Jove's high counsels nursed by Proserpine,
And born the dread of all the powers divine:
Come, blessed power, regard thy suppliant's voice,
Propitious come, and in these rites rejoice.

FROM "HYMN TO DIONYSUS"

Lady Margaret Sackville (1881–1963)

Lady Margaret Sackville was a poet, feminist, and ardent campaigner against World War I. Here she suggests that Dionysus is the antidote for the poison of an unfulfilling life.

How in our hearts is madness brought to birth,
O Dionysus! We who all day long
Spun out our lives like a monotonous song,
Holding our tedious hours of little worth,
Now gaining from our servitude reprieve,
Rise from moldering feasts of pleasure and grief,
By strange and unfamiliar voices led;
Casting our old lives, like garments shed,
Far from us, and all chains that mar and bind. …

CHORUS FROM *THE FROGS*

Aristophanes (ca. 446–ca. 386), translated by Benjamin Rogers

Another prayer to Dionysus as Iacchus.

Come, arise, from sleep awaking,
Come the fiery torches shaking,
O Iacchus! O Iacchus!
Morning Star that shinest nightly.
Lo, the mead is blazing brightly,
Age forgets its years and sadness,
Agèd knees curvet for gladness,
Lift thy flashing torches o'er us,
Marshal all thy blameless train,
Lead, O, lead the way before us. …

BACCHUS

André Chénier (1762–1794), translated by B. Nolan

"Minos' daughter" is Ariadne, princess of Crete, whom Dionysus rescued after the hero Theseus abandoned her on the shore of Naxos. Thyoneus, Evian, Iacchus, Evius, and Lenaeus are epithets of the god. Sylvanus is the god of the woods, while Silenus is the wine-loving tutor of Dionysus.

Come O divine Bacchus, O youthful Thyoneus,
O Dionysus, Evius, Iacchus and Lenaeus,
Come as you appeared in the deserts of Naxos
When your voice spoke soothingly to Minos' daughter. . . .
Garlanded with grape-studded vines,
The tiger with its flanks criss-crossed with stripes,
And the starry lynx, the feral panther,
Wandered with you in your course along the shore.
Gold glittered everywhere on the axles of your chariots.
The Maenads ran with their long, entangled hair
And sang Evius, Bacchus, and Thyoneus,
And Dionysus, Iacchus and Lenaeus,
And all the beautiful names Greece had for you.
And the voice of the rocks repeated their songs,
And the raucous drum, the sonorous cymbals,
The tortuous oboes, and the double rattlesnakes
Who waved in the dance along your boisterous way.
The faun, the satyr and the young Sylvanus,
Gathered haphazardly around old Silenus,
Who, his cup in hand, from the Indian shore,
Still drunk, still stupefied, tottering,
Rode step by step on his indolent donkey.

CHORUS FROM *THE BACCHAE*

Euripides (480–406 BCE), translated by T. A. Buckley

The Bacchae *won third place in the Dionysia of 405 BCE. It is a strange, beautiful, violent play, full of wonder and terror, as powerful today as it was two thousand four hundred years ago. This excerpt describes the double birth of Dionysus. Bromios is one of the god's many titles. The* bacchae *(sometimes called maenads) are the female followers of Dionysus. Hellas is Greece, while Phrygia is part of what is now Turkey. A thyrsos or thyrsus is the staff borne by the followers of Dionysus.*

Blessed is he who, being fortunate and knowing the rites of the gods, keeps his life pure and has his soul initiated into the Bacchic revels, dancing in inspired frenzy over the mountains with holy purifications, and who, revering the mysteries of great mother Kybele, brandishing the thyrsos, garlanded with ivy, serves Dionysus.

Go, Bacchae, go, Bacchae, escorting the god Bromius, child of a god, from the Phrygian mountains to the broad streets of Hellas—Bromius, whom once, in the compulsion of birth pains, the thunder of Zeus flying upon her, his mother cast from her womb, leaving life by the stroke of a thunderbolt. Immediately Zeus, Kronos' son, received him in a chamber fit for birth, and having covered him in his thigh shut him up with golden clasps, hidden from Hera.

And he brought forth, when the Fates had perfected him, the bull-horned god, and he crowned him with crowns of snakes. . . .

FROM "PAEAN TO DIONYSUS"

Philodamus (ca. 340 BCE), version by B. Nolan

A dithyramb is a song in honor of Dionysus, though it has come to mean any impassioned piece of poetry or music; hence Dionysus is here called Dithyrambus. *Paeans were more traditionally written to honor either Asclepius or Apollo, who both bore the title Paean, but Philodamus is breaking with tradition here to give the title and the lyric poem to Dionysus instead, although he does tie in Apollo and the Muses. This may be because this piece was originally performed at the Oracle of Apollo at Delphi.*

Thyone is another name for Semele, mother of Dionysus. Parnassus was both a mountain sacred to Dionysus and the place where Apollo is said to have given Orpheus his lyre. Pieria is the home of the Muses.

Come, lord Dithyrambus, Bacchus . . . ivy-crowned, Bull, Roarer, come to us in sacred springtime. . . . Thyone of the beautiful children bore you to Zeus, and all the divinities danced on that day. O Paean, come, savior, graciously preserve our city with a blessed time of abundance.

On that day there was frenzied dancing in the famous land of Cadmus ... and there was dancing in Delphi's sacred, blessed precincts, which overflowed with hymns. And you, with your starry form, took your place on the peaks of Parnassus with the women of Delphi. O Paean, come, savior, kindly preserve our city with a blessed time of abundance.

With your night-banishing torch in your hand, in the grip of divine frenzy you went to the flower-studded valleys of Eleusis, where all the people of the whole land ... called upon you as Iacchus. You have given to suffering mortals a haven without pain. O Paean, come, savior, happily preserve our city with a blessed time of abundance.

From rich Eleusis you travelled to the cities of Thessaly and to the sacred bounds of Olympus and famous Pieria, and immediately the maidenly Muses crowned themselves with ivy, dancing in a circle and singing your praises, with Apollo leading them in song. O Paean, come, savior, mercifully preserve our city with a blessed time of abundance.

From *Oedipus Rex*

Lucius Annaeus Seneca (ca. 4 BCE–65 CE), translated by Frank Justus Miller

Seneca was a Romano-Spanish Stoic philosopher and author, and for a time an adviser of Emperor Nero.

 Thebes is the traditional birthplace of Dionysus, but Nysa is the name of the place where he grew up, which is why the thyrsus—his pinecone-studded staff—is called "Nysaean" here. The Araxes is a river in modern Turkey, while the Bears are the constellations Ursa Major and Ursa Minor. Nereus is a god of the sea, while Erebus is the god of shadows and darkness. The "stepdame" of Dionysus is Hera. Lyaeus is another title of Dionysus, meaning "deliverer from care."

 Dionysus's androgynous nature is emphasized in this piece.

Bind your streaming locks with the nodding ivy, and in your soft hands grasp the Nysaean thyrsus!

Bright glory of the sky, come here to the prayers. ... Here turn with favor your virginal face; with your star-bright countenance drive away the clouds, the grim threats of Erebus, and greedy fate. You it becomes to circle your locks with flowers of the springtime, you to cover your head with Tyrian purple turban, or your smooth brow to wreathe with the ivy's clustering berries; now to fling loose thy lawless-streaming locks, again to bind them in a knot close-drawn; in such guise as when, fearing your stepdame's wrath, you did grow to manhood with false-seeming limbs, a pretended maiden with golden ringlets, with saffron girdle binding your garments. So thereafter this soft vesture has pleased you, folds loose hanging and the long-trailing mantle. Seated in your golden chariot, your lions with long trappings covered, all the vast coast of the Orient saw you, both he who drinks of the Ganges and whoever breaks the ice of snowy Araxes.

While the bright stars of the ancient heavens shall run in their courses; while the ocean shall encircle the imprisoned earth with its waters; while the full moon gather again her lost radiance; while the Day Star shall herald the dawn of the morning and while the lofty Bears shall know naught of caerulean Nereus; so long shall we worship the shining face of beauteous Lyaeus.

APRIL

April is a month of goddesses, of Venus, Queen of Love; Cybele, the Great Mother; and Ceres, Nourisher of All. As the sun and the spring begin their show of force, the glorious goddesses who embody all the joyful possibilities of the world are honored in a round of happy celebrations.

APRIL 1: VENERALIA

On the first of April it's time to say, with the poet Rimbaud, "I believe! I believe in you! divine mother,/Sea-born Aphrodite!" The Veneralia was the Roman feast day of Venus, the counterpart of the Greek Aphrodite and the Near Eastern Ishtar, Astarte, and Inanna. But the Veneralia, despite its association with the goddess of love, was not primarily a tribute to unbridled sensuality (that comes later in the year, with the Aphrodisia). Instead, the Veneralia was a time to celebrate Venus as the divine Mother. At this time of year she was also called Venus Verticordia, Venus Heart-Changer, because she had the power to help suppliants change damaging behavior (especially sexual behavior). Now is the time to get rid of that bad relationship or bad habit! Otherwise, offer up prayers to the goddess whose desire is the origin of all life.

FROM "EPITHALAMION"

e e cummings (1894–1962)

Venus is often referred to as Cytherea *or* Cytherean *because, according to legend, she was born from the foam on the shore of Cythera, one of the Ionian islands.*

imperial Cytherea, from frail foam
sprung with irrevocable nakedness
to strike the young world into smoking song—
as the first star perfects the sensual dome
of darkness, and the sweet strong final bird
transcends the sight, O thou to whom belong
the hearts of lovers!—I beseech thee bless
thy suppliant singer and his wandering word.

FROM *THE VIGIL OF VENUS*

Anonymous (second–fifth century CE),
translator unknown (nineteenth century)

This poem was written in honor of the Veneralia; it was composed right on the borderline of the ancient and medieval worlds, when Paganism was still practiced openly by a diminishing minority. Here Venus, the "queen of love and light," is also referred to as Dione, "The Goddess." The "strange horses of the main" are the ocean's waves.

He that never loved before,
Let him love to-morrow!
He that hath loved o'er and o'er,
Let him love to-morrow!

Spring, young Spring, with song and mirth,
Spring is on the newborn earth.
Spring is here, the time of love—
The merry birds pair in the grove,
And the green trees hang their tresses,
Loosened by the rain's caresses.

Tomorrow is the day when first
From the foam-world of Ocean burst,

Like one of his own waves, the bright
Dione, queen of love and light,
Amid the sea-gods' azure train,
'Mid the strange horses of the main.

She it is that lends the hours
Their crimson glow, their jewel-flowers:
At her command the buds are seen,
Where the west-wind's breath hath been,
To swell within their dwellings green. . . .

Venus still through vein and soul
Bids the genial current roll;
Still she guides its secret course
With interpenetrating force,
And breathes through heaven, and earth, and sea,
A reproductive energy.

FROM "VENUS DE MILO"
Leconte de Lisle (1818–1894), translated by B. Nolan

Charles Leconte de Lisle, a prolific nineteenth-century French writer, was a member of the Académie Française.

Hail! At the sight of you the heart beats faster. . . .
You move, naked and proud, and the world skips a beat
And the world is yours, voluptuous Goddess!

FROM *DE RERUM NATURA*
Lucretius (99–ca. 55 BCE),
translated by John Selby Watson, modernized by B. Nolan

Lucretius, the founder of Epicurean philosophy, opened his philosophical poem On the Nature of Things *with this hymn to Venus as the mother of all life.*

Favonius, the equivalent of the Greek Zephyr, is a god of the wind.

O bountiful Venus, mother of the [Romans], delight of gods and men, who, beneath the gliding constellations of heaven, fill with life the ship-bearing sea and the fruit-producing earth...by your influence every kind of living creature is conceived, and, springing forth, hails the light of the sun. You, O goddess, you the winds flee; before you, and your approach, the clouds of heaven disperse; for you the variegated earth puts forth her fragrant flowers; on you the waters of the ocean smile, and the calmed heaven beams with effulgent light. For, as soon as the vernal face of days is unveiled, and the genial gale of Favonius exerts its power unconfined, the birds of the air first, O goddess, testify of you and your coming, smitten in heart by your influence. Next, the wild herds bound over the joyous pastures, and swim across the rapid streams. So all kinds of living creatures, captivated by your charms and allurements, eagerly follow you wherever you proceed to lead them....[T]hroughout seas, and mountains, and whelming rivers, and the leafy abodes of birds, and verdant plains, you, infusing balmy love into the breasts of all, cause them eagerly to propagate their races after their kind.

ORPHIC HYMN TO APHRODITE

Anonymous (ca. 200 CE), translated by B. Nolan

Adonis is a dying god, the personification of love and beauty, who came to Greece from what is now Lebanon. He is the beloved of Aphrodite. The Loves are the little winged gods who follow in the train of the goddess.

Heavenly, much-sung Aphrodite, laughter-loving, foam-born, life-giving goddess, you who love the pleasures of the night, venerable, nocturnal, you who make all beings mate, cunning mother of necessity; the whole world exists because of you, you've subdued the universe and rule over all that is in heaven, upon the abundant earth, and in the depths of the sea. O sacred companion of Bacchus, mother of the Loves, you delight in weddings, Persuader of the marriage-bed, and you grant your grace in secret. You are seen and yet invisible, lovely-locked daughter of a kingly father. With a scepter you attend the weddings of the gods, you she-wolf, lover of men and beloved of men, sought-after source of life. Your intoxicating love-spells bind mortals, and ensnare all the beasts in heedless lust. Come, Cyprian goddess, be favorable to us, beautiful queen, whether you are enthroned in heaven, delighting in your beautiful countenance; or dwelling in your palace in Syria, abundant in frankincense; or whether you are driving in your chariot of gold over the plains; or whether you are beside the sacred life-giving river of Egypt; or riding over the ocean waves in your chariot drawn by swans, rejoicing with the sea-creatures as they dance in circles, or playing with the dark-eyed nymphs as they nimbly frolic on the sandy shores. Come, even from Cyprus, land where you were raised, where beautiful maidens and chaste wives sing your praises all year long, as they chant to sweet, sacred Adonis. Come, beloved goddess, with your beautiful form; with a pure heart and holy words I call you.

FROM "ISHTAR"

Alfred Henry Hyatt (1911)

Ishtar is one of the Mesopotamian counterparts of Aphrodite.

Ishtar! more glorious than the stars thine eyes;
Thy voice more sweet than songs of breeze that rise
To fill the night with happy melody;
Come forth, belov'd, and speak thy words to me!

FROM "A HYMN TO APHRODITE"

John Warren, Baron de Tabley (1835–1895), modernized by B. Nolan

Aphrodite Urania means "Heavenly Aphrodite."

Uranian Aphrodite, fair
    From ripples of the ocean spray:
Sweet as the sea-blooms in your hair,
    Rosed with the blush of early day. …
Give us the treasures of your rest;
Take us as children to your breast.

       ****

Yours are the seasons past and dumb,
And yours the unborn years to come.

FROM A HYMN TO APHRODITE

Proclus Lycaeus (410–485 CE), translated by B. Nolan

I sing the famous one, the foam-born one, the magnificent source from which all the divine winged Cupids fly forth, some of them shooting their unearthly arrows at mortal souls, so that, having been struck by the uplifting point of desire, those souls want nothing more than to see the burning palace of Love's mother. … Oh, goddess—because you can hear everything, everywhere—whether you wrap your embrace around lofty heaven, because, as it is said, you give the unending universe its immortal soul, or whether you inhabit the airy place above the edges of the seven planets while you pour forth an uncontrollable power in your train, oh please listen, Lady, and, with your sacred arrows of fire, guide the struggles of my life, taking me away from the cold comfort of base desire.

FROM "THE HIPPOLYTUS OF EURIPIDES"

Hilda Doolittle (1886–1961)

Kupris is a variant of Cypris, *one of the titles of Aphrodite. This excerpt is from a loose translation of Euripides's play* Hippolytus. *Eros is the son of Aphrodite, the equivalent of the Roman Cupid. Helios is the sun.*

Men you strike
and the gods'
dauntless spirits alike,
and Eros helps you, O Kupris,
with wings' swift
interplay of light:
now he flies above earth,
now above sea-crash
and whirl of salt:
he enchants beasts
who dwell in the hills
and shoals in the sea-depth:
he darts gold wings
maddening their spirits:
he charms all born of earth,
(all whom Helios visits,

fiery with light)
and men's hearts:
you alone, Kupris,
creator of all life,
reign absolute.

TO VENUS

Francis Beaumont (1584–1616), John Fletcher (1579–1625)

Beaumont and Fletcher were a team of popular English playwrights during the reign of James I. "The seven" here are the seven heavenly bodies known to the ancients: the Moon, Mercury, Venus, the Sun, Mars, Jupiter, and Saturn.

O divine star of Heaven,
Thou in power above the seven;
Thou, O gentle Queen, that art
Curer of each wounded heart,
Thou the fuel, and the flame;
Thou in heaven, and here, the same;
Thou the wooer, and the wooed;
Thou the hunger, and the food;
Thou the prayer, and the prayed;
Thou what is or shall be said.

INCANTATION TO ISHTAR

Anonymous (ancient Mesopotamia), translated by H. W. F. Saggs

A personal, magical prayer to Ishtar, from ancient Mesopotamia (although the scholar who translated it did not assign it a firm date). Sin is the Mesopotamian god of the moon, Ningal is the goddess of reeds, and Enlil is a storm god, the cognate of Zeus. Shedu and lamassu *are guardian spirits, sometimes depicted as winged bulls with human heads; they are often seen in art from the region.*

O Heroic One, Ishtar; Immaculate One of the goddesses,
Torch of heaven and earth, Radiance of the continents, Goddess Lady-of-Heaven, First-begotten of Sin, Firstborn of Ningal,

Twin-sister of … the hero Shamash [the Sun god];

O Ishtar, you are Anu [the supreme god], you rule the heavens;

With Enlil the Counsellor you advise mankind; …

Where conversation takes place, you, like Shamash, are paying attention, …

You alter the Fates, and an ill event becomes good; …

Before you is a *shedu*, behind you a *lamassu*;

At your right is Justice, at your left Goodness,

Fixed on your head are Audience, Favor, Peace,

Your sides are encompassed with Life and Wellbeing;

How good it is to pray to you, how blessed to be heard by you!

Your glance is Audience, your utterance is Light.

Have pity on me, Ishtar! Ordain my prospering! …

I have sought your brightness; may my face be bright.

I have turned to your dominion; may it be life and wellbeing for me. …

Lengthen my days, bestow life!

Let me live, let me be well, let me proclaim your divinity.

Let me achieve what I desire. …

(At the end of the prayer comes the instruction:

You shall set a censer with juniper-wood before Ishtar: you shall pour a gruel-libation, you shall recite the 'hand-raising' three times, you shall do obeisance.)

ORPHIC HYMN TO EROS

Anonymous (ca. 200 CE), translated by Thomas Taylor

Eros is the son of Aphrodite. His name means desire, *but here, in keeping with the ancient spirit of the Veneralia, he is called upon here to keep "mad desires" at bay.*

   Tartarus is a place of punishment in the Greek afterlife.

I call great Eros, source of sweet delight,

holy and pure, and lovely to the sight;

Darting, and winged, impetuous fierce desire,

with Gods and mortals playing, wandering fire:

Cautious, and two-fold, keeper of the keys

of heaven and earth, the air, and spreading seas;

Of all that Demeter's fertile realms contains,

by which the all-parent Goddess life sustains,
Or dismal Tartarus is doomed to keep,
widely extended, or the sounding, deep;
For you, all Nature's various realms obey,
who rules alone, with universal sway.
Come, blessed power, regard these mystic fires,
and far avert unlawful mad desires.

IN PRAISE OF APHRODITE

Philippus of Thessalonica (first century CE), translated by B. Nolan

Paphos is a city on the island of Cyprus, believed to be the birthplace of Aphrodite; therefore, she is sometimes referred to as "Paphian."

Greetings, Paphian goddess! All mortals, who live but for a moment, forever honor your power, your deathless beauty, and your sensual majesty, through words and works of beauty. In all times and to everyone you make known your renown.

MUSE OF THE GOLDEN THRONE

Helen Bantock (1868–1961)

These verses, which were set to music by British composer Granville Bantock, are an English tribute to the poetry of Sappho, the ancient Greek poet. Helen Bantock was the composer's wife, who often wrote the texts her husband set to music.

Muse of the golden throne, O raise that strain,
Which once thou used to sweetly sing:
Come, Cyprian Goddess, and in cups of gold
Pour forth thy nectar of delight,
Thou and thy servant, Love!

Come, rosy-armed, pure Graces,
sweet-voiced maidens, come
With winged feet, dance round the altar fair,
Trampling the fine soft bloom of the grass.

Hither now, Muses, hither, come!

FROM A HYMN TO INANA

Enheduanna (ca. 2334–2154 BCE) , translated by J. A. Black, G. Cunningham,
J. Ebeling, E. Flückiger-Hawker, E. Robson, J. Taylor, and G. Zólyomi

*Enheduanna, daughter of King Sargon of Akkad, lived about four thousand five hundred years ago
in what is now Iraq. A priestess of the goddess Inanna, she is the world's first named poet. Her most
famous work is her long hymn to Inanna or Inana, from which the excerpts below are taken.*

*The Anuna are a powerful group of Mesopotamian deities. An is the sky god, Sin is the moon
god, and Enlil is the storm god.*

The great-hearted mistress, the impetuous lady, proud among the Anuna gods and preeminent in all lands, the great daughter of Sin, exalted among the Great Princes, the magnificent lady who gathers up the divine powers of heaven and earth and rivals great An,
is mightiest among the great gods—she makes their verdicts final. The Anuna gods crawl
before her august word whose course she does not let An know; he dares not proceed
against her command.

At her loud cries, the gods of the Land become scared. Her roaring makes the Anuna
gods tremble like a solitary reed. At her rumbling, they hide all together. Without Inanna
great An makes no decisions, and Enlil determines no destinies. Who opposes the mistress who raises her head and is supreme over the mountains? She can make cities become
ruin mounds and haunted places, and shrines become waste land. ... She stirs confusion
and chaos against those who are disobedient to her, speeding carnage and inciting the
devastating flood, clothed in terrifying radiance. ... Clothed in a furious storm, a whirl-
wind ... Inanna sits on harnessed lions, she cuts to pieces him who shows no respect ... the
mistress is a great bull trusting in its strength; no one dares turn against her. ... The mistress, a leopard among the Anuna gods, full of pride, has been given authority.

You ride on seven great beasts as you come forth from heaven. ... The great gods kissed
the earth and prostrated themselves. The high mountain land, the land of cornelian and
lapis lazuli, bowed down before you. ... Without you no destiny at all is determined, no
clever counsel is granted favor. To run, to escape, to quiet and to pacify are yours, Inana.
To rove around, to rush, to rise up, to fall down ... are yours, Inana. To open up roads and
paths, a place of peace for the journey, a companion for the weak, are yours, Inana. To
keep paths and ways in good order, to shatter earth and to make it firm are yours, Inana.
To destroy, to build up, to tear out and to settle are yours, Inana. To turn a man into a

woman and a woman into a man are yours, Inana. Desirability and arousal, goods and property are yours, Inana. Gain, profit, great wealth and greater wealth are yours, Inana. Gaining wealth and … financial loss and reduced wealth are yours, Inana. … Assigning virility, dignity, guardian angels, protective deities and cult centres are yours, Inana … mercy and pity are yours, Inana. To cause the … illnesses are yours, Inana. Neglect and care, raising and bowing down are yours, Inanna. To build a house, to create a woman's chamber, to possess implements, to kiss a child's lips are yours, Inanna. To run, to race, to desire and to succeed are yours, Inana. To interchange the brute and the strong and the weak and the powerless is yours, Inana. To interchange the heights and valleys … is yours, Inanna. To give the crown, the throne and the royal sceptre is yours, Inanna. To gather the dispersed people and restore them to their homes, are yours, Inanna.

You are the lady of heaven and earth! … You alone are magnificent. You are the great cow among the gods of heaven and earth, as many as there are. When you raise your eyes they pay heed to you, they wait for your word. The Anuna gods stand praying in the place where you dwell. Great awesomeness, glory. … May your praise not cease! Where is your name not magnificent?

Once you have made a decision …, it cannot be changed in heaven and earth. Once you have specified approval of a place, it experiences no destruction. Once you have specified destruction for a place, it experiences no approval.

Your divinity shines in the pure heavens. … Your torch lights up the corners of heaven, turning darkness into light. … You exercise full ladyship over heaven and earth; you hold everything in your hand. Mistress, you are magnificent, no one can walk before you. You dwell with great An in the holy resting-place. … You are magnificent, your name is praised, you alone are magnificent!

FROM A HOMERIC HYMN TO APHRODITE

Anonymous (700–500 BCE), translated by Hugh G. Evelyn-White

Orichalc is an old term for a shining metal, probably an alloy of brass. Cytherea is, of course, a title of Aphrodite.

I will sing of stately Aphrodite, gold-crowned and beautiful, whose dominion is the walled cities of all sea-set Cyprus. There the moist breath of the western wind wafted her over the waves of the loud-moaning sea in soft foam, and there the gold-filleted Hours welcomed her joyously. They clothed her with heavenly garments: on her head they put a fine, well-wrought crown of gold, and in her pierced ears they hung ornaments of orichalc and precious gold, and adorned her with golden necklaces over her soft neck and snow-white breasts, jewels which the gold-filleted Hours wear themselves whenever they go to their father's house to join the lovely dances of the gods. And when they had fully decked her, they brought her to the gods, who welcomed her when they saw her, giving her their hands. Each one of them prayed that he might lead her home to be his wedded wife, so greatly were they amazed at the beauty of violet-crowned Cytherea.

Hail, sweetly-winning, coy-eyed goddess!

STANZAS FROM "A HYMN TO ASTARTE"

John Warren, Baron de Tabley (1835–1895)

Here Astarte, as Ishtar was known among the Canaanites, is associated, like Venus, with the morning star, "Time's early born daughter." Quick is used here in the archaic sense of "living." Rood means a small piece of land, less than half an acre.

Empress of earth, and queen
    Of cloud: Time's early born
Daughter, enthroned between
    Grey Sleep and emerald Morn;
    Ruler of us who fade:
    God, of the gods obeyed!

Queen of the roses' wood
    Where blighted lovers weep:
Queen of the cypress rood
    Where bygone lovers sleep.
    The quick thy slaves abide:
    The dead thy servants died.

APRIL 4: MEGALESIA

Cybele, the Great Mother or Mother of the Gods, originally hails from Phrygia, in what is now Turkey. The Romans began to worship her in 205 BCE, after being commanded to do so by a prophecy from the Sibyl at the Oracle of Apollo at Dardania. Cybele's statue was brought into Rome with much fanfare in early April of that year, and the Megalesia commemorates this event. Along with her worship, that of her son Corybas and her husband/son Attis also entered into Rome.

Cybele, as the primal mother and nature goddess, is the cognate of the Greek Rhea and the Roman goddess Ops (Plenty). In antiquity, her retinue included her (probably transgender) priests, the *galli*, who dressed as women and frequently practiced self-castration.

The ancient Megalesia was celebrated with a procession, horse racing and theatrical performances during the day, while in the evening dinner parties would be held in honor of the goddess—a tradition in which any modern Pagan can participate.

FROM "CYBELE"

Leconte de Lisle (1818–1894), translated by B. Nolan

The Korybantes or Corybantes were the sons of the Muses and followers of Cybele; they were known for their dances and the armor they wore when performing them. The Pactolus is a river in what is now Turkey.

Along the sounding shores of the azure seas,
By the great woods full of pious cries,
You pass slowly by, ancient Mother of the Gods,
On the back of savage lions.
Furious with foam and bathed in sweat
The Nymphes of Ida, the holy Korybantes,
Tear their falling clothes
And dance with frantic leaps. …

They run to you who were born first,
who preside over a thousand weddings!
Majestic maiden, wonder-worker,
Who give your gifts to both gods and men,
You give the divine milk from which life flows,
Glowing dew in which the universe swims,
Spilling on the ravished land
Splendid summers and winters!

Cybele, seated in the immovable center of the world,
Queen of the kindly eyes, surrounded by great towers,
Hail, source of goodness and long life.
Cybele, O fertile nurse!
In the breast of the golden Pactolus
Where your palaces are, Goddess!
You give strength and wisdom to mortals,
You breathe the incense of the favorite temple.
Shaking from your dress a cloud of roses,
In the splendid Aethyr without end
You unroll a chorus of things
Obedient to the divine order!

Under the yoke of their Destinies,
All the wan humans through the fleeting years
Cry out to you under the weight of their burdens;
And in their wounded hearts, O Wise One, you mix in
With the dark fears of their travails
The immortal Hopes:
The world clings, Goddess, to your breasts,
And from the fold of your dress it dreams of new days.

FROM *HYMN TO THE MOTHER OF THE GODS*

Julian (331–363 CE), translated by Wilmer Cave Wright; modernized by B. Nolan

Flavius Claudius Julianus Augustus, better known as Julian the Apostate, was the last Pagan emperor of Rome. Raised a Christian, he converted to Paganism at the age of twenty. During his brief, eighteen-month reign, he fought to reestablish Paganism as the dominant religion of the Roman Empire. This effort was cut short when, at the age of thirty-two, he died of wounds sustained in battle. The Christian legend that he was assassinated by friendly fire from one of his own Christian soldiers is unfounded, as is the legend that he acknowledged Christ's triumph in his final moments: he was fatally wounded by a Persian soldier, and died a believing Pagan.

Attis is the son and husband of Cybele.

O Mother of gods and men, you that are the assessor of Zeus and share his throne, O source of the intellectual gods. ... O life-giving goddess that are the counsel and the providence and the creator of our souls; O you that love great Dionysus, and saved Attis when exposed at birth, and led him back when he had descended into the cave of the nymph; O you that give all good things to the intellectual gods and fill with all things this sensible world, and with all the rest give us all things good! Grant to all men happiness, and that highest happiness of all, the knowledge of the gods. ... And for myself, grant me as fruit of my worship of you that I may have true knowledge in the doctrines about the gods. Make me perfect in theurgy. And in all that I undertake ... grant me virtue and good fortune, and that the close of my life may be painless and glorious, in the good hope that it is to you, the gods, that I journey!

FROM "SUN AND FLESH (CREDO IN UNAM)"
Arthur Rimbaud (1854–1891), translated by B. Nolan

I long for the time of great Cybele,
Who was said to travel, gigantic and beautiful,
In a great brazen chariot, through magnificent cities;
Her two breasts poured, in endless abundance,
The pure streams of everlasting life.
Mankind suckled, happy, at her blessed nipple,
Like a small child, playing on her knees.
—Because he was strong, Man was chaste and gentle.

ORPHIC HYMN TO THE MOTHER OF THE GODS
Anonymous (ca. 200 CE), translated by Asphodel P. Long

Here Cybele is equated with Hestia or Vesta, the goddess of the hearth, the home, and the state.

Asphodel P. Long, author of In a Chariot Drawn by Lions, *was an influential member of the Goddess movement in Great Britain in the 1970s.*

Divinely honored, mother of the deathless gods, nurse of all,
Look in our direction; accomplishing Goddess, thou Lady, be with us.
Your fast-running chariot is drawn by bull-killing lions.
You carry the scepter of common, the famous axis of the sky, thou, many-named, majestic.
Your throne is in the center of the world, and therefore
Yours is the earth, gently granting nourishment to mortals.
From you the race of immortals and mortals poured out.

From you grew mighty rivers and all the oceans.

Once you were called Hestia, now we name you Giver of Prosperity

Because you graciously provide all good things to mortals.

Attend our Mysteries, Lady who loves the drumbeat.

All-subduer, Phrygian, Savior, Bedfellow of time,

Celestial, ancient, life-gathering, frenzy-loving.

Come in joy, Agreeable one, to our holy celebrations.

FROM *DE RERUM NATURA*

Lucretius (99–ca. 55 BCE), translated by John Selby Watson, modernized by B. Nolan

Here the Curetes or Kouretes, whom we met during Mars's birthday in March, are described as followers of the great Mother Goddess. They are Dictaean *because they helped hide the infant Zeus, or Jupiter, in the Dictaean Cave in order to keep him safe from his murderous father Saturn. The Curetes are said to have covered his cries with the clash of their bronze—or* brazen—*weapons.*

Cybele's "mural crown" represented a tower, or city walls. She is called "Idaean" because she was closely associated with Mount Ida in modern Turkey.

…[T]he earth alone [Cybele] is called the great mother of the gods, and mother of beasts, and parent of the human race.

The old and learned poets of the Greeks sang that she, in her seat on her chariot, drives two lions yoked together; signifying that the vast earth hangs in the open space of the air, and that one earth cannot stand upon another earth. They added the lions, because any offspring, however wild, ought to be softened, when influenced by the good offices of parents. And they surrounded the top of her head with a mural crown, because the earth, fortified in lofty places, sustains cities; distinguished with which decoration the image of the divine mother is borne, spreading terror through the wide world. Her various nations, according to the ancient practice of their worship, call the Idæan mother, and assign her bands of Phrygians as attendants, because they say that from those parts corn first began to be produced, and from there was diffused over the globe of the earth. …

As soon, therefore, as, riding through great cities, she … bestows a silent blessing on mortals, they strew the whole course of the road with brass and silver, enriching her with munificent contributions; while they diffuse a shower of roses, overshadowing the mother and her troop of attendants. Here the armed band, whom the Greeks call by the name of Phrygian Curetes, dance round vigorously with ropes, and leap about to their tune, streaming with blood. Shaking the terrible crests on their heads as they nod, they represent the Dictaean Curetes, who are formerly said, in Crete, to have concealed that famous infant-cry of Jupiter, when the armed youths, in a swift dance around the child, struck, in tune, their brazen shields with their brazen spears, lest Saturn, having got possession of him, should devour him, and cause an eternal wound in the heart of his mother. Either for this reason, therefore, armed men accompany the great mother; or else because the priests thus signify that the goddess admonishes men to be willing to defend the land of their country with arms and valor, and to prepare themselves to be a protection and honor to their parents.

FROM "APOLLO"

Eugene Lee-Hamilton (1805–1907)

In this prayer, a reminder that communion with the gods is never free from danger.

I come, I come,
O Cybele, great Cybele, that hast
Thy chief throne here, I come to thee at last!
From my far home
I bring at last to thy deep rustling grove
The wild pent fire that in my bosom strove;
I come to lift thy praise to heaven's dome;
Perchance to die, on tasting thy dread love.

CHORUS FROM *PHILOCTETES*

Sophocles (ca. 497/6–406/5 BCE), translated by Lewis Campbell

The Mother referred to here is Cybele, whose chariot is drawn by a team of lions; she is often equated with Rhea, the mother of Zeus.

Mother of mightiest Zeus,
Feeder of all that live,
Who from thy mountainous breast
Rivers of gold dost give!
… Thou, whom bull-slaughtering lions yoked bear,
O mighty mother, hear!

LATE APRIL: CEREALIA

The festival of Ceres, the Roman grain goddess and equivalent of Demeter, was celebrated in late April, though the exact date is unknown; modern Pagans could choose any convenient day at this time of year. Traditionally, offerings of grain, salt, milk, honey, wine, and incense were offered to the goddess, and theatrical performances were given.

Ceres has given us the word with which we describe things associated with grain: cereal. And, because of her association with prosperity, the goddess has remained something of a popular icon, at least in America; currently she can be found on the state seals of New Jersey and Virginia, on top of the state capitols of Vermont and Missouri, and on the Chicago Board of Trade Building.

"O CERES AND LIBERA" FROM *AGAINST VERRES*
Cicero (106–43 BCE), translated by C. D. Yonge

Marcus Tullius Cicero was the greatest orator of ancient Rome. A lawyer, he used his verbal gifts to fight his way up from relative obscurity to the highest levels of Roman society; it's no accident that Ciceronian *is a synonym for "eloquent." This prayer to Ceres and Libera, a Roman fertility goddess who was sometimes supposed to be Ceres's daughter, is taken from one of his famous courthouse speeches.*

And you, O Ceres and Libera, whose sacred worship, as the opinions and religions of all men agree, be contained in the most important and most abstruse mysteries; you by whom the principle of life and food, the examples of laws, customs, humanity, and refinement are said to have been given and distributed to nations and to cities … you again and again I appeal to, most holy goddesses … you whose invention and gift of corn, which you have distributed over the whole earth, inspire all nations and all races of men with reverence for your divine power.

THE OAK OF CERES
André Chénier (1762–1794), translated by B. Nolan

The Graeco-French poet André Chénier died by the guillotine in the very last days of the Reign of Terror. Here, however, he writes of a Pagan world far removed from Revolutionary France, where offerings to Ceres—bouquets and crowns—adorn an oak tree that has received her favor.

Let us sing, sitting in the holy woods,
Under this proud oak, favorite of Ceres,
Who far around casts an immense shadow,
You see, hanging from its leaves on all sides,
Crowns and headbands and piled-up bouquets,
Sweet remembrances of wishes by Ceres granted.

In this shade often the woodland nymphs
Come to trace the steps of their light dances;
To measure his trunk and its vast outline,
Their interlaced hands entwine around him:
And with outstretched arms almost twenty dryads
Press against this gnarled trunk, of which Ceres is so proud.

FROM *THE FASTI*

Ovid (43 BCE–17/18 CE), version by B. Nolan

Here the "partners in work" are Ceres and Earth. Darnel is a common name for Eurasian rye-grass, which is not edible. There was an ancient belief that before Ceres gave the gift of grain to humankind, acorns were our primary food. (Though edible, acorns must be very carefully prepared to remove potentially lethal toxins.)

Partners in work, you who, in the distant past, replaced the acorns of the oak with better food, please grant the wishes of the farmers with abundant crops, that they may reap the rewards of their labors. Grant the new seeds unhindered growth, and keep the sprouting shoots from being bitten by cold snows. Let the sky be clear and the winds gentle when we sow, but after the seeds are planted let the soft rain fall. Don't let the birds, the pests of farms, destroy the fields of corn with their avaricious flocks. O ants, may you too leave alone the seeds—if you do you will have more loot after the harvest. But for now let no mildew afflict the growing plants nor bad weather sicken them; may they not dry up nor grow so fast they are choked back by their own exuberance. Let the fields be free from unsightly darnel, and no wild oats grow in tilled fields. Let the farm yield, with great interest, wheat, barley, and spelt. ...

I offer up these prayers for you, farmers, and you should pray, as well. May the two goddesses grant our prayers. ... Peace is the guardian of Ceres, and Ceres is the child of Peace.

FROM "PERSEPHONE"

Edgar Lee Masters (1868–1950)

Best known as the author of the Spoon River Anthology, *Edgar Lee Masters was a Midwestern poet and lawyer. Demeter is the Greek form of Ceres.*

Then dawn came up as fresh as jonquils;
There were blossoms in coverts, fields and hills;
There were songs in the sky;
There were musical tongues in the teeming sea
That chanted hymns to the April morn.
For Demeter walked with Persephone
Over the land of the springing corn,
And men rejoiced, they sang believing
In Earth from Heaven life receiving,
In life that does not die.

TO CERES

Henry James Pye (1744–1813)

A prayer to Ceres and her daughter for protection.

To bright-haired Ceres, and the lovely maid
Proserpina, my votive verse be paid.
List to my song, and with propitious powers
From every hostile inroad guard these towers.

FROM "THREE PRAYERS TO CERES"

Freda Kirchwey (1893–1976)

Here Ceres is asked to give her blessings to lovers in the spring.

Goddess … rapt mistress of the Earth,
Languorous, longing, sweet and full of fire,
Goddess of clinging peace, of passionate mirth,
Yielding, yet ever quickening desire,
Take those to your great heart and soothe and bless

—O Maker of the madness of the Spring—
Who hold the breathless, fainting happiness
That only lovers know and lovers sing.

"CERES' BLESSING" FROM *THE TEMPEST*
William Shakespeare (1564–1616)

Shakespeare, like all other literate people of his day, was well acquainted with classical deities, and in The Tempest *he imagines Ceres blessing a newly married couple.* Foison *is an archaic word for a harvest, while a* garner *is a granary.*

Earth's increase, foison plenty,
Barns and garners never empty,
Vines and clustering bunches growing,
Plants with goodly burthen bowing;
Spring come to you at the farthest
In the very end of harvest!
Scarcity and want shall shun you;
Ceres' blessing so is on you.

FROM "THE COMPLAINT OF CERES"
Friedrich Schiller (1759–1805), translated by B. Nolan

Schiller, best known today for having written the words to Beethoven's "Ode to Joy," here writes from the point of view of Ceres; her "joy and despair" refer to the abduction and release of her daughter. Iris is the goddess of the rainbow, while Aurora is the goddess of the dawn.

Joy to you, children of the reborn fields.
Let your cups overflow with the pure nectar that is the dew.
I will stream rays of light upon you,
I will paint your petals with
The most beautiful colors of Iris' bow,
Like the face of Aurora.
In the bright splendor of spring
And the dying wreath of autumn,
All tender hearts may clearly read
My joy and my despair.

From "Invocation to Ceres"

Herman Charles Merivale (1839–1906)

Goddess of the golden horn,
Plenty's Queen when man was born,
Hear us where we bend the knee
To thine high divinity. …
    Shed thy store o'er field and town,
    Ceres, send thy blessing down.

MAY

May is a season of flowers and fertility—indeed, the month takes its name from the Greek goddess Maia, whose name means "growth." Now the hours of daylight lengthen, carrying with them the promise of a warm and fertile summer, and animal life flourishes. The month begins with the ancient Celtic fertility festival of Bealtaine or Beltane, an extremely popular celebration that lasted, as May Day, long after the arrival of Christianity. Later in the month Maia's trickster son, Hermes or Mercury, is honored during his own holiday, the Mercuralia.

MAY 1: MAY DAY

May Day, known in Irish as *Lá Bealtaine* and in Scottish Gaelic as *Là Bealltainn* (frequently Anglicized as Beltane) is an ancient pan-European agricultural festival, celebrated for thousands of years from Scandinavia to Spain, Ireland to Russia. The holiday survived the Christian conversion, however, and in fact it has been celebrated as a secular festival down to the present day, by Christians and Pagans alike (not to mention Communists, who observe it as International Workers' Day).

In the British Isles, May Day festivities have traditionally included bonfires, maypoles, and songs and dances by mummers, although the purely religious aspects of the holiday have been lost in the mists of history: we do not know for sure which deities were worshipped on this day, or what prayers they were offered. In the classical world, however, the first of May was the day the Romans honored the goddess Maia, mother of Hermes, who gave her name to the month; Maia's holiday came right after the festival of the goddess Flora, deity of flowers, at the very end of April, and the two were eventually conflated.

Here, prayers to Maia and Flora, Celtic deities like the goddess Danu, the Norse goddess Freya, and various other fertility goddesses and gods have been combined to provide prayers for this most far-flung of Pagan holidays.

FROM *A MAY-DAY INTERLUDE*

Gerald Bishop (1904)

On this May-day, (in form we cannot see,)
The Winter God may Northward speeding be,
Driven by the warm breath of the Summer God
Who comes all sweetly clad in palest green.
Let us believe our fathers then were right
And pay them homage due. It may do good,
Secure us from the Winter God's return,
Bring us warm sun, soft rain, and plenteous fruits. …

BELTANE BLESSING

Traditional Scottish, translated by Alexander Carmichael

This traditional Scottish rune, collected in the nineteenth century, keeps to the old Celtic Pagan calendar, asking for blessings "from Hallow Eve (November 1st) to Beltane Eve." (I've added in another line to make the blessing complete throughout the year; it seems clear to me the charm must originally have had something like it.) This is another case where the unnamed "Three" can reasonably be interpreted as the Threefold Goddess. A sheiling is a Scottish mountain pasture.

Bless, O Threefold true and bountiful,
Myself, my spouse, and my children,
My tender children and their beloved mother at their head.
On the fragrant plain, on the gay mountain sheiling,
    On the fragrant plain, on the gay mountain sheiling.
Everything within my dwelling or in my possession,
All kine and crops, all flocks and corn,
From Hallow Eve to Beltane Eve,
[From Beltane Eve to Hallow Eve],
With goodly progress and gentle blessing,
From sea to sea, and every river mouth,
    From wave to wave, and base of waterfall.

FROM "MAY-DAY"

Ralph Waldo Emerson (1803–1882)

For hundreds of years, humans have celebrated May Day by taking to the fields and woods. Up and away!

Where shall we keep the holiday,
And duly greet the entering May?
Too strait and low our cottage doors,
And all unmeet our carpet floors;
Nor spacious court, nor monarch's hall,
Suffice to hold the festival.
Up and away! where haughty woods
Front the liberated floods:
We will climb the broad-backed hills,
Hear the uproar of their joy;
We will mark the leaps and gleams
Of the new-delivered streams,
And the murmuring rivers of sap
Mount in the pipes of the trees,
Giddy with day, to the topmost spire,
Which for a spike of tender green
Bartered its powdery cap;
And the colors of joy in the bird,
And the love in its carol heard,
Frog and lizard in holiday coats,
And turtle brave in his golden spots;
While cheerful cries of crag and plain
Reply to the thunder of river and main.

"COMMAND OF THE SUMMER QUEEN" FROM *A MAY-DAY INTERLUDE*

Gerald Bishop (1904)

Here the Summer Queen—i.e., the goddess of summer—commands us to celebrate her holiday with revelry and greenery.

Good merry folks, in each degree,
Pray you of your jollity,
Bring your gifts to the May Sprite,
Then go dance till morning light.
Feast and revel, fair and free,
Foot it lightly, hearts a-glee,
Carry joy to every one,
Winter's gone, Summer's begun.
Hang the green on every door,
Summer brings you plenty more.
Hang the green on every table,
Hang the green on byre and stable,
Hang the green where'er you go :
Indoors, outdoors, high and low,
Let the Summer sign be seen,
Thus I rule it, Summer's Queen.

PRAYER TO FREYA

Galina Krasskova (twenty-first century)

Freya is the Norse goddess of love, fertility, and beauty—as well as war. She could be honored alongside Aphrodite or Ishtar, as they have many similarities, but May Day is also a suitable time to honor her.

The Vanir *are one of two groups of Norse gods.*

Hail to the Lady of amber.
Hail to the Lady of steel.
Hail to the Lady of passion,
Bringer of luck,

Bestower of wealth.
You are the envy of all the Gods,
the treasure of the nine sacred worlds.

Freya, mighty and magnificent,
We praise Your name this Beltane.
Ignite within us an awareness
of our own creative fire.
Ignite within us a passion,
to burn through the pale shadows of our lives
and find integrity:
in all we do, in all we dream, in all we are.
Bless us, Freya, Lady of the Vanir,
and we shall hail You,
always.

HYMNS TO FREYJA

Rebecca Buchanan (twenty-first century)

Njord is the god of the sea, father of Freya and her brother Frey. Odr is the often-absent husband of Freya. Hildisvini is Freya's boar, Brisingamen is her golden neck-ring, and Valshamr is her cloak of feathers.

I

Sea-Bright daughter of Njord
Flaxen-haired wife of Odr
forever mourning
lashes glittering
with gold-rich tears
wandering mountains
steep shores
dark bogs
wide meadows
ever searching
ever seeking

Weeping Lady
tears the hidden treasure of the world

II

Sea-Bright Goddess
Flaxen hair braided with gold
amber
falcon feathers
Mistress of the Honored Dead
Who chooses heroes
to feast in her many-seated hall
Who rides into battle
on the broad back of Hildisvini
gold-bristled boar
Who parades in glory in her chariot
drawn by great-eared lynxes
Freyja
Great Lady

III

Amber Lady
Bearer of Brisingamen
forged with love and skill
Bearer of Valshamr
cloak of stealth and transformation
Mistress of the Valkyries
chooser of the noble dead
Bountiful Giver
Great Sow
Honored in many lands
by many names
But known by all
as Goddess Most Fair

FROM "FOR THE VANADÍS"

Gudrun of Mimirsbrunnr (twenty-first century)

Vanadís is an epithet of Freya.

Hail to the Laughing Dancer
on Beltane morning
as she weaves the maypole's ribbons
and the wombs of women are filled
as they lie with their loves on the turned earth.
O Freya bright in green and gold
fill me with life like the pealing waterfall,
for I am dull and dry with years of thirsting
and I have forgotten the mystery of the branching trees.

DANA

AE (1867–1935)

Danu or Dana was the mother of the Irish gods, known as the Tuatha Dé Dannan *or Tribe of the Goddess Danu. Little mention of her survives in Irish literature, but she is the Irish version of the ancient Indo-European water goddess Danu, mentioned in the* Rig Veda, *who gave her name to the rivers Danube, Dniester, Don, and Dee, among others.*

Irish Theosophist and mystical poet AE (George William Russell) here writes of Danu as the "mother of all"—which is, of course, exactly what water is.

I am the tender voice calling "Away,"
Whispering between the beatings of the heart,
And inaccessible in dewy eyes
I dwell, and all unkissed on lovely lips,
Lingering between white breasts inviolate,
And fleeting ever from the passionate touch,
I shine afar, till men may not divine
Whether it is the stars or the beloved
They follow with rapt spirit. And I weave
My spells at evening, folding with dim caress,
Aerial arms and twilight dropping hair,

The lonely wanderer by wood or shore,
Till, filled with some deep tenderness, he yields,
Feeling in dreams for the dear mother heart
He knew, ere he forsook the starry way,
And clings there, pillowed far above the smoke
And the dim murmur from the duns of men.
I can enchant the trees and rocks, and fill
The dumb brown lips of earth with mystery,
Make them reveal or hide the god. I breathe
A deeper pity than all love, myself
Mother of all, but without hands to heal:
Too vast and vague, they know me not. But yet,
I am the heartbreak over fallen things,
The sudden gentleness that stays the blow,
And I am in the kiss that foemen give
Pausing in battle, and in the tears that fall
Over the vanquished foe, and in the highest,
Among the Danaan gods, I am the last
Council of mercy in their hearts where they
Mete justice from a thousand starry thrones.

From "The Love-Song of Drostan"

William Sharp (1855–1905)

Another paean to Danu or Dana, from Scotland this time.

In the days of the Great Fires when the hills were aflame,
Aed the Shining God lay by a foamwhite mountain,
The white thigh of moon-crown'd Dana, Beautiful Mother.
And the wind fretted the blue with the tossed curling clouds
Of her tangled hair, and like two flaming stars were her eyes
Torches of sunfire and moonfire: and her vast breasts
Heaved as the sea heaves in the white calms, and the wind of her sighs
Were as the winds of sunrise soaring the peaks of the eagles—
Dana, Mother of the Gods, moon-crowned, sea-shod, wonderful!

THE WIFE OF LLEW

Francis Ledwidge (1887–1917)

According to The Mabinogion, *the medieval Welsh narrative that contains much of what remains of the Welsh mythological cycle, the Welsh goddess Blodeuwedd ("Flower-faced") was made of flowers by the gods Math and Gwydion when they learned that Gwydion's nephew Llew Llaw Gyffes was forbidden to take a wife of any tribe that existed at that time in the world. Irish poet Francis Ledwidge recounts that creation in this short poem, written before his untimely death during World War I.*

Although little of Blodeuwedd's story remains, she was clearly a goddess associated with love, beauty, and fertility—though she does cut down her husband at the turning of the seasons. Here in spring, however, there is no sign of the trouble to come.

And Gwydion said to Math, when it was Spring:
"Come now and let us make a wife for Llew."
And so they broke broad boughs yet moist with dew,
And in a shadow made a magic ring:
They took the violet and the meadow-sweet
To form her pretty face, and for her feet
They built a mound of daisies on a wing,
And for her voice they made a linnet sing
In the wide poppy blowing for her mouth.
And over all they chanted twenty hours.
And Llew came singing from the azure south
And bore away his wife of birds and flowers.

FROM "THE SONG OF BLODEUWEDD ON MAY MORNING"

Hilary Llewellyn-Williams (1984)

And now the goddess speaks in her own voice.

The poet notes that the lines "With calmness, with care/with breast milk, with dew" come from the chanting of Maria Sabina, a Mazatec wise woman.

Skilful woman am I
and dancing woman am I
turning and turning on the green

skin of the dawn fields:
woman of light am I, my morning eyes
too clear, too bright for you.

With calmness, with care,
with breast milk, with dew,
my web I weave
my spell I cast on you.

With calmness, a still point
that the world spins around,
I am pulled up out of the ground
my spell has found you.

Beauty above and below me,
beauty behind me and before me,
beauty surrounds me
and I sound, I resound like a drum.
I am making my magic, my power;
flying woman who soars to the sun
am I, lovely goddess woman
covered in rainbows, in feathers, in flowers.
dark my mind with visions of stars
of the night I have seen, where I have been:
See! I have chosen you.

Strong young man, a man of trees
of river-shadows, of hills, of horns;
all new and secret, my moon-mate,
I await you on the cold breeze,
that brings you to me stumbling warm
from your bed, oh yes, with care
with milk and with dew
I draw you to me on my white thread.

When you hear my voice, my cry,
when you see the oak blossoming

when you feel the owls pass by
fetch your staff and rn from your door—
it is I, woman of flowers, who calls,
who holds wide her wings for you.
with beauty behind, with beauty before;
with calmness, with care
with breast milk, with dew,
this stone I place: I bathe my face
and I wait for you.

GREEN MAN

William Anderson (1935–1997)

The Green Man, who appears throughout the British Isles carved in stone, painted on pub signs, and as a character in mumming, is the spirit of the plants. Here British writer William Anderson gives voice to him.

Like antlers, like veins in the brain, the birches
Mark patterns of mind on the red winter sky;
"I am thought of all plants," says the Green Man,
"I am thought of all plants," says he.
The hungry birds harry the last berries of rowan
But white is her bark in the darkness of rain;
"I rise with the sap," says the Green Man,
"I rise with the sap," says he.
The ashes are clashing their bows like sword-dancers
Their black buds are tracing wild faces in the clouds;
"I come with the wind," says the Green Man.
"I come with the wind," says he.
The alders are rattling as though ready for battle
Guarding the grove where she waits for her lover;
"I burn with desire," says the Green Man,
"I burn with desire," says he.
In and out of the yellowing wands of the willow
The pollen-bright bees are plundering the catkins;

"I am honey of love," says the Green Man,
"I am honey of love," says he.
The hedges of quick are thick will May blossom
As the dancers advance on their leaf-covered king;
"It's off with my head," says the Green Man,
"It's off with my head," says he.
Green Man becomes grown man in flames of the oak
As its crown forms its mask and its leafage his features;
"I speak through the oak," says the Green Man,
"I speak through the oak," says he.
The holly is flowering as hay fields are rolling
Their gleaming long grasses like waves of the sea;
"I shine with the sun," says the Green Man,
"I shine with the sun," says he.
The hazels are rocking the cups with their nuts
As the harvesters shout when the last leaf is cut;
"I swim with the salmon," says the Green Man,
"I swim with the salmon," says he.
The globes of the grapes are robing with bloom
Like the hazes of autumn, like the Milky Way's stardust;
"I am crushed for your drink," says the Green Man,
"I am crushed for your drink," says he.
The aspen drops silver on leaves of earth's salver
And the poplars shed gold on the young ivy flower heads;
"I have paid for your pleasure," says the Green Man,
"I have paid for your pleasure," says he.
The reed beds are flanking in silence the islands
Where meditates Wisdom as she waits and waits;
"I have kept her secret," says the Green Man,
"I have kept her secret," says he.
The bark of the elder makes whistles for children
To call to the deer as they rove over the snow;
"I am born in the dark," says the Green Man,
"I am born in the dark," says he.

FROM "A POET'S CALENDAR"

Henry Wadsworth Longfellow (1807–1882)

The Hesperides is a name given to both the mythical Fortunate Isles and the nymphs that inhabit them.

Hark! The sea-faring wild-fowl loud proclaim
    My coming, and the swarming of the bees.
These are my heralds, and behold! my name
    Is written in blossoms on the hawthorn-trees.
I tell the mariner when to sail the seas;
    I waft o'er all the land from far away
The breath and bloom of the Hesperides,
    My birthplace. I am Maia. I am May.

FRAGMENT OF AN ODE TO MAIA, WRITTEN ON MAY-DAY 1818

John Keats (1795–1821)

Two hundred years ago, the English Romantic poet Keats celebrated May Day by writing this little poem in honor of the goddess Maia. Baiae is a town on the Gulf of Naples.

Mother of Hermes! and still youthful Maia!
    May I sing to thee
As thou wast hymned on the shores of Baiae?
    Or may I woo thee
In earlier Sicilian? or thy smiles
Seek as they once were sought, in Grecian isles,
By bards who died content on pleasant sward,
    Leaving great verse unto a little clan?
O give me their old vigor! and unheard
    Save of the quiet primrose, and the span
        Of heaven, and few ears,
Rounded by thee, my song should die away
        Content as theirs,
Rich in the simple worship of a day.

FROM THE HOMERIC HYMN TO HERMES

Anonymous (ca. 700–500 BCE), translated by Hugh G. Evelyn-White

Maia does not have her own Homeric hymn, but she is remembered in the long hymn honoring her son Hermes.

Hermes, the son of Zeus and Maia … whom Maia bare, the rich-tressed Nymph, when she was joined in love with Zeus—a shy goddess, for she avoided the company of the blessed gods, and lived within a deep, shady cave. There the son of Cronos used to lie with the rich-tressed nymph, unseen by deathless gods and mortal men, at dead of night while sweet sleep should hold white-armed Hera fast. And when the purpose of great Zeus was fulfilled, and the tenth moon with her was fixed in heaven, she was delivered and a notable thing was come to pass. For then she bare a son, of many shifts, blandly cunning, a robber, a cattle driver, a bringer of dreams, a watcher by night, a thief at the gates, one who was soon to show forth wonderful deeds among the deathless gods.

FROM "AN HYMN TO MAY"

William Thompson (1746)

Come, bounteous May! in fullness of thy might
Lead, briskly, on the mirth-infusing hours,
All-recent from the bosom of delight,
With nectar, nurtured, and involved in flowers:
By spring's sweet blush, by nature's teeming womb;
By Hebe's dimply smile, by Flora's bloom,
By Venus' self (for Venus' self demands thee), come!

FROM "ARCADIAN HYMN TO FLORA"

Richard Henry Stoddard (1825–1903)

Flora, the Roman goddess of flowers and spring , needs little introduction to English speakers, since her name is everywhere in our language: flora, floral, florist, and so on. The Romans celebrated her festival in the last days of April, so her worship is a fitting part of the May Day holiday.

O Flora! sweetest Flora, goddess bright,
Impersonation of selectest things,
The soul and spirit of a thousand Springs,

Bodied in all their loveliness and light,

A delicate creation of the mind,

Fashioned in its divinest, daintiest mould,

In the bright age of gold,

Before the world was wholly lost and blind,

But saw and entertained with thankful heart

The gods as guests. ...

MAY 15: MERCURALIA

Midway through the month of May comes the Mercuralia, the festival of Maia's son Mercury, god of communication, commerce, boundaries, theft—and magic. The great trickster of the Western world, Mercury (or Hermes, as the Greeks knew him) is also a benefactor of humankind, giving us the gift of music and guiding the souls of the dead to the Underworld. It's also clear that he, the divine messenger whose winged sandals can carry him around the world in the blink of an eye, is the patron of electricity, the telephone, and the internet, and so perhaps the foremost deity of the modern world.

FROM "VALERIE'S RHYMING INVOCATIONS TO THE FOUR QUARTERS"
Starhawk / Valerie Walker (1979)

This invocation, from the seminal The Spiral Dance: A Rebirth of the Ancient Religion of the Great Goddess (1979), *summons Mercury, the quicksilver messenger, to guard the eastern quarter of the circle. It can also be used as a stand-alone prayer.*

Quicksilver messenger

Master of the crossroads

Springtime step lightly

Into my mind

Golden One whisper

Airy ferryman

Sail from the East on the wings of the wind.

HERMES

Greek Magical Papyri (by 500 CE) translated by G. R. S. Mead

Making connections between deities from different cultures is not just a modern practice; it was widespread in the ancient world. In Egypt, large Greek and Roman communities embraced Thoth the Thrice-Great, the ibis- or baboon-headed god of writing, wisdom, knowledge, and magic (who, like Mercury and Hermes, plays a role in the journey of the soul after death) as the equivalent of Mercury/Hermes. The Egyptian influence is clear in this magical invocation of Hermes from late antiquity. "Hermes' city" is Hermopolis, a city in central Egypt; it was a major cult-center of Thoth. The wood referred to here is ebony, according scholar Hans Dieter Betz, while "your tree" may be the olive. The different forms of the god include the ibis and the baboon, traditional animals of Thoth, as well as the serpent and the wolf.

Come unto me, Lord Hermes, even as into women's wombs [come] babes!
Come unto me, Lord Hermes, who dost collect the food of gods and men!
Lord Hermes, come to me, and give me grace,
[and] food, [and] victory, [and] health and happiness, and cheerful countenance, beauty and powers in sight of all!
I know your Name that shines forth in heaven; I know your forms as well; I know your tree; I know your wood as well.
I know you, Hermes, who you are, and whence you are, and what your city is.
I know your names in the Egyptian tongue, and your true name as it is written on the holy tablet in the holy place at Hermes' city, where you had your birth.
I know you, Hermes, and you [know] me; [and] I am you, and you are I.
Come unto me; fulfil all that I crave; be favorable to me together with good fortune and the blessing of the Good.

FROM "HYMN TO MERCURY"

Percy Bysshe Shelley (1792–1822)

Shelley reworked a number of the Homeric hymns into English verse. This is the opening of his version of the hymn to the "Herald-child," Hermes or Mercury, who celebrated his own birth by inventing the lyre, and then promptly crept off to steal the god Apollo's cattle.

Sing, Muse, the son of Maia and of Jove,
The Herald-child, king of Arcadia
And all its pastoral hills, whom in sweet love
Having been interwoven, modest May

Bore Heaven's dread Supreme. An antique grove
Shadowed the cavern where the lovers lay
In the deep night, unseen by Gods or Men,
And white-armed Juno slumbered sweetly then.

Now, when the joy of Jove had its fulfilling,
And Heaven's tenth moon chronicled her relief,
She gave to light a babe all babes excelling,
A schemer subtle beyond all belief;
A shepherd of thin dreams, a cow-stealing,
A night-watching, and door-waylaying thief,
Who 'mongst the Gods was soon about to thieve,
And other glorious actions to achieve.

The babe was born at the first peep of day;
He began playing on the lyre at noon,
And the same evening did he steal away
Apollo's herds;—the fourth day of the moon
On which him bore the venerable May,
From her immortal limbs he leaped full soon,
Nor long could in the sacred cradle keep,
But out to seek Apollo's herds would creep.

FROM THE HOMERIC HYMN TO HERMES

Anonymous (ca. 700–500 BCE), translated by Hugh G. Evelyn-White

This excerpt from "The Homeric Hymn to Hermes" describes the reconciliation that took place between Hermes and his half-brother Apollo after the day-old Hermes stole Apollo's cattle. Hermes soothed Apollo's anger with the gift of the lyre, which he had just invented, and the pair swore eternal friendship.

"Son of Leto" and the "Far-shooter" are epithets of Apollo. Hermes is the "son of Maia," and Zeus is the "Son of Cronos."

…Hermes…held out the lyre: and Phoebus Apollo took it, and readily put his shining whip in Hermes' hand, and ordained him keeper of herds. The son of Maia received it joyfully, while the glorious son of Leto, the lord far-working Apollo, took the lyre upon his left arm and tried each string with the key. Awesomely it sounded at the touch of the god, while he sang sweetly to its note.

Afterwards they two, the all-glorious sons of Zeus, turned the cows back towards the sacred meadow, but themselves hastened back to snowy Olympus, delighting in the lyre. Then wise Zeus was glad and made them both friends. And Hermes loved the son of Leto continually, even as he does now, when he had given the lyre as token to the Far-shooter, who played it skilfully, holding it upon his arm. But for himself Hermes found out another cunning art and made himself the pipes whose sound is heard afar.

Then the son of Leto said to Hermes: "Son of Maia, guide and cunning one, I fear you may steal from me the lyre and my curved bow together; for you have an office from Zeus, to establish deeds of barter amongst men throughout the fruitful earth. Now if you would only swear me the great oath of the gods, either by nodding your head, or by the potent water of Styx, you would do all that can please and ease my heart."

Then Maia's son nodded his head and promised that he would never steal anything of all the Far-shooter possessed, and would never go near his strong house; but Apollo, son of Leto, swore to be fellow and friend to Hermes, vowing that he would love no other among the immortals, neither god nor man sprung from Zeus, better than Hermes: and the Father sent forth an eagle in confirmation. And Apollo swore also: "Verily I will make you only to be an omen for the immortals and all alike, trusted and honored by my heart. Moreover, I will give you a splendid staff of riches and wealth: it is of gold, with three branches, and will keep you scatheless, accomplishing every task, whether of words or deeds that are good, which I claim to know through the utterance of Zeus...."

So he spake. And from heaven father Zeus himself gave confirmation to his words, and commanded that glorious Hermes should be lord over all birds of omen and grim-eyed lions, and boars with gleaming tusks, and over dogs and all flocks that the wide earth nourishes, and over all sheep; also that he only should be the appointed messenger to Hades, who, though he takes no gift, shall give him no mean prize.

Thus the lord Apollo showed his kindness for the Son of Maia by all manner of friendship: and the Son of Cronos gave him grace besides. He consorts with all mortals and immortals: a little he profits, but continually throughout the dark night he cozens the tribes of mortal men.

HERMES
Francis Thompson (1859–1907)

Hermes was sometimes understood to possess both a male and female aspect, and here English poet Francis Thompson compares that duality to Hermes's wand, the caduceus, with its two separate but intertwined serpents. Hermes's large, round hat and winged sandals (talaria) are also mentioned, as is his mother Maia ("the maiden May").

Soothsay. Behold, with rod twy-serpented,
Hermes the prophet, twining in one power
The woman with the man. Upon his head
The cloudy cap, wherewith he hath in dower
The cloud's own virtue—change and counterchange,
To show in light, and to withdraw in pall,
As mortal eyes best bear. His lineage strange
From Zeus, Truth's sire, and maiden May—the all-
Illusive Nature. His fledged feet declare
That 'tis the nether self trans-deified,
And the thrice-furnaced passions, which do bear
The poet Olympus-ward. In him allied
Both parents clasp; and from the womb of Nature
Stern Truth takes flesh in shows of lovely feature.

TO HERMES
Alcaeus of Mytilene (ca. 625 / 620–ca. 580 BCE), translated by James S. Easby-Smith

Alcaeus was a poet from the island of Lesbos. He was a contemporary of Sappho and there is specu-lation that he may have been her lover.

Hermes is "Cyllenean" because, according to legend, he was born on Mount Cyllene. Zeus is "the son of Cronos."

Cyllenean Ruler and Lord, a paean
Raise I now. Beloved of the son of Cronos,
Maia brought thee forth on the sacred mountain's
    Loftiest summit.

ORPHIC HYMN TO HERMES

Anonymous (ca. 200 CE), translated by B. Nolan

Here Hermes is referred to as "Corycian" because he was worshipped near the town of Corycus in modern-day Turkey. He killed Argus, the giant with the hundred eyes, at the behest of Zeus (after Argus's death, the goddess Hera transformed him into the peacock with a hundred eyes in its tail).

Hear me, Hermes son of Maia, messenger of Zeus, great-hearted lord of humankind, you who preside over contests, trickster, negotiator, killer of Argus. You wear the winged sandals, the *talaria*, O friend of humankind, spirit of eloquence. Lover of life, you rejoice in gymnastics and in trickery and lies. Universal interpreter, you love gain and dispel cares. You carry in your hands the unassailable rod of peace, Corycian lord, blessed, many-tongued and skillful, and you help mortals with their labors and their necessities, wielding your speech as a weapon. Hear me, Hermes, and grant me good works, graceful speech, a good memory, and a merciful death.

FROM "THE ADVENT OF HERMES"

J. B. McConnell (1871)

Who comes like the brightening morn?
   Who comes like the light to the leaves—
Like the sun to the ripening corn—
   Like the wind to the rustling sheaves?
'Tis Hermes, the Messenger God!—'tis Hermes, the Prince of the Thieves!

Speak, Hermes, that we may rejoice,
   Oh, open thine eloquent mouth!
We have longed for the sound of thy voice
   As the flowers for the gales of the south—
As the earth for the soft-falling showers, in the season of drought!

ODE TO MERCURY

Horace (65–8 BCE), translated by B. Nolan

Mercury's maternal grandfather was the Titan Atlas, who bears the world on his shoulders.

Mercury, persuasive grandson of Atlas, giver of language and the customs of the gymnasium, clever shaper of the wild ways of primal humanity,

I sing of you, great Jove's messenger and the messenger of all the gods, inventor of the curved lyre, how cunningly you hide whatever you take with tricks and jokes!

Once, when you were only a baby, Apollo yelled at you to give back the cows you had stolen from him; then he found himself without his quiver, and laughed.

You guide good souls to their joyful spaces, with a golden staff you shepherd the weightless throng, you are at ease with the gods above and the gods below.

THE EMERALD TABLET

Pseudo-Apollonius of Tyana (ca. 700 CE), version by Sir Isaac Newton

From the Arab world comes this fascinating and influential text, which, according to its unknown author, was originally discovered under a statue of Hermes in Tyana, in what is now Turkey. Although scholars have their doubts about this account, the text of the tablet, translated from the Arabic, became an influential alchemical text in medieval and Renaissance Europe, where it was believed to be a coded recipe for transmuting base metal into gold. Be that as it may, the text also offers a fairly good introduction to Pythagorean philosophy, which had an enormous influence on the Paganism of late antiquity (as well as nascent Christianity). The "one thing" may refer to the Pythagorean monad, the totality of all divinity, and the "separate the earth from fire" instruction may refer to the purification of the soul in order that it may unite with God.

The chances are good that you already know the tablet's most famous line, "That which is below is like that which is above and that which is above is like that which is below," which is most succinctly translated as "As above, so below." Trismegist or, more properly, Trismegistus, means "Thrice-great."

The translation given here was done by Isaac Newton, developer of the theory of gravity as well as much of modern optics and calculus—and an ardent alchemist.

'Tis true without lying, certain and most true.

That which is below is like that which is above
and that which is above is like that which is below
to do the miracles of one only thing

And as all things have been and arose from one by the mediation of one:
so all things have their birth from this one thing by adaptation.

The Sun is its father,
the moon its mother,
the wind hath carried it in its belly,
the earth is its nurse.
The father of all perfection in the whole world is here.
Its force or power is entire if it be converted into earth.

Separate thou the earth from the fire,
the subtle from the gross
sweetly with great industry.
It ascends from the earth to the heaven
and again it descends to the earth
and receives the force of things superior and inferior.

By this means you shall have the glory of the whole world
and thereby all obscurity shall fly from you.

Its force is above all force,
for it vanquishes every subtle thing and penetrates every solid thing.

So was the world created.

From this are and do come admirable adaptations
where of the means is here in this.

Hence I am called Hermes Trismegist,
having the three parts of the philosophy of the whole world.

That which I have said of the operation of the Sun is accomplished and ended.

FROM *THE FASTI*

Ovid (43 BCE–17/18 CE), translated by B. Nolan

Ovid here explains the origin of the Mercuralia as the day that a great temple to Mercury was founded in Rome. Maia, the mother of Mercury, was one of the Pleiades—that is, one of the daughters of the ocean nymph Pleione.

Come, renowned grandson of Atlas, whom one of the Pleiades bore to Jupiter long ago, in the mountains of Arcadia. Giver of peace and war to the gods of heaven and of the underworld, you who race along on your winged feet, who love the music of the lyre, and love the gymnasium, glistening with oil—you who teach mortals to speak most beautifully. The Senate built you a temple … since its opening that day has been your holiday. All merchants burn incense to you, begging that you will give them wealth.

HERMES OF THE WAYS

Anyte of Tegea (ca. third century BCE), translated by Richard Aldington

This ancient poem refers to a herm, or statue of Hermes, which were frequently placed on roads and boundaries. Anyte of Tegea was a Greek poet known as "the female Homer," though little of her work has survived.

I, Hermes, stand here at the cross-roads by the wind-beaten orchard, near the hoary-grey coast;
And I keep a resting-place for weary men. And the cool stainless spring gushes out.

FROM "HERMES"

Juanita Tramana (1916)

A devotion before an image of the god.

Before your pagan form divine
　　My soul in rapture kneels;
I kiss your dreamy mystic face,
　　To which the sun-god steals

To kiss it too, before he goes
　　Into the realm of night,
To dream in darkness of the world
　　To which you bring the light.

An Invocation of Hermes as the Good Mind

Anonymous (before 500 CE), translated by G. R. S. Mead, modernized by B. Nolan

In this hymn from the Graeco-Egyptian world, Hermes is the Good Daimon, or Spirit. The "eight Wardens" are the Ogdoad, the eight primeval deities worshipped in Hermopolis.

Come unto me, O you of the four winds, almighty one, who breathe spirit into men to give them life;

Whose name is hidden, and beyond the power of men to speak; no prophet [even] can pronounce it; even daimons, when they hear your name, are fearful!

O you, whose tireless eyes are sun and moon—[eyes] that shine in the pupils of the eyes of men!

O you, who have the heaven for head, æther for body, [and] earth for feet, and for the water round you ocean's deep! You the Good Daimon are, who are the sire of all things good, and nurse of the whole world.

Your everlasting revelling-place is set above.

Yours the good emanations of the stars—those daimons, fortunes, and those fates by whom are given wealth, good blend [of nature], and good children, good fortune, and good burial. For you are lord of life—

You who are king of heavens and earth and all that dwell in them;

Whose Righteousness is never put away; whose Muses hymn your glorious name; whom the eight Wardens guard—you the possessor of the Truth pure of all lie!

Your Name and Spirit rest upon the good.

O may you come into my mind and heart for all the length of my life's days, and bring unto accomplishment all things my soul desires!

For you are I, and I am you. Whatever I speak, may it for ever be; for that I have your Name to guard me in my heart.

And every serpent 1 roused shall have no power over me, nor shall I be opposed by any spirit, or daimonial power, or any plague, or any of the evils in the Unseen World; for that I have your Name within my soul.

You I invoke; come unto me, Good, altogether good, [come] to the good—you whom no magic can enchant, no magic can control, who gives me good health, security, good store, good fame, victory, [and] strength, and cheerful countenance!

Cast down the eyes of all who are against me, and give me grace on all my deeds!

FROM *SAPPHO*

Bliss Carman (1861–1929)

O Hermes, master of knowledge,
Measure and number and rhythm,
Worker of wonders in metal,
Moulder of malleable music,
So often the giver of secret
    Learning to mortals!

JUNE

Summer is finally here! The month of June, named for the Roman goddess Juno, starts with a festival in honor of the great Queen of Heaven, mother of the gods. Then, as the days lengthen and the heat increases, it's time to celebrate Vesta, goddess of fire, and the Summer Solstice, the longest day of the year. It's a month of sun and light and flowers, but it closes with the feast day of the goddess Fortuna—a reminder that the Wheel of the Year is always turning and summer will not last forever.

JUNE 1: FEAST OF JUNO

Juno, Queen of Heaven, sister and wife of Jove, and patron goddess of the Roman state, is worshipped on the first day of the month that bears her name. Ancient Romans celebrated her on this day in her role as Juno Moneta, the divine protectoress; her temple on the Capitoline Hill watched over the city, and the precious metals used to mint coins were stored there for safety.

Juno is, like her Greek equivalent Hera, the goddess of wives (thus June is the traditional wedding season) and of mothers, which may explain how June—a month of luxuriant growth—became sacred to her.

HOMERIC HYMN TO HERA

Anonymous (ca. 700–500 BCE), trans by Hugh G. Evelyn-White

Mother of both Hera and Zeus, Rhea is a Titaness, one of the divine race which gave birth to the Olympian gods.

I sing of golden-throned Hera whom Rhea bare. Queen of the immortals is she, surpassing all in beauty: she is the sister and the wife of loud-thundering Zeus—the glorious one whom all the blessed throughout high Olympus reverence and honor even as Zeus who delights in thunder.

FROM "BUT WHAT AT SACRED JUNO'S FEET"

Aphra Behn (1640–1689)

Aphra Behn was one of the first professional female authors in the English language. She rose from poverty and obscurity to become a popular playwright of the Restoration stage.

But what at Sacred Juno' s feet
Shall the adoring nymphs present?
Juno charming, chaste and sweet,
The refuge of the innocent:
The business of our pious themes,
Our waking bliss, our joy in dreams;
The president of virtuous wives,
The bright example of the fair,
Whence virgins learn their modest lives;
And saints their pure devotion there:
And all the goddesses of less degree
Take a peculiar majesty.

PSYCHE'S PRAYER TO HERA

Lucius Apuleius Madaurensis (ca. 124–170 CE), translated by B. Nolan

This excerpt is from the wonderful Roman novel The Golden Ass, *which describes the supernatural travails of one Lucius Apuleius and his eventual rescue by the goddesses Isis, who releases him from a spell which has transformed him into a donkey. It is also our earliest source for the well-known story of Cupid and Psyche.*

Here, the still-mortal Psyche invokes the aid of Juno the Protectress. Zygia was a Taurian goddess, worshipped in what is now Crimea, while Lucina ("Light") is used as an epithet of both Juno and Diana. Samos is an island in the Aegean Sea, while the Inachus is a river in southern Greece.

Beloved wife and sister of great Jove, you who may be found in the ancient temple at Samos, where you were born and shed your first tears and grew to maidenhood, or at your splendid temple in high Carthage, where you are worshipped as a maiden riding the lion through the heavens, or at the famous citadel of Argus on the banks of the Inachus, where you are named the Thunderer's Bride and the Queen of the Gods, you who are adored as Zygia in the East and Lucina in the West, be in my great need Juno the Savior. …

From "The Nuptials of Juno"

Thomas Wade (1825)

Here English poet Thomas Wade emphasizes the majesty and power of Juno in her role of heavenly sovereign. Hebe is the goddess of youth.

Fair Infant of Samos! to thee it is given
To be Queen of the Earth—to be Mistress of Heaven;
The souls of the mighty, the hearts of the proud
Down—down to the dust at thy footstool have bowed;
The Monarchs of Earth and the Gods of the sky
Shall shake at a glance of thy far-beaming eye,
And maidens, to quench burning passion's wild flame,
Will kneel ere they slumber, and worship thy name!
Mother of Hebe! Mother of Mars!
Ruler of Earth! and Queen of the Stars!

Orphic Hymn to Hera

Anonymous (ca. 200 CE), translated by B. Nolan

This hymn equates Hera's nature with that of the element of air, perhaps reflecting the idea that as the Great Mother, she penetrates all of nature.

O Hera, Queen of the Universe, blessed wife of Zeus, clothed in the blue of heaven, airy in form and in nature, you send mortals gentle breezes which nourish life. Mother of rain, mother of wind, from you alone all things come. Everything is a part of you, everything is ruled by you. Your breath inspires the world. Come, holy, joyful goddess of many names, come to us kindly and serene.

JUNO'S SONG FROM *THE TEMPEST*
William Shakespeare (1564–1616)

Honor, riches, marriage-blessing,
Long continuance, and increasing,
Hourly joys be still upon you!
Juno sings her blessings upon you.

LADY HERA
Sappho (ca. 630–ca. 570 BCE), translated by B. Nolan

"The Atreídai" refers to the Greek warriors who fought the Trojan War; in that conflict, Juno famously sided with the Greeks against the Trojans, who were aided by Zeus. (Husbands, take note: Juno won that marital battle.) "Thyone" is another name for Semele, whose son is Dionysus.

Come to me now, Lady Hera, you who answered the Atreídai, princes of undying fame, who fought for many things at Troy and on the ocean, when they sailed toward Lesbos and found the sea-road barred until they called on you, as well as on Zeus the merciful and Dionysus, Thyone's beautiful child; be kind to me, goddess, help me as you helped them.

FROM "HERA PARTHENIA"
Frederic Manning (1882–1935)

The Greek title Parthenia *means "maiden." Juno is famously a wife, but the title was given to her even in antiquity. Here Australian poet Frederic Manning may be suggesting that the seasons follow the development of the goddess, from spring maiden to mother to crone.*

Lo! she awakens again, the flowery Hera, the Maiden:
Break the bewildering beauty, and wonder, and grace of the Spring,
Leading the months of fair colors, wild March with his daffodils laden;
April of the blossoming boughs, fragrant, where nightingales sing
From the deep peace of the woods; and valleys, where glimmering reaches
Of radiance lie on the lakes, and the cold crests of the hills
Are white with the foam of her flowers, that is fairer than breaks on the beaches:
All now she clothes with her joy, all with her music fulfills.

Laughs the green earth, and the ocean, exultant with thunder, rejoices;

Loud is the choir of the winds, sweeping the harp of the woods;

Filled with her manifold praises are the earth's multitudinous voices,

Rain, and the streaming of snows, falling in vehement floods:

Yea, as she cometh the odor of orchard and garden is shaken

Out of the folds of her raiment, blue as the seas and the skies:

She, who had left us, of sunlight and breath of the flowers, forsaken,

Bends once again upon earth, mild and benignant, her eyes.

FROM "ON JUNO"
Nicholas Billingsley, (1658)

Saturn and Ops, parents of Juno and Jove, are the Roman equivalents of the Greek Cronos and Rhea.

The sceptred Queen of heaven, to thundering Jove

Sister and wife, of marriage does approve.

Goddess of riches, ever counted mild

And helpful unto woman great with child;

Saturn and Ops, her parents; she was bred

Up by the flowers, and by the sea-nymphs fed. ...

In a rich chariot, stately to behold,

Of beaten silver and of burnished gold,

A yoke of yellow lions draws her round

Her vast dominions; spangled star-paved ground.

JUNE 7–15: VESTALIA

In the second week of June comes the festival of the goddess Vesta (Hestia to the Greeks). A quiet goddess, keeper of sacred fire, she rules over both the domestic hearth and the hearth of the state. Her gentle nature, however, cloaks an awesome power, a power that was reflected in the status of her ancient priestesses, the Vestal Virgins. Although their cloistered lives were strictly regulated, they were greatly honored in Rome: the word of a Vestal was accepted on any matter without the necessity of swearing an oath, and they had the power to free slaves or rescue condemned criminals from execution simply by touching them. In antiquity, Vesta was rarely depicted in anthropomorphic form. Instead, she was embodied in the living flame which was never allowed to die out in her temple—a recognition, perhaps, that her primordial power could never be adequately represented by the works of humankind.

Normally, the Temple of Vesta was closed to protect the peace of the cloistered Vestals, but on the first day of the Vestalia it was opened to women for worship. Men were forbidden to enter the Temple except for the Pontifex Maximus, the chief priest of Roman religion—and even he was only allowed in at certain times. But ancient men could and did pray to Vesta: according to Cicero, every prayer and sacrifice should conclude with an acknowledgement of her.

Vesta was worshipped with offerings of food during this week. Modern Pagans might perhaps also consider donating to local homeless shelters or food banks in honor of the goddess of homes.

HOMERIC HYMN TO HESTIA

Anonymous (ca. 700–500 BCE), translated by Hugh G. Evelyn-White

Here Hestia, protector of the home, is closely linked with Hermes (Slayer of Argus, Son of Zeus and Maia), protector of travelers. Like Zeus, Hestia is a child of Cronos.

Hestia, in the high dwellings of all, both deathless gods and men who walk on earth, you have gained an everlasting abode and highest honor: glorious is your portion and your right. For without you mortals hold no banquet where one does not duly pour sweet wine in offering to Hestia both first and last.

And you, Slayer of Argus, Son of Zeus and Maia, messenger of the blessed gods, bearer of the golden rod, giver of good, be favorable and help us, you and Hestia, the worshipful and dear. Come and dwell in this glorious house in friendship together; for you two, well knowing the noble actions of men, aid in their wisdom and their strength.

Hail, Daughter of Cronos, and you also, Hermes, bearer of the golden rod!

FROM *THE VESTAL*

Victor-Joseph Étienne de Jouy (1764–1846),
translated by B. Nolan

This prayer is taken from La Vestale *or* The Vestal, *a popular opera from the early nineteenth century.*

Daughter of heaven, eternal Vesta,
Spread here your immortal light,
Keep in the hands of your faithful maidens
The divine fire that was kindled by your breath.

Fire of creation, soul of the world,
Immortal symbol of life,
May your flame live and grow
Shining forever on your altar.

ORPHIC HYMN TO HESTIA

Anonymous (ca. 200 CE), translated by B. Nolan

Lady Hestia, daughter of mighty Cronos, undying flame, you are the center of every home. May you bless the initiates of your holy rites, granting them strength, wisdom, and wealth. Home of the great gods, fortress of humankind, ever-living, variable, slender, and beloved; graciously, O holy queen, accept these offerings, and grant us health and prosperity.

FROM "HOMERIC HYMN TO APHRODITE"

Percy Bysshe Shelley (1792–1822)

Shelley here describes Vesta's decision to remain a virgin, and the honors she is granted by gods and men. Fane *is an archaic word for a temple.*

… Saturn's first-born daughter, Vesta chaste,
Whom Neptune and Apollo wooed the last,
Such was the will of ægis-bearing Jove;
But sternly she refused the ills of Love,
And by her mighty father's head she swore

An oath not unperformed, that evermore
A virgin she would live 'mid deities
Divine: her father, for such gentle ties
Renounced, gave glorious gifts; thus in his hall
She sits and feeds luxuriously. O'er all
In every fane, her honors first arise
From men—the eldest of Divinities.

HYMN TO HESTIA
Aristonoos from Corinth (fourth century BCE), translated by B. Nolan

The navel of the world is the symbolic center; the Greeks tended to think of it as being located at the Oracle of Apollo in Delphi. The Pythoness was the high priestess of the Oracle.

Sing to holy Hestia, Queen of Sanctity! You rule eternally over Olympus and the navel of the world and the laurel at Delphi, you dance in the high temple of Apollo, delighting in the prophetic voice of the Pythoness, and the music of the seven strings of Apollo's golden lyre, when, with you, he sings the praises of the revelling gods. Hail, child of Rhea and Cronos, you who bring fire to the holy altars of the gods! Hestia, in return for our prayers, grant us wealth without wickedness. Allow us to dance forever around your glittering throne.

FROM *THE FASTI*
Ovid (43 BCE–17/18 CE), translated by B. Nolan

Ops is the Roman goddess equivalent to the Greek Rhea, while Saturn is the equivalent of Cronos.

Vesta is the same as Earth. An eternal fire burns under both of them, while the earth and the hearth are both symbols of the home.... Vesta's temple conceals an undying fire, but there is no image of Vesta nor of the fire there.

It's said that Juno and Ceres were born of Ops by Saturn, and their third daughter was Vesta. The other two got married and had children, but Vesta refused to submit herself to a husband.... But remember that Vesta is the living flame, and that flames may not give birth to flesh. Vesta is a true virgin who neither takes seeds nor gives them, and she dearly loves her virgin companions.

SECOND HOMERIC HYMN TO HESTIA

Anonymous (ca. 700–500 BCE), translated by Hugh G. Evelyn-White

Hestia's Homeric hymns are short, but she does get two of them. Pytho is an archaic name for Delphi, site of the Oracle of Apollo. The "soft oil" in Hestia's hair is probably a reference to ambrosia, the sacred liquid of immortality.

Hestia, you who tend the holy house of the lord Apollo, the Far-shooter at goodly Pytho, with soft oil dripping ever from your locks, come now into this house, come, having one mind with Zeus the all-wise—draw near, and withal bestow grace upon my song.

LATE JUNE: SUMMER SOLSTICE

Here comes the sun! As the longest day of the year, the summer solstice is celebrated in virtually every culture as the triumph of light over darkness—since all humans rely on the sun for survival and most experience some seasonal lengthening and diminution of daylight. The importance of the summer solstice to ancient humans is well-known, but it has never ceased to be a time associated with thanksgiving, reverence, and the joy invoked by the light and warmth of the sun's rays.

For this happy season, here is a collection of hymns, prayers, and poems in honor of fiery solar gods.

HYMN TO THE SUN

Casimir Delavigne (1793–1843), translated by B. Nolan

This hymn to the sun, penned by French poet Casimir Delavigne, was set to music by composer Lili Boulanger in 1912.

Let us bless the power of the reborn sun!
With the universe let us celebrate his return.
Crowned with splendor, he rises in strength;
The awakening of the earth is a hymn of love.
Seven coursers whose fire the god fights to restrain
Light up the horizon with their burning breath.

O life-giving Sun, you appear!
With the fields in flower, mountains, and deep forests,

The vast ocean blazes with your fire;
The universe, grown younger and fresher,
Glitters with dewdrops through the morning clouds.

FROM THE HOMERIC HYMN TO HELIOS

Anonymous (ca. 700–500 BCE), translated by Hugh G. Evelyn-White

Euryphaessa is another name for the Titaness Theia, goddess of the ether and mother of Helios, Greek god of the sun; Hyperion is the god of heavenly light. Eos is the goddess of the dawn, and Selene is a goddess of the moon. Calliope is the muse of epic poetry.

A distinction is made here between the Titans and the (Olympian) gods; Helios is a Titan. From the human point of view, however, this is a distinction without much of a difference, since both groups are immortal beings possessed of awe-inspiring powers.

And now, O Muse Calliope, daughter of Zeus, begin to sing of glowing Helios whom mild-eyed Euryphaessa, the far-shining one, bare to the Son of Earth and starry Heaven. For Hyperion wedded glorious Euryphaessa, his own sister, who bare him lovely children, rosy-armed Eos and rich-tressed Selene and tireless Helios who is like the deathless gods. As he rides in his chariot, he shines upon men and deathless gods, and piercingly he gazes with his eyes from his golden helmet. Bright rays beam dazzlingly from him, and his bright locks streaming from the temples of his head gracefully enclose his far-seen face: a rich, fine-spun garment glows upon his body and flutters in the wind: and stallions carry him. Then, when he has stayed his golden-yoked chariot and horses, he rests there upon the highest point of heaven, until he marvelously drives them down again through heaven to Ocean.

Hail to you, lord! Freely bestow on me substance that cheers the heart. ...

TO THE SUN

Christoph August Tiedge (1752–1841), translated by B. Nolan

The sun is most often conceived of as a male divinity, but here German poet Christoph Tiedge lauds the sun as a goddess, in keeping with the Germanic tradition.

Franz Schubert set the German text of this poem to music as "An die Sonne" (D 439).

Royal sun of morning,
Hail to you in your happiness,

Hail to you in your splendor.
Your golden robe is already flowing
Around the hills; the forests come alive with birds.

All things feel your blessings;
The fields sing to you;
All things unite in harmony.
You listen with delight to the merry forest;
O listen to me, hear my praise, too.

Great goddess, I welcome you
Into my solitude with a joyful song.
The first full-blown rose glows in the caress
Of your rays, awakening me
From my dreams.

With a brilliant face I stand in your radiance.
Your smile warms the world like
Divinity, your clearness illuminating
Delirium here, truth there—
More tolerant than humanity.

Your overflowing godhood illuminates my stillness
Like pageantry in the halls of princes.
May you be sung, sung loudly!
Greatly praised by the tongues
Of every hill, of every valley!

ORPHIC HYMN TO HELIOS

Anonymous (ca. 200 CE), translated by B. Nolan

Here Helios is equated with his father Hyperion, "the high one."

Hear me, blessed one, all-seeing, eternal eye, glittering golden Titan, Hyperion, ceaseless heavenly light, you who are sweetness to all living creatures! To the right you bring forth morning, on your left night. King of seasons, driving steeds with sounding hooves, you race, powerful, all fire and brightness, through your endless heavenly course. Enemy of the vicious, you lead the pious to good, maintaining, with your golden lyre, the harmony of the world. You inspire good deeds, lord, as you lead the cosmos playing your pipes, circling around in your fiery course, shedding shimmering light, life-giving, ever-young, ever-clear King of Time. Eternal Zeus, bright light encompassing the world, you see all at both sunset and sunrise. O summit of justice, water-loving lord, safeguard of every oath, most powerful of protectors, eye of justice, life-light, great charioteer, your crackling whip goads on your fiery team of horses. Hear me, I beg you, and grant a sweet and pious life to your followers.

SONG FROM *DEMETER, A MASK*

Robert Bridges (1844–1930)

With music endeth night's prisoning terror,
With flow'ry incense: Haste to salute the sun,
That for the day's chase, like a huntsman,
With flashing arms cometh o'er the mountain.

HYMN TO HELIOS

Emperor Julian (331/332–363 CE), translated by Wilmer Cave Wright

I pray that Helios, the King of the All, may be gracious to me in recompense for this my zeal; and may he grant me a virtuous life and more perfect wisdom and inspired intelligence, and, when fate wills, the gentlest exit that may be from life, at a fitting hour; and that I may ascend to him thereafter and abide with him, for ever if possible, but if that be more than the actions of my life deserve, for many periods of many years.

FROM "ODE TO THE SUN"

Eloise Bibb Thompson (1878–1928)

Here African-American writer and teacher Eloise Bibb Thompson calls upon the sun to illuminate her life.

Shine on, majestic one!
Shine on, O glorious sun!
And never fail to cheer
My life so dark and drear.

Whene'er thou shinest bright,
And show thy brilliant light,
The cares I know each day
Silently steal away.

CHORUSES FROM "THE SUN-GOD'S RETURN"

Joseph Bennett (1831–1911)

Joseph Bennett, in this libretto for the cantata "The Sun-God's Return" by Alexander Mackenzie, identifies the sun with the Norse god Baldur, more commonly known as the god of spring and regeneration. The "towers of Asgard" are the home of some members of the Norse pantheon.

Lo, the sun-god at hand!
The glory increases,
And touches with radiance
The towers of Asgard.
It floods earth and ocean
With celestial splendor!

Behold him resplendent
With light re-created.
Scarce can our weary eyes,
Weakened with watching,
Endure the effulgence.

All hail to thee, Baldur,
Lord of life and the living!
Those whom thy passing
Left weeping in darkness
With thee have arisen.
Hearken the world-cry:
"Welcome, O Baldur!
Lord of life and the living!
Lord of light and gladness,
Lord of the joys that now are
And of delights that shall be hereafter."

HYMN TO THE SUN

Mesomedes of Crete (second century CE),
translated by B. Nolan

Here the Sun is the father of Dawn, rather than her brother. Olympos here is not the mountain of
the gods but rather the ether or space through which the planets move.

Father of pale-lidded dawn, you drive your rose-colored chariot behind the soaring steps
of your steeds, rejoicing in your glittering hair, twining your far-reaching rays through
the endless height of heaven, enveloping the entire earth in your expanding radiance as
rivers of fire give birth to beautiful day. In your honor, Lord of Olympus, the chorus of
the untroubled stars dances, always singing their tranquil song, loving Phoebus Apollo's
lyre, and before them the crystal Moon leads the months and seasons, drawn by her white
goats. And your kindly heart is happy as the richly-clad universe revolves around it.

FROM *DAPHNE*

Ottavio Rinuccini (1562–1621), translated by B. Nolan

Here the sun is equated with Apollo of the bow, an identification which became common in antiq-
uity, although Apollo and Helios were originally separate deities.

This is an excerpt from the very first opera ever performed: the Daphne *of Jacopo Peri, which*
was performed in Florence in 1598. Opera was originally intended to be a re-creation of ancient
Greek tragedy (which was religious in its origin and chanted or sung rather than spoken) and, as a
result, many early operas were written on classical themes.

Noble god, you circle the heavens
in your burning chariot,
Dressing the day in a golden cloak.
If between the awful, icy shadows
The sky is illuminated with glorious light,
The glory and the honor belong to you.
If leaves sprout, and flowers,
Woods, and meadows, and if
The wide earth renews her beautiful dress,

If each plant becomes lovely with
Its sweet adornments,
The glory and the honor belong to you.

Everything the human eye can see
Lives and flourishes only through you.
O Lord of the eternal chariot,
Only of thy bow and arrow let
The praise resound to high heaven—
Let all other praises be soft.

"O FAIR-FACED SUN" FROM *ATALANTA IN CALYDON*

Algernon Charles Swinburne (1837–1909)

O fair-faced sun killing the stars and dews
And dreams and desolation of the night!
Rise up, shine, stretch thine hand out, with thy bow
Touch the most dimmest height of trembling heaven,
And burn and break the dark about thy ways,
Shot through and through with arrows; let thine hair
Lighten as flame above that flameless shell
Which was the moon, and thine eyes fill the world
And thy lips kindle with swift beams; let earth
Laugh, and the long sea fiery from thy feet
Through all the roar and ripple of streaming springs
And foam in reddening flakes and flying flowers
Shaken from hands and blown from lips of nymphs
Whose hair or breast divides the wandering wave
With salt close tresses cleaving lock to lock,
All gold, or shuddering and unfurrowed snow;
And all the winds about thee with their wings,
And fountain-heads of all the watered world. . . .

THEIA

Pindar (ca. 518–438 BCE), translated by B. Nolan

Because no god is complete without his mother, here is a little hymn for Theia (also known as Eury-phaessa), mother of Helios. In antiquity, gold was sometimes believed to have come from the sun.

Mother of Helios, many-named Theia, for your sake humankind honors gold as a power beyond all others. In your honor, great queen, ships racing across the sea in rivalry and chariot-teams whirling around the track to win are made wonderful.

HYMN AT SUNRISE

Leyden Papyrus I: 350, New Kingdom, translated by John Foster

The Ennead, or Nine, are among the primary gods of ancient Egypt, roughly equivalent to the Olympians of Greece.

The Nine Great Gods are come forth from Chaos
    to gather to see you, O great of majesty
Lord of Lords, who fashioned himself by himself,
    Lord of the Goddesses—He is the Lord!

Those who were dreaming, he shines for them all
    to brighten their faces in another of his Forms;
His eyes are gleaming, his ears are listening,
    and all his body is clothed in light.

The sky is like gold, the primeval waters are lapis lazuli blue,
    and the Southland is turquoise, as he rises among them.
The gods are watching, their temples are open,
    and people appear, to marvel and look at him.

The trees sway their bodies before him,
    turned toward the One, their arms wide with blossoms;
The scaley ones dart about in the water,
    come out of hiding for love of him;
The small beasts leap before him,
    birds dance with extended wings.

The creatures all know him at this, his loveliest moment,
    it is life to them to see him each day.
They are in his hand, stamped with his seal,
    and never a god shall open them except for his Majesty.
There is nothing created without him,
the great God, life of the Ennead.

"HYMN OF THE SUN" FROM *IRIS*

Luigi Illica (1857–1919), translated by B. Nolan

This text is from an opera by Italian composer Pietro Mascagni.

It is I! I am Life!
I am infinite beauty, and light and warmth.
Love, o World! I say:
I am the new god and the ancient god,
I am Love!
Through me the birds have songs,
The flowers their perfume and their magic.
The scent of the flowers,
The dawn the color of roses,
And everything pulses with the heart of life.

SUN HAIL

Hilla Stormbringer (twenty-first century)

Hail to the Sun!
Hail to her rising,
Hail to the bright and shining Day!
Hail to her setting,
Hail to her light along our way!

Early in the morning
The foaming waves are grey and cold.
At the beginning of the story
I stand and watch the dawn unfold.

See her dancing on the water
On a path of shining gold,
Like a kindled fire in winter,
A brilliant glory to behold!

Hail to the Sun!
Hail to her rising,
Hail to the bright and shining Day!
Hail to her setting,
Hail to her light along our way!

Through the day she watches
As she travels in the skies.
Stretching to the far horizons,
Fair the world below her lies.
Warmth she gives to all earth's creatures,
Light to all that lives and dies.
Bright her coming and her going,
How bright the sunshine in our eyes!

Hail to the Sun!
Hail to her rising,
Hail to the bright and shining Day!
Hail to her setting,
Hail to her light along our way!

HYMN TO THE SUN

Augusta Holmès (1847–1903), translated by B. Nolan

Augusta Holmès was a French composer and poet of Irish descent.

Sacred sun! Splendor! Love!
Arise from the darkness, O ruby-red King!
The heavens smile on your return,
The sea blazes when you awake!
The meadow is coated with color;

Oak and undergrowth,
The wood quivers
To see you again!
The horizon smokes
In the distance, the mist
Trembles and is illuminated,
Vast censer!
The dreamy darkness lulled our hearts;
A black blindfold covered our eyes;
Banish dreams and terrors,
Rekindle in us joyous hope!
Demons without number
From the dark night
Flee, in the hurrying shadows!
O glorious day!
Evil and criminality
Die in the abyss
Of your brightness!

FROM "FOR THE VANADÍS"

Gudrun of Mimirsbrunnr, (twenty-first century)

A final Solstice prayer not to the sun but to the goddess of gold.

Hail to the Summer Queen
on the solstice morning
as she turns the head to love
and the body to loving,
and opens hearts with a touch.
O Freya with tongue and thighs of honey,
open me up like a ripe fruit
for I am dull and withered with years of hunger
and I have forgotten the mystery of the tender blossom.

JUNE 24: FORS FORTUNA

Right after the Solstice comes the festival of the Roman goddess Fortuna (Greek Tyche), Queen of Luck and ruler of fortune both good and bad. Her power needs no explication: it is she who can make or break the life of a human or a civilization in a moment. Often depicted with her Wheel of Fortune, she also sometimes carries a rudder, since she ultimately decides the course of the Ship of State—and of the individual human life.

FROM "O FORTUNA"

Anonymous (thirteenth century), translated by B. Nolan

This text was made famous by the choral work Carmina Burana. *Although the poem is a complaint against the writer's bad fortune, it opens with this striking address to the power of the goddess.*

O Fortuna, you
are like the moon:
always changing,
always waxing
or waning;
painful life
now oppresses
then soothes,
playing with the mind;
poverty,
power—
she melts them like ice.

ORPHIC HYMN TO TYCHE

Anonymous (ca. 200 CE?), translated by B. Nolan

Here Tyche is equated with Artemis, presumably because the moon and human fortune both wax and wane. The name Eubouleus is a bit unclear: it may be an epithet of Dionysus, or it may refer to a separate deity now lost to us.

I invoke you, great Tyche, kind goddess of the roads, for great wealth, as Artemis the guide, daughter of renowned Eubouleus—wise, invisible, wandering, praised by the songs of humankind. From you comes the great variety of lives: to some you grant riches and blessings in plenty, but you offer only hateful want to those who have angered you. O goddess, be here now and be merciful, and grant me happiness and wealth.

FORTUNE

Anonymous (ca. 500 CE), translated by B. Nolan

Fortune, you who are the beginning and end of humankind, you sit on the throne of Wisdom and honor the worthy actions of humans. More goodness comes from you than evil, and your scale is weighted towards what is best; goodness glitters about your golden wings. O most marvellous of divinites, you break through the barriers of misfortune and illuminate the darkness.

FORTUNE

Nonnus of Panopolis, (ca. 500 CE), translated by B. Nolan

Fortune, how many forms you put on, how you toy with the race of humankind! Be merciful to me, you who conquer all!

FROM "ODE TO FORTUNE"

John Warren, Baron de Tabley (1835–1895)

A hymn to the awe-inspiring power of the goddess, from a reclusive English nobleman.

Demon or goddess, who dost sway
    The changes of our mortal state:
Before whose footstep fades away,
    As snow, the grandeur of the great.

Thou art almighty in thy might.
    Heaven fades before thy fiery breath.
The giant planets of the night
    Fall, if thy hand decree their death.

Wisdom is but a little child,
    Before the breath of thy command:
And Virtue, broken and beguiled,
    Rests in the hollow of thy hand.

From "Olympian Ode 12"

Pindar (ca. 518–438 BCE), translated by B. Nolan

Daughter of liberating Zeus, our savior Tyche, I ask protection for my city, and that you cause it to flourish in strength. You who steer ships as they race across the sea, you rule over the outbreaks of cruel war on land, and you govern the meetings of sage law-givers.

JULY

As the sun shines bright in a summer sky, we celebrate a month of the glittering gods and goddesses: Apollo, the shimmering god of light; Aphrodite, the glamorous lady of beauty; and Poseidon, god of the shining sea. July is a time of fine weather, beauty, and leisure, when beneficent gods are blessed for their kindness toward the world.

JULY 6–13: GAMES OF APOLLO

Phoebus Apollo ("Bright Apollo"), is the Graeco-Roman god of light, poetry, healing, archery, music, herdsmen, and prophecy. The son of Zeus and the Titaness Leto, Apollo was traditionally honored for a week every July when the sun is at its zenith. This likely aided his identification with the sun, a gradual process that took place throughout antiquity—and a natural one, considering that Apollo's twin sister, Artemis, is a moon goddess.

The Games of Apollo, which commemorate the help Apollo gave the Roman people during an invasion, traditionally featured horse-racing and dramatic performances. While it's difficult for the modern Pagan to stage horse races in honor of the gods, it is easy for us to give performances: because Apollo is a god of poetry both in his own right and as a consort of the Muses, poets throughout the ages have written hymns in his honor, a selection of which appears in the following pages.

Second Delphic Hymn to Apollo

Limēnios son of Thoinos, ca. 128 BCE, translated by Richard Hooker

Parnassus is the mountain of the Muses, and the Pierian Spring was one of their sacred sites. Apollo is "Pythian" because he slew the great Python at Delphi. Leto, mother of Apollo, was said to have given birth to him on the island of Delos. The olive is the gift of Pallas Athena to humankind.

Oh, come now, Muses,
and go to the craggy sacred place
upon the far-seen, twin-peaked Parnassus,
celebrated and dear to us, Pierian maidens.
Repose on the snow-clad mountain top;
celebrate the Pythian Lord
with the golden sword, Phoebus,
whom Leto bore unassisted
on the Delian rock surrounded by silvery olives,
the luxuriant plant
which the Goddess Pallas
long ago brought forth.

From "Ode to Apollo"

John Keats (1795–1821)

Apollo as leader of the nine Muses was a popular image in nineteenth-century England, and many paeans were written to him by poets hoping to capture a little of his divine luster. "Erst" means "long ago." "Adamantine" means "diamond."

In thy western halls of gold
When thou sittest in thy state,
Bards, that erst sublimely told
Heroic deeds, and sang of fate,
With fervor seize their adamantine lyres,
Whose chords are solid rays, and twinkle radiant fires.

But when Thou joinest with the Nine,
And all the powers of song combine,
We listen here on earth:
The dying tones that fill the air,
And charm the ear of evening fair,
From thee, great God of Bards, receive their heavenly birth.

FROM "TO APOLLO"

Horace (65–8 BCE), translated by Christopher Smart

Horace was perhaps the greatest lyric poet of the early Roman Empire. Here he asks, while offering wine as a libation to Apollo, that the god grant him a simple life and a healthy mind.

Poignantly, this translation was done in the eighteenth century by the half-Welsh, half-mad poet Christopher Smart, who is now mostly remembered for his "For I Will Consider My Cat Jeoffry," an ode to the cat who kept him company in the mental asylum where he was involuntarily confined.

Grant, God of song, this humble lot,
But to enjoy what I have got,
And I beseech thee keep my mind entire
In age without disgust, and with the cheerful lyre.

HYMN TO CALLIOPE AND APOLLO

Mesomedes of Crete (second century CE), translated by B. Nolan

Apollo, son of Leto, is referred to as "Delian" because he was born on the island of Delos. "Paian" or "Paean" is another of his titles, which he shares with his son Asclepius; it refers to his skill as a healer. Over time, it came to be a term for a lyric poem. Calliope is the muse of epic poetry.

O wise Calliope,
And you, leader of the graceful Muses
And sage initiate in the mysteries,
Son of Leto, Paian, Delian:
Come to me with favor.

FROM "APOLLO"

Henry Bernard Carpenter (1840–1890)

Carpenter was an Irish Unitarian minister.

God of the lyre! to thee thy poets owe
All kindling sounds that through their kingdom go.
Glory to thee, to whom for aye belong
The world's wide harp and thought's fire-shafted bow—
Paian Apollo, Lord of light and song!

FROM THE HOMERIC HYMN TO APOLLO

Anonymous (ca. 700–500 BCE), translated by Hugh G. Evelyn-White

This selection from the Homeric hymn recounts the birth of Apollo. Eilithyia is a goddess of child-birth; Delos is one of the Cyclades islands; and Ortygia, where Artemis was born, is part of Sicily.

I will remember and not be unmindful of Apollo who shoots afar. As he goes through the house of Zeus, the gods tremble before him and all spring up from their seats when he draws near, as he bends his bright bow. But Leto alone stays by the side of Zeus who delights in thunder; and then she unstrings his bow, and closes his quiver, and takes his archery from his strong shoulders in her hands and hangs them on a golden peg against a pillar of his father's house. Then she leads him to a seat and makes him sit: and the Father gives him nectar in a golden cup welcoming his dear son, while the other gods make him sit down there, and queenly Leto rejoices because she bare a mighty son and an archer. Rejoice, blessed Leto, for you bare glorious children, the lord Apollo and Artemis who delights in arrows; her in Ortygia, and him in rocky Delos. . . .

How, then, shall I sing of you who in all ways are a worthy theme of song? For every-where, O Phoebus, the whole range of song is fallen to you, both over the mainland that rears heifers and over the isles. All mountain-peaks and high headlands of lofty hills and rivers flowing out to the deep and beaches sloping seawards and havens of the sea are your delight. Shall I sing how at the first Leto bare you to be the joy of men, as she rested against Mount Cynthus in that rocky isle, in sea-girt Delos . . . ?

. . . [A]s soon as Eilithyia the goddess of sore travail set foot on Delos, the pains of birth seized Leto, and she longed to bring forth; so she cast her arms about a palm tree and kneeled on the soft meadow while the earth laughed for joy beneath. Then the child leaped forth to the light, and all the goddesses raised a cry. Straightway, great Phoebus, the goddesses washed you purely and cleanly with sweet water, and swathed you in a white garment of fine texture, new-woven, and fastened a golden band about you.

Now Leto did not give Apollo, bearer of the golden blade, her breast; but Themis duly poured nectar and ambrosia with her divine hands: and Leto was glad because she had borne a strong son and an archer. But as soon as you had tasted that divine heavenly food, O Phoebus, you could no longer then be held by golden cords nor confined with bands, but all their ends were undone. Forth-with Phoebus Apollo spoke out among the deathless goddesses:

"The lyre and the curved bow shall ever be dear to me, and I will declare to men the unfailing will of Zeus."

So said Phoebus, the long-haired god who shoots afar and began to walk upon the wide-pathed earth; and all the goddesses were amazed at him. Then with gold all Delos was laden, beholding the child of Zeus and Leto, for joy because the god chose her above the islands and shore to make his dwelling in her: and she loved him yet more in her heart. She blossomed as does a mountain-top with woodland flowers.

And you, O lord Apollo, god of the silver bow, shooting afar, now walked on craggy Cynthus, and now kept wandering about the islands and the people in them. Many are your temples and wooded groves, and all peaks and towering bluffs of lofty mountains and rivers flowing to the sea are dear to you, Phoebus, yet in Delos do you most delight your heart....

And now may Apollo be favorable and Artemis.... I will never cease to praise far-shooting Apollo, god of the silver bow, whom rich-haired Leto bare.

FROM "CHANT OF APOLLO'S PRIESTESS"

Emanuel von Bodman (1874–1946), translated by B. Nolan

In this poem, which was set to music by Richard Strauss, priestesses of Apollo pursue knowledge beyond that of this world.

Today every single sorrow is forgotten.
Dear Sisters, hark: the holy one draws near.
The cypresses rustle as he goes by,
And our duty beckons us forward.

We sing to him an echoing song of darkness
So his beautiful rays will shine down warmly,
We move through this pale hall
Dressed as the brides of the god.

All mortals rejoice, and all pluck
The great joy-blossoms of the world,
We alone gather the golden fruit
That falls in the space between sleeping and waking.

FROM "THE LAST ORACLE"

Algernon Charles Swinburne (1837–1909)

Swinburne here is referring to the famous last oracle given by Apollo's priestess at Delphi in 393 CE, which declared the ancient oracle finished; however, Swinburne refuses to accept that Apollo no longer rules in this world.

Day by day thy shadow shines in heaven beholden,
    Even the sun, the shining shadow of thy face:
King, the ways of heaven before thy feet grow golden;
    God, the soul of earth is kindled with thy grace.
In thy lips the speech of man whence Gods were fashioned;
    In thy soul the thought that makes them and unmakes;
By thy light and heat incarnate and impassioned,
    Soul to soul of man gives light for light and takes
As they knew thy name of old time could we know it,
    Healer called of sickness, slayer invoked of wrong,
Light of eyes that saw thy light, God, king, priest, poet,
    Song should bring thee back to heal us with thy song.
        For thy kingdom is past not away,
            Nor thy power from the place thereof hurled;
        Out of heaven they shall cast not the day,
            They shall cast not out song from the world.
        By the song and the light they give
        We know thy works that they live;
            With the gift thou hast given us of speech

We praise, we adore, we beseech,
We arise at thy bidding and follow,
   We cry to thee, answer, appear,
O father of all of us, Paian, Apollo,
   Destroyer and healer, hear!

FROM THE HOMERIC HYMN TO THE MUSES AND APOLLO

Anonymous (ca. 700–500 BCE), translated by Hugh G. Evelyn-White

I will begin with the Muses and Apollo and Zeus. For it is through the Muses and Apollo that there are singers upon the earth and players upon the lyre; but kings are from Zeus. Happy is he whom the Muses love: sweet flows speech from his lips.

Hail, children of Zeus!

FROM "APOLLO"

Callimachus (ca. 310/305–ca. 240 BCE), adapted from the translation by A. W. Mair

Lycoreia was a town on the side of Mount Parnassus, home of the Muses and sometimes of Apollo. "Pytho" refers to Delphi, where the Oracle of Apollo would be established. Hië is an exclamation, similar to io *or* oh!

How the laurel branch of Apollo trembles! How trembles all the shrine! Away, away, he that is sinful! Now surely Phoebus knocks at the door with his beautiful foot. … The Delian palm nods pleasantly of a sudden and the swan in the air sings sweetly. Of yourselves now you bolts be pushed back, pushed back of yourselves, you bars! The god is no longer far away. And you, young men, prepare for song and for the dance.

Not unto everyone does Apollo appear, but unto him that is good. Who has seen Apollo, he is great; who has not seen him, he is of low estate. We shall see you, O Archer, and we shall never be lowly. Let no the youths keep silent lyre or noiseless step, when Apollo visits his shrine, if they think to accomplish marriage and to cut the locks of age, and if the wall is to stand upon its old foundations. …

Be hushed, you that hear, at the song to Apollo; yea, hushed is even the sea when the minstrels celebrate the lyre or the bow, the weapons of Lycoreian Phoebus. …

Apollo will honor the choir, since it sings according to his heart; for Apollo has power, for that he sits on the right hand of Zeus. Nor will the choir sing of Phoebus for one day only. He is a copious theme of song; who would not readily sing of Phoebus?

Golden is the tunic of Apollo and golden his mantle, his lyre and his ... bow and his quiver: golden too are his sandals; for rich in gold is Apollo, rich also in possessions. ... And ever beautiful is he and ever young: never on the girl cheeks of Apollo has come so much as the down of manhood. His locks distil fragrant oils upon the ground; not oil of fat do the locks of Apollo distil but the very Healing of All. And in whatsoever city those dews fall upon the ground, in that city all things are free from harm.

None is so abundant in skill as Apollo. To him belongs the archer, to him the minstrel; for unto Apollo is given in keeping alike archery and song. His are the lots of the diviner and his the seers; and from Phoebus do leeches know the deferring of death.

And Phoebus it is that men follow when they map out cities. For Phoebus himself does weave their foundations. ... Lord of many prayers, your altars wear flowers in spring, even all the ... flowers which the Hours lead forth when Zephyrus breathes dew, and in winter the sweet crocus. Undying evermore is your fire. ...

FROM "APOLLO AND HYACINTHUS"

Rufinus Widl (1731–1798), translated by B. Nolan

This is an excerpt from the libretto of Apollo et Hyacinthus, *an opera composed by Mozart when he was eleven years old.*

God, son of Leto,
Hear the prayers of your supplicants,
Who try to worthily honor you
Who are most deserving of praise.
With your kindly favor, bless
All those who are present here.

"FATHER PHOEBUS" FROM THE *THEBAID*

Papinius Statius (ca. 45–ca. 96 CE), translated by B. Nolan

Patara was a city in Lycia, a region in what is now Turkey. The Castalian Spring is the spring near the Oracle of Apollo at Delphi.

O Father Phoebus, whether you are busied in the woods of Patara or the icy highlands of Lycia, or are joyfully bathing your golden hair in the pure water of Castalia…to you belong the bow bent against savage enemies, to you belong the arrows. Your heavenly parents gave you ever-youthful cheeks. You are able to read the threads of the Fates, and the destiny beyond them, and the will of great Jove: to whom will come war or plagues, what kingdoms will be overthrown by which comets.…Oh, come, remember our hospitality, grant your love and grace to Juno's fields.…

TO APOLLO (EPIGRAM FROM BOOK 9)

The Greek Anthology (ca. 100 BCE), translated by W. R. Paton

Apollo is "Clarian" because he had a large temple complex at Claros, on the Ionian coast.

Let us hymn Paean the great god, Apollo;
Immortal, gloriously formed, unshorn, soft-haired,
Stern-hearted, king, delighting in arrows, giver of life,
Joyous, laughing, slayer of giants, sweet-hearted,
Son of Zeus, slayer of the dragon, lover of the laurel,
Sweet of speech, of ample might, far-shooter, giver of hope,
Creator of animals, divine, Jove-minded, giver of zeal,
Mild, sweet-spoken, sweet-hearted, gentle-handed,
Slayer of beasts, blooming, charmer of the spirit, soft speaking,
Shooter of arrows, desirable, healer, charioteer,
Weaver of the world, Clarian, strong-hearted, father of fruits,
Son of Leto, pleasant, delighting in the lyre, resplendent,
Lord of the mysteries, prophet, magnanimous, thousand-shaped,
Lover of the bow-string, wise, stiller of grief, sober,
Lover of community, common to all, taking thought for all, benefactor of all,

Blessed, making blessed, Olympian, dweller on the hills,
Gentle, all-seeing, sorrowless, giver of wealth,
Savior from trouble, rose-coloured, man-breaker, path-opener,
Glittering, wise, father of light, saviour,
Delighting in the dance, Titan, initiator, revered,
Chanter of hymns, highest, stately, of the height,
Phoebus, purifier, lover of garlands, cheerer of the spirit,
Utterer of oracles, golden, golden-complexioned, golden-arrowed,
Lover of the lyre, harper, hater of lies, giver of the soul,
Swift-footed, swift-voiced, swift of vision, giver of seasons.
Let us hymn Paean the great god, Apollo.

SONG TO APOLLO

John Lyly (1554–1606)

Aurora is the goddess of dawn. Apollo here is "Delian" because he was born on Delos, and his laurel crown is "Daphnean" because the nymph Daphne became a laurel tree in order to elude his desire. "Physic" is used here in the archaic sense of "medicine."

Sing to Apollo, god of day,
Whose golden beams with morning play
And make her eyes so brightly shine,
Aurora's face is called divine;
Sing to Phœbus and that throne
Of diamonds which he sits upon.
    Io, pæans let us sing
    To Physic's and to Poesy's king!

Crown all his altars with bright fire,
Laurels bind about his lyre,
A Daphnean coronet for his head,
The Muses dance about his bed;
When on his ravishing lute he plays,
Strew his temple round with bays.
    Io, pæans let us sing
    To the glittering Delian king!

FROM "THE FIRST DELPHIC HYMN TO APOLLO"

Athenaios (ca. 128 BCE), English version by May Sinclair

In this ancient hymn, found inscribed on a wall in the town of Delphi, the poet Athenaios first calls upon the Muses (who sometimes live on Mount Helicon, and sometimes Mount Parnassus—both mountains are in the same range), encouraging them to praise Apollo. The "Pythian priestess" is the priestess of Apollo at Delphi, who acted as his oracle, while the Castalian Spring is where the priestesses washed themselves before performing their rites. "Loxias" was a title of Apollo at Delphi. Apollo is "Cynthian" because Mount Cynthus is an important feature of the island of Delos, where he was born.

Come, all ye Muses,
Praise him with singing,
Praise him, your brother,
Golden-haired Phoebus,
Cynthian, Delian,
    Paian Apollo!
Praise him, the holy
Haunter of hill-tops,
Who on the twin-peaked
Rocky Parnassus
Chooseth his high seat;
Who with the Pythian
Priestess and maiden
Guards the Castalian
Virginal waters.
Praise him who dwells by
Sweet-springing fountains,
Loxias! Delphian!
Biding for ever
High on the frowning
    Oracular steep.

APOLLO

Aristonoos from Corinth (fourth century BCE),
translated by William D. Furley and Jan Maarten Bremer

The "holy Pythian oracle" is the Oracle at Delphi, the most famous oracle in the ancient world, where the high priestess, the Pythia or Pythoness, spoke with the voice of Apollo; Pytho was the city nearby. The names come from the Python, an enormous serpent which was said to live at Delphi before Apollo slew it and established his shrine there. Because the Python was a child of Gaia, however, Apollo had to be purified after he killed it; he went to the Vale of Tempe in Thessaly and was purified in the river there. His half-sister Athena then took him to Delphi to found the famous temple.

Permanent occupant of the holy Pythian oracle, founded by gods on the mountain flanking Delphi, Apollo—O hail Paean—Apollo, pride and joy of Leto, Coeus' daughter, and by the will of Zeus, supreme among the gods—O Paean.

There from your prophetic seat waving fresh-cut laurel sprigs, you pursue the art of prophecy—O hail Paean—from the awesome inner temple: the sacred course of the future with oracles and melodious chords on the lyre—O Paean.

Purged in the Vale of Tempe by the will of Zeus on high, helped by Pallas on your way to Pytho—O hail Paean—you talked Gaia, the flower-nurse, and Themis of the lovely hair, into giving you the perfumed seat of power—O Paean.

So, as gods know gratitude, you grant Athena pride of place at the threshold of your holy temple—O hail Paean—you thank her for her kindness, the kindness she showed long ago you remember always: sumptuous is her honor—O Paean.

The gods make generous donations: Poseidon a most religious site, the Nymphs a grotto called Corycian—O hail Paean—Dionysus torch-lit mountain revels. Stern Artemis patrols the land with her well-trained pack of guard-dogs—O Paean.

So you who beautify your body in the gushing waters of Castalia from the slopes of Mount Parnassus, I beseech you—O hail Paean—receive with grace the hymn we sing, grant us wealth with decency for ever, protect us with your presence—O Paean.

LORD PHOEBUS

Theognis (ca. sixth century BCE), translated by B. Nolan

Lord, son of Leto, born of Zeus, my chant will never forget you … you will always be my first, my last … but turn toward me, hear me, be kind to me.

Mighty Phoebus, when the great goddess Leto, clasping the palm-tree with her slender arms, gave birth to you, the most beautiful of gods, beside the round lake, the whole island of Delos was filled with holy perfume, the wide earth smiled, and the vast deeps below the white-capped waves rejoiced.

FROM "APOLLO"

Edmund Clarence Stedman (1833–1908)

At last the god cometh!
The air runs over with splendor;
The fire leaps high on the altar;
Melodious thunders shake the ground.
Hark to the Delphic responses!
Hark! it is the god!

JULY 23: NEPTUNALIA

The Neptunalia is the celebration of the Roman sea god Neptune, known in Greece as Poseidon; both gods are the equivalent of the Gaelic deity Manannán mac Lir. These gods, along with their wives and extended families (including allied water gods like Proteus and Oceanus) rule over the watery depths. And, because the ancients understood that earthquakes often originate from deep within the ocean (though the discovery of tectonic plates was still millennia away), they also have dominion over earthquakes.

Curiously enough, Neptune, Poseidon, and Manannán are also lords of horses, perhaps because of the way a running horse recalls the swiftness and smoothness of a breaking wave. Indeed, in Ireland waves are still remembered as the "horses of Manannán." In Greece, Poseidon was regarded as the "lord of Helicon," a mountain associated with horses in general and with Pegasus, the winged horse, in particular.

Not much is known about how this holiday was celebrated in antiquity, but it was surely a time when worshippers flocked to the seaside, where the sun and the waves are still able to excite feelings of thanksgiving. Whether or not you make it to the beach, there are a plethora of ocean-inspired prayers to choose from to honor the sea-gods today.

FROM THE HOMERIC HYMN TO POSEIDON

Anonymous (ca. 700–500 BCE), translated by Hugh G. Evelyn-White

Here Poseidon is hailed as the lord of a mountain (Helicon) as well as of a sea (Aegean).

I begin to sing about Poseidon, the great god, mover of the earth and…sea, god of the deep who is also lord of Helicon and wide Aegaen. A two-fold office the gods allotted you, O Shaker of the Earth, to be a tamer of horses and a savior of ships!

Hail, Poseidon, Holder of the Earth, dark-haired lord! O blessed one, be kindly in heart and help those who voyage in ships!

A HYMN IN PRAISE OF NEPTUNE

Thomas Campion (1567–1620)

The English composer Thomas Campion penned this little hymn to Neptune during the English Renaissance; the English, as islanders, have often claimed a special relationship with Neptune. "Sea-dog" here refers not to an old sailor but a mythical doglike animal; the Tritons are minor sea gods in the retinue of Poseidon. The "scaly nation" refers to fish and other sea creatures. The Sirens mentioned here are the same ones who tempted Odysseus and his crew. "Empery" means "dominion."

Of Neptune's empire let us sing,
At whose command the waves obey;
To whom the rivers tribute pay,
Down the high mountains sliding:
To whom the scaly nation yields
Homage for the crystal fields
   Wherein they dwell:
And every sea-dog pays a gem
Yearly out of his wat'ry cell
To deck great Neptune's diadem.

The Tritons dancing in a ring
Before his palace gates do make
The water with their echoes quake,

Like the great thunder sounding:
The sea-nymphs chant their accents shrill,
And the sirens, taught to kill
    With their sweet voice,
Make ev'ry echoing rock reply
Unto their gentle murmuring noise
The praise of Neptune's empery.

ORPHIC HYMN TO POSEIDON

Anonymous (ca. 200 CE?), translated by Patrick Dunn

The "third share" refers to the oceans, which, when the sons of Cronos were dividing the world, fell to Poseidon by lot (his brothers Zeus and Hades received the heavens and the underworld in the same drawing).

Hear me, Poseidon, who protects the earth,
the dark-haired horseman, bearing in your hand
a bronze trident, you who dwell in the low
foundations of the deep-chested ocean.
Loud-thundering lord of the briny sea,
earth-shaker and joy-giver, blossoming
in the waves through which you drive your four-horsed
chariot, splashing through the salty sea.
You won the third share, the deepest currents
of the sea. You delight in waves and beasts
of the water, daimon of the deep. Save
the foundations of the earth, and the ships,
running fast in their advance. Bring us peace,
health, and wealthy happiness without blame.

ORPHIC HYMN TO TETHYS

Anonymous (ca. 200 CE?), translated by B. Nolan

Tethys is the wife of Neptune or Poseidon, and goddess of fresh water, as well. Here she is named the mother of Aphrodite, who was famously born from the ocean.

Silver-eyed Tethys, bride of the Sea-King, I call upon you! Queen veiled in darkness, whose sweet breath exhaling through the earth drives the frothy waves to break upon the rocks, you rejoice in ships and guard the sea-roads, and you nourish the creatures of the deep. Mother of Aphrodite and of dark clouds, Mother of the filtering springs, hear me, most holy one! Be kind to me, blessed one, and send fair winds to sailing ships.

FROM *ISIS*

Philippe Quinault (1635–1688), translated by B. Nolan

This ode to Neptune comes from the French Baroque opera Isis, *which was in turn based on Ovid's* Metamorphoses.

The God of the waters will appear.
Let us stand beside our Master,
Let's hold back the most violent winds;
May the noise of the waves give way to our songs. . . .

Celebrate his great name on earth and on the waves,
May it not be bounded by the most vast ocean.
Let it fill the entire world,
May it last as long as the universe.

FROM *THE VOYAGE OF BRAN*

Anonymous (eighth cen. CE), translated by Kuno Meyer

In this medieval Irish piece, the ancient Gaelic sea god Manannán mac Lir (or Ler) explains to the hero Bran, who is sailing across the ocean, that what appears to Bran to be water is, to Manannán's eyes, a fair and fertile land. Here two separate realities, human and divine, mundane and other-worldly, are able to coexist simultaneously—one of the hallmarks of Irish thought.

When he had been at sea two days and two nights, [Bran] saw a man in a chariot coming towards him over the sea. That man . . . made himself known to him, and said that he was Manannán the son of Ler. . . . So [Manannán] sang these . . . quatrains to him:

"Bran deems it a marvellous beauty
In his coracle across the clear sea:
While to me in my chariot from afar
It is a flowery plain on which he rides about.

"What is a clear sea
For the prowed skiff in which Bran is,
That is a happy plain with profusion of flowers
To me from the chariot of two wheels.

"Sea-horses glisten in summer
As far as Bran has stretched his glance:
Rivers pour forth a stream of honey
In the land of Manannán son of Ler.

"Speckled salmon leap from the womb
Of the white sea, on which thou lookest:
They are calves, they are colored lambs
With friendliness, without mutual slaughter.

"Though (but) one chariot-rider is seen
In Mag Mell of many flowers,
There are many steeds on its surface,
Though them thou seest not.

"The size of the plain, the number of the host,
Colors glisten with pure glory,
A fair stream of silver, cloths of gold,
Afford a welcome with all abundance.

"A beautiful game, most delightful,
They play (sitting) at the luxurious wine,
Men and gentle women under a bush,
Without sin, without crime.

"Along the top of a wood has swum
Thy coracle across ridges,
There is a wood of beautiful fruit
Under the prow of thy little skiff.

"A wood with blossom and fruit,
On which is the vine's veritable fragrance,
A wood without decay, without defect,
On which are leaves of golden hue."

ORPHIC HYMN TO NEREUS

Anonymous (ca. 200 CE), translated by B. Nolan

Nereus is another ancient sea god, father of the Nereid nymphs.

Lord whose kingdom reaches to the roots of the ocean, you who reside in the realm of azure darkness under the foam of the waves, rejoicing in your fifty maiden daughters—O Nereus, god of great renown, you are the foundation of the sea, the limit of earth, the ruler of all. The sacred throne of Demeter shakes when you engulf the hurricane winds in your hidden depths. Blessed one, save us from earthquakes, and grant to your followers happiness, peace, health, and riches.

"HYMN TO THETIS" FROM *AETHIOPICA*

Heliodorus of Emesa (ca. 300 CE), anonymous translation (1897)

Heliodorus of Emesa came from a priestly family in Syria who, as his name suggests, worshipped the Sun. Here he honors Thetis, one of the Nereids, and her grandson Neoptolemus, who seems, like his father Achilles, to have inherited semidivine status through his grandmother's line (his grandfather, King Peleus, was a mortal).

I sing of Thetis, Thetis with the golden hair, immortal daughter of Nereus of the sea, wedded to Peleus by the will of Jupiter, glory of the seas, our Venus of Paphos. She it was who bore the mighty, the hero of battle, the divine Achilles, whose glory reaches the heavens. The son of Achilles and Pyrrha was Neoptolemus, who destroyed the city of Troy and defended the Greeks. Be thou propitious to us, O hero, son of Achilles, blessed Neoptolemus ... receive this sacrifice favourably and drive away fear from our city. I sing of Thetis, Thetis with the golden hair.

FROM THE ORPHIC HYMN TO THE NEREIDS

Anonymous (ca. 200 CE), translated by B. Nolan

Here the Tritons, immortal followers of Poseidon, seem to be in the shape of dolphins, or perhaps whales, although the Tritons were often depicted as mermen. Triton (singular) refers to the son of Poseidon.

Fair-faced, pure nymphs, robust daughters of deep-sea Nereus, you love to dance across the ocean floor, fifty maidens revelling in the water. You rejoice in the company of the Tritons, the gods in the shapes of the sea-nourished beasts, and the other dwellers of the deep, subjects of Triton. Leaping and jumping through the waves, you are like blue dolphins diving through dark waters. I beg you to bring happiness to your followers. ...

"POSEIDON" FROM *THE KNIGHTS*

Aristophanes (ca. 446–ca. 386 BCE), anonymous translation (1912)

Poseidon, god of the racing steeds, I salute you, you who delight in their neighing and in the resounding clatter of their brass-shod hoofs, god of the swift galleys, which, loaded with mercenaries, cleave the seas with their azure beaks, god of the equestrian contests, in which young rivals, eager for glory, ruin themselves for the sake of distinction with their chariots in the arena, come and direct our chorus; Poseidon with the trident of gold, you, who reign over the dolphins. ... I salute you!

ORPHIC HYMN TO OCEANUS

Anonymous (ca. 200 CE?), translated by Thomas Taylor

Oceanus is, despite his name, the god of all freshwater rivers, especially those that drain to the sea.

Ocean I call, whose nature ever flows,
from whom at first both Gods and men arose;
Sire incorruptible, whose waves surround,
and earth's concluding mighty circle bound:
Hence every river, hence the spreading sea,
and earth's pure bubbling fountains spring from thee:
Hear, mighty fire, for boundless bliss is thine,
whose waters purify the powers divine:
Earth's friendly limit, fountain of the pole,
whose waves wide spreading and circumfluent roll.
Approach benevolent, with placid mind,
and be for ever to thy mystics kind.

"POSEIDON" FROM *ON ANIMALS*

Aelian (ca. 175–ca. 235 CE), translated by B. Nolan

Lord of the ocean, great among the gods, Earth-Shaker Poseidon of the golden trident, of the salty swelling sea-waves: the finned animals of the deep swim and dance around you, leaping lightly and gracefully. . . .

ORPHIC HYMN TO PROTEUS

Anonymous (ca. 200 CE?), translated by Thomas Taylor

Proteus is the original Old Man of the Sea, the god of the changing mood of the waters: his name means "firstborn." He is usually described as Poseidon's firstborn son, but it is quite possible that he is an older god who was grafted onto the family tree at a later date.

Our English word protean *comes from this god, recalling his nature which, like the sea itself, is ever-changing.*

Proteus I call, whom Fate decrees, to keep
the keys which lock the chambers of the deep;
First-born, by whose illustrious power alone
all Nature's principles are clearly shown:
Matter to change with various forms is thine,
matter unformed, capacious, and divine.
All-honored, prudent, whose sagacious mind
knows all that was, and is, of every kind,
With all that shall be in succeeding time;
so vast thy wisdom, wondrous, and sublime:
For all things Nature first to thee consigned,
and in thy essence omniform confined.
Come, blessed father, to our rites attend,
and grant our happy lives a prosperous end.

HYMN TO NEPTUNE

Herman Charles Merivale (1839–1906); slightly modernized by B. Nolan

Aegae is, according to Homer, Poseidon's underwater palace. According to one legend Poseidon built the walls of Troy. Saturn, or Cronos, ate all of his divine children except Jove, of Zeus; the latter eventually forced his father to release his brothers and sisters, including Poseidon, from his belly.

God of the steed and the spear and the Ocean,
    Speed you our barks o'er the wandering foam;
Steer us by reef, and by headland and island,
    Outward and onward, and inward and home;
Hail to you, Neptune! great Neptune, all hail!

Shaker of Earth and upheaver of Water,
    Father of Triton and brother of Jove,
You at whose bidding Troy rose as a palm-tree,
    Under whose branches her warriors strove,
Hail to you, Neptune! great Neptune, all hail!

Saturn begat you, and Saturn devoured you,
    But to restore thee to mystical birth;
Neptune some style you, some call you Poseidon,
    Many your names as the races of Earth:
Hail to you, Neptune! great Neptune, all hail!

Deep in the sea lies your palace at Ægæ,
    Whence you arisest to ride on the wave,
Yoking your golden-maned, brazen-hoofed coursers,
    Mighty to ruin, but powerful to save;
Hail to you, Neptune! great Neptune, all hail!

Clouds as you biddest them gather and scatter,
    Come at your whisper and fly at your nod;
Look then on us that bow down at your altars,
    King of the Ocean, the Mariners' God!
Hail to you, Neptune! great Neptune, all hail!

LATE JULY: APHRODISIA

The moveable feast called the Aphrodisia honors Aphrodite, Greek goddess of love, beauty, and fertility. In antiquity, goddesses' temples were cleaned and reconsecrated on this day, and their statues were taken down to the sea to be washed, much as statues of Durga or Ganesha are immersed in rivers or oceans in India today. Then offerings of flowers and incense would be made, along with the sacred fire.

While the Aphrodisia definitely has a sensual side, Aphrodite also has an aspect, known as *Aphrodite Pandemos* ("Aphrodite of all the people") that emphasizes social harmony and cohesion—in other words, the mystical art of getting along with other people, even those very different from oneself (Aphrodite was, after all, well-known for her ability to charm anyone). This Aphrodisia, choose whichever aspect of the goddess is most appropriate for your situation.

A number of prayers to Adonis, the dying god and doomed lover of Aphrodite, are also featured here. Adonis had his own festival in antiquity, but the date is uncertain; some sources state that it was at the height of summer, others in the spring. Since the matter is still unsettled and since Adonis is now mostly remembered because he was beloved of Aphrodite, it seemed appropriate to include him during the Aphrodisia. Also included are a number of hymns to Near Eastern goddesses who are aligned with Aphrodite: Inanna, Ishtar, and Astarte, as well as a few hymns to Eros, the goddess's mischievous, love-bringing son.

HYMN TO ASTARTE

Pierre Louÿs (1870–1925), translated by B. Nolan

Astarte was the Canaanite version of the goddess Ishtar or Inanna, and so is a cognate of Aphrodite/Venus.

Louÿs was a French Decadent poet who is best remembered today as the author of texts set to music by Claude Debussy.

Mother inexhaustible, incorruptible, creative,
first-born, born of yourself,
conceived of yourself, coming from yourself alone
and rejoicing in yourself, Astarte!

O ever-fertile, O maiden
and nourisher of all, chaste and lustful,

pure and erotic, ineffable, nocturnal, sweet,
fire-breather, foam of the sea!

You who secretly grant grace,
you who unite, you who love, you who grip
in a furious desire the multiplying races
Of wild beasts, and join the sexes in the forests.

O Irresistible Astarte, hear me, take me,
own me, o Moon! and thirteen times, each year,
snatch from my insides the libation of my blood!

FROM *SAPPHO*

Estelle Lewis (1875)

Celestial goddess, daughter of great Jove!
Fair Queen of Love, and mother of sweet Hymen,
Whose beauty draws all heaven into thy train,
And holds the conquering gods in hopeless bonds,
Give ear. …

Beautiful queen, my soul falls at thy feet,
And all the portals of my heart are open;
Enter, blest giver of most blissful joys!
Allay the fever of its wild desires,
And throne in it the idol of my dream.

FROM "HYMN TO APHRODITE"

Laurent Tailhade (1854–1919), translated by B. Nolan

Aphrodite, immortal goddess of beautiful laughter,
Who find pleasure in the woeful songs of the wood-pigeon,
You make mortal hearts sing for you like harps,
And your arms make the paleness of the apple-trees pall.

Hail, imperial granter of life,
You make wild beasts submit to your yoke,
You make lip brush against delighted lip,
Hail, bright Cypris, Queen of Pleasure!

It's because of you that, under the fortunate myrtle,
Happy lovers sweetly intertwine at night,
And that, beside rivers and at the edge of cliffs,
The children of love sob in the darkness.

It's because of you that, aflame with intoxication,
The wild rose paints herself with sweet-smelling blood,
And the maiden, overjoyed and blushing,
Carries her crown and her heart into her lover's arms.

It's you who, in the rhythm of the divine stars,
Makes the heart of the universe beat,
So the harmony with which you reveal yourself may
Make poets of unsullied men.

FROM "A ROYAL HYMN TO ISHTAR"

Anonymous (ca. 2000–1600 BCE), translated by Alan Lenzi

Ishtar is the love goddess of ancient Mesopotamia, and preeminent among the Igigi, the gods of Mesopotamia.

Sing of the goddess, the most awe-inspiring of the goddesses,
Let the lady of the people, the great one of the Igigi be praised!
    Sing of Ishtar, the most awe-inspiring of the goddesses,
    Let the lady of the women, the great one of the Igigi be praised!
She of excitement, clothed with sexual charm,
She is adorned with sexual allure, attraction, and appeal.
Ishtar of excitement, clothed with sexual charm,
She is decorated with sexual allure, attraction, and appeal.
    With regard to (her) lips she drips honey, her mouth vivacity,
    Smiles flourish upon her face.
She is resplendent, loveliness is set upon her head,
Her tones are beautiful, her eyes colorful (and) iridescent.

The goddess—counsel is with her,
    She holds the destinies of everything in her hand.
At her glance happiness is engendered,
Dignity, splendor, a protective spirit (and) guardian.
She loves attention, passion, (and) contentedness,
And she controls concord.
The young woman who ... has been abandoned obtains a
mother (in her),
One invokes her among women/people, one calls her name.
    Who can rival her greatness? Who? ...
Ishtar—who can rival her greatness? ...

She is the one whose position is foremost among the gods,
Her word is respected, it prevails over theirs.
    Ishtar, whose position is foremost among the gods,
    Her word is respected, it prevails over them/theirs.
She is their queen, they discuss her utterances,
    All of them kneel before her.
They go to her (in) her luminescence,
Women and men fear her.

FROM "INANNA AND THE KING"

Anonymous (ca. 2000 BCE), translated by Samuel Noah Kramer

*This hymn celebrates the sacred marriage between the Sumerian goddess Inanna and the king of the
land, which allows the earth to blossom.*

    The sun has gone to sleep, the day has passed,
    As in bed you gaze (lovingly) upon him,
    As you caress the lord,
    Give life unto the lord,
    Give the staff and crook unto the lord.

She craves it, she craves it, she craves the bed,
She craves the bed of the rejoicing heart, she craves the bed,

She craves the bed of the sweet lap, she craves the bed,
She craves the bed of kingship, she craves the bed,
She craves the bed of queenship, she craves the bed.
By his sweet, by his sweet, by his sweet bed,
By his sweet bed of the rejoicing heart, by his sweet bed,
By his sweet bed of the sweet lap, by his sweet bed,
By his sweet bed of kingship, by his sweet bed,
By his sweet bed of queenship, by his sweet bed,
He covers [the bed]… for her, covers the bed for her,
He covers [the bed]… for her, covers the bed for her.

———

May the Lord whom you have called to (your) heart,
The king, your beloved husband,
   enjoy long days at your holy lap, the sweet,
   Give him a reign favorable (and) glorious
   Give him the throne of kingship on its enduring foundation.…

From (where) the sun rises, to (where) the sun sets,
From south to north.…
May he make productive the fields like the farmer,
May he multiply the sheepfolds like a trustworthy shepherd.

Under his reign may there be plants, may there be grain,
At the river, may there be overflow,
In the field may there be late-grain,
In the marshland may the fish
   (and) birds make much chatter,
   In the canebrake may the 'old' reeds,
   the young reeds grow high.…
In the forests may the deer and the wild goats multiply,

May the watered garden produce honey (and) wine,

In the trenches may the lettuce and cress grow high,

In the palace may there be long life.

Into the Tigris and Euphrates may flood water be brought,

On their banks may the grass grow high,

may the meadows be covered,

May the holy queen of vegetation

pile high the grain heaps and mounds,

O my queen, queen of the universe,

the queen who encompasses the universe,

May he enjoy long days [at your holy] lap.

HYMN TO VENUS

Augusta Holmès (1847–1903), translated by B. Nolan

Oh, Venus, so fair and beautiful,

I sigh at your bare feet!

Lily of heaven, froth of the wave,

Unknowable rose, O Venus!

Your voice burned my life

With unslaked ardor,

And for your eyes

Of radiant blue

I have suffered

The beautiful weakness.

Oh, Venus, love divine,

Open your arms, O Blessed One!

Your sweetness allows

The earth to bear,

Your splendor ravishes

The heavens!
Your beauty intoxicates me
And changes me
Like forbidden fruit!

In the exile where my soul cries out
My whole being reclaims you!
To clasp you,
Tender flower of desire,
I consent to dark death.
O Venus! Love divine!
Grant to me one happy hour.

CHORUS FROM *HIPPOLYTUS*

Euripides (ca. 480–ca. 406 BCE), translated by Gilbert Murray

Cypris *and* Cyprian *are both titles of Aphrodite, who was born off the shore of the island of* Cyprus. *Her winged companion here is Eros.*

Thou comest to bend the pride
Of the hearts of God and man,
Cypris; and by thy side,
In earth-encircling span,
He of the changing plumes,
The Wing that the world illumes,
As over the leagues of land flies he,
Over the salt and sounding sea.

For mad is the heart of Love,
And gold the gleam of his wing;
And all to the spell thereof
Bend, when he makes his spring;
All life that is wild and young
In mountain and wave and stream,
All that of earth is sprung,
Or breathes in the red sunbeam;
Yea, and Mankind. O'er all a royal throne,
   Cyprian, Cyprian, is thine alone!

FROM "HYMN TO INANA AS NINEGALA"

Anonymous (ca. 1894–ca. 1595 BCE), translated by J. A. Black, G. Cunningham,
J. Ebeling, E. Flückiger-Hawker, E. Robson, J. Taylor, and G. Zólyomi

*Ninegala is an epithet of Inana or Inanna; her spouse is Dumuzid or Tammuz, a vegetation god.
An is the sky god, and Eridu is one of the oldest cities in the world.*

Great light, heavenly lioness, always speaking words of assent! Inana, great light, lioness of heaven, who always speaks words of assent! Ninegala! As you rise in the morning sky like a flame visible from afar, and at your bright appearance in the evening sky, the shepherd entrusts (?) the flocks of Sumer to you. Celestial sign, … glory of heaven! … Inana, you are the lady of all the divine powers, and no deity can compete with you. Here is your dwelling, Ninegala; let me tell of your grandeur!

… You are the good woman who spreads a sense of awe perceptibly throughout the Land. Inana, you are the lady of all the divine powers, and no deity can compete with you. Here is your dwelling, Ninegala; let me tell of your grandeur!

After the first watch of the night has passed, as like a shepherd you get up from the grass, you seize your battle-mace like a warrior, you fasten the … cloth on your arms, and you bind on your indefatigable strength. Thus you appear brilliantly, together with An, in the city. On earth, Inana, you emit awe-inspiring splendour from the holy dais. Your feet are placed on seven dogs, your seat is set upon a lion and a leopard. …

Inana, you are the lady of all the divine powers, and no deity can compete with you. Here is your dwelling, Ninegala; let me tell of your grandeur!

When you act as a shepherd with the herdsman, when … with the cowherd you throw the halters on the cows, when you mix the butter, when you purify the milk, when you find joy in the embrace of your spouse Dumuzid, when you have pleasure in the embrace of your spouse Dumuzid, when you take your seat on the high dais in the great hall in your Kura-igijal where judgment is passed, then the people of the holy *uzga* stand there at your service. …

They cannot compete with you, Inana. As a prostitute you go down to the tavern and, like (?) a ghost who slips in through the window, you enter there.

Inana, you are the lady of all the divine powers, and no deity can compete with you. Here is your dwelling, Ninegala; let me tell of your grandeur!

When the servants let the flocks loose, and when cattle and sheep are returned to cow-pen and sheepfold, then, my lady, like the nameless poor, you wear only a single garment. The pearls of a prostitute are placed around your neck, and you are likely to snatch a man from the tavern. As you hasten to the embrace of your spouse Dumuzid, Inana, then the seven paranymphs share the bedchamber with you.

Inana, you are the lady of all the divine powers, and no deity can compete with you. Here is your dwelling, Ninegala; let me tell of your grandeur!

In the evening, when the stars return together again and when Utu enters into his chamber, when in heaven, Inana, you diffuse awesomeness like fire, and when on earth, Ninegala, you screech like a falcon. . . . You go from moonlight to star, you go from star to moonlight.

Inana, you are the lady of all the divine powers, and no deity can compete with you. Here is your dwelling, Ninegala; let me tell of your grandeur!

The levy of troops is brought into the broad square like a crouching dragon. The young man who has come to know your eminence makes a gesture of obeisance.

Inana, you are the lady of all the divine powers, and no deity can compete with you. Here is your dwelling, Ninegala; let me tell of your grandeur!

ETERNAL EROS

Bertel Gripenberg (1878–1947), version by B. Nolan

Eternal Eros, god of fire,
Still I love the sound of your voice.
Long for you I lived and endured;
Life's path winds slowly down.

The flashing fire
Of the eternal stars,
The far-off land of
Longing's promise,

Are lit for us
By you only, Eros.

Delight and pain,
Sorrow and lust,
Are all sent as gifts from
That far shore.
The enchanted glow
of poetry and dreams,
These are the gifts
Of your abundance.

FROM "HYMN TO APHRODITE"

Sappho (ca. 630–ca. 570 BCE), translated by Elizabeth Vandiver

The great female poet Sappho—"the Tenth Muse," as she was known in antiquity—here begs Aphrodite for help with her unrequited love in her famous hymn to the goddess.

Iridescent-throned Aphrodite, deathless
Child of Zeus, wile-weaver, I now implore you,
Don't—I beg you, Lady—with pains and torments
Crush down my spirit,

But before if ever you've heard my pleadings
Then return, as once when you left your father's
Golden house; you yoked to your shining car your
Wing-whirring sparrows;

Skimming down the paths of the sky's bright ether
On they brought you over the earth's black bosom,
Swiftly—then you stood with a sudden brilliance,
Goddess, before me;

Deathless face alight with your smile, you asked me
What I suffered, who was my cause of anguish,
What would ease the pain of my frantic mind, and
Why had I called you

To my side: "And whom should Persuasion summon
Here, to soothe the sting of your passion this time?

Who is now abusing you, Sappho? Who is
Treating you cruelly?

Now she runs away, but she'll soon pursue you;
Gifts she now rejects—soon enough she'll give them;
Now she doesn't love you, but soon her heart will
Burn, though unwilling."

Come to me once more, and abate my torment;
Take the bitter care from my mind, and give me
All I long for; Lady, in all my battles
Fight as my comrade.

FROM "THE RETURN OF APHRODITE"
Grant Allen (1848–1899)

Deep in Cythera a cave,
    Pealing a thunderous pæan,
Roars, as the shivering wave
    Whitens the purple Ægean:
There to astonish the globe,
    Terrible, beautiful, mighty,
Clad with desire as a robe,
    Rose Aphrodite.

Never again upon earth
    Like her arose any other;
Got without labor or birth,
    Sprung without father or mother:
Zeus, from his aery home,
    Seeing the roseate water
Lift her aloft on its foam,
    Hailed her his daughter.

FROM A HOMERIC HYMN TO APHRODITE

Anonymous (ca.700–500 BCE), translated by Hugh G. Evelyn-White

Of Cytherea, born in Cyprus, I will sing. She gives kindly gifts to men: smiles are ever on her lovely face, and lovely is the brightness that plays over it.

Hail, goddess, queen of well-built Salamis and sea-girt Cyprus.…

GENTLE ADONIS IS DYING

Sappho (ca. 630–ca. 570 BCE), translated by Edwin Marion Cox

In this poem Aphrodite, or Cythera, commands mortal women to mourn for Adonis, the lost god of the flowers. Adonis angered the goddess Artemis by his hubris over his skill in hunting; as a result, she sent a boar to gore him to death. He died in Aphrodite's arms, and his blood became the anemone, or windflower.

Gentle Adonis is dying, O Cythera, what shall we do?
Beat your breasts, O maidens, and rend your garments.

Gentle Adonis wounded lies, dying, dying.
What message, O Cythera, dost thou send?
Beat, beat your breasts, O ye weeping maidens,
And in wild grief your mourning garments rend.

FROM "LAMENT FOR ADONIS"

Elizabeth Barrett Browning, after Bion of Smyrna (ca. 100 BCE)

This song, a loose translation by British poet Elizabeth Barrett Browning of an ancient poem, commemorates the pain of Aphrodite at the annual death of her lover Adonis. Cypris, Cytherea, and the Paphian are epithets of Aphrodite. The Loves are the winged gods who follow her.

I.

I mourn for Adonis—Adonis is dead!
Fair Adonis is dead, and the Loves are lamenting.
Sleep, Cypris, no more, on thy purple-strewed bed;
Arise, wretch stoled in black,—beat thy breast unrelenting,
And shriek to the worlds, "Fair Adonis is dead."

II.

I mourn for Adonis—the Loves are lamenting.
He lies on the hills, in his beauty and death,—
The white tusk of a boar has transpierced his white thigh;
And his Cypris grows mad at the thin gasping breath,
While the black blood drips down on the pale ivory:
And his eye-balls lie quenched with the weight of his brows.
The rose fades from his lips, and, upon them just parted,
The kiss dies which Cypris consents not to lose,
Though the kiss of the Dead cannot make her glad-hearted—
He knows not who kisses him dead in the dews.

III.

I mourn for Adonis—the Loves are lamenting.
Deep, deep in the thigh, is Adonis's wound;
But a deeper, is Cypris's bosom presenting—
The youth lieth dead, while his dogs howl around,
And the nymphs weep aloud from the mists of the hill,—
And the poor Aphrodite, with tresses unbound,
All dishevelled, unsandalled, shrieks mournful and shrill
Through the dusk of the groves. The thorns, tearing her feet,
Gather up the red flower of her blood, which is holy,
Each footstep she takes; and the valleys repeat
The sharp cry which she utters, and draw it out slowly. …

VI.

Ah, ah, Cytherea! Adonis is dead,—
She wept tear after tear, with the blood which was shed;
And both turned into flowers for the earth's garden-close;
Her tears, to the wind-flower,—his blood, to the rose.

VII.

… Love him still, poor Adonis! cast on him together
The crowns and the flowers! since he died from the place
Why let all die with him—let the blossoms go wither;

Rain myrtles and olive-buds down on his face:
Rain the myrrh down, let all that is best fall a-pining,
For thy myrrh, his life, from thy keeping is swept!—
—Pale he lay, thine Adonis, in purples reclining—
The Loves raised their voices around him and wept.
They have shorn their bright curls off to cast on Adonis:
One treads on his bow,—on his arrows, another,—
One breaks up a well-feathered quiver; and one is,
Bent low on a sandal, untying the strings;
And one carries the vases of gold from the springs,
While one washes the wound; and behind them a brother
Fans down on the body sweet airs with his wings.

VIII.

… The Fates mourn aloud for Adonis, Adonis,
Deep chanting! he hears not a word that they say:
He would hear, but Persephone has him in keeping.
—Cease moan, Cytherea—leave pomps for to-day,
And weep new when a new year refits thee for weeping.

SEARCHING FOR ADONIS

Mikhail Kuzmin (1872–1936), version by B. Nolan

Searching for Adonis, the Cytherian
Prowls along the shore like a lioness.
The Cyprian goddess is tired, can't sleep—
She sees pale Adonis, his bright gaze frozen,
Dead. Venus jumps up, scarcely breathing,
Forgetting her exhaustion. She runs
Right to the place where the body of Adonis
Lays by the sea. Loudy, loudly, does
The Cyprian weep, and the waves
Murmur along with her,
Echoing her grief.

FROM "A LAMENT FOR ADONIS"

John Warren, Baron de Tabley (1835–1895)

Here Aphrodite is consoled with the reminder that, although Adonis may die, her kingdom will stand forever.

Tithonus was the mortal lover of Eos, the dawn; blessed (or cursed) with immortality, he nonetheless continued to age and shrink until, in some versions, he became a cicada. Myrtle is sacred to Aphrodite.

Lament not, Queen of love, lament no more:
Nature and Love alone are ageless powers;
Thy queendom, Aphrodite, shall not fail.
The reign of might shall fail, the wisdom fail
That wrought out heavenly thrones: the weary clouds
Shall not sustain them longer: only Love
And Nature are immortal. Nature sealed
Adonis' eyes: the kindly hand forgave
The creeping years that held Tithonus old
Before her eyes who loved and saw him fade.

Have comfort; and our homeward choir shall hymn
Thy godhead thro' the cedarn labyrinths.
Till they emerge upon the flushing sheet
Of sunset: on those waters many an isle
And cape and sacred foreland ripe with eve,
Cherish thy myrtle in delicious groves:
Infinite worship at this hour is thine.
They name thee Aphrodite, and the name
Blends with the incense towards the crimson cloud.

FROM "THE PSALM OF ADONIS" (IDYLL XV)

Theocritus (ca. 270 BCE), translated by Andrew Lang, modernized by B. Nolan

The dying god returns! Here Adonis is compared to many heroes—among them Agamemnon, who led the Greeks to Troy, and Hector—and is found superior to them all. Acheron is a river in the Underworld, and Ida is a mountain famous in mythology.

O Queen … O Aphrodite … from the stream eternal of Acheron they have brought back to you Adonis … they have brought him, the dainty-footed Hours. … Before him lie all ripe fruits that the tall trees' branches bear, and the delicate gardens, arrayed in baskets of silver, and the golden vessels are full of incense of Syria. And all the dainty cakes that women fashion in the kneading-tray, mingling blossoms manifold with the white wheaten flour, all that is wrought of honey sweet, and in soft olive oil, all cakes fashioned in the semblance of things that fly, and of things that creep, lo, here they are set before him.

Here are built for him shadowy bowers of green, all laden with tender anise, and children flit overhead—the little Loves—as the young nightingales perched upon the trees fly forth and try their wings from bough to bough. …

Another bed is strewn for beautiful Adonis, one bed Cypris keeps, and one the rosy-armed Adonis. A bridegroom of eighteen or nineteen years is he, his kisses are not rough, the golden down being yet upon his lips! And now, good-night to Cypris, in the arms of her lover! But lo, in the morning we will all of us gather with the dew, and carry him forth among the waves that break upon the beach, and with locks unloosed, and ungirt raiment falling to the ankles, and bosoms bare will we begin our shrill sweet song.

You only, dear Adonis, so men tell, you only of the demigods visits both this world and the stream of Acheron. … Be gracious now, dear Adonis, and propitious even in the coming year. Dear to us has your advent been, Adonis, and dear shall it be when you come again.

AUGUST

August marks the beginning of the season of harvest. It opens with the celebration of Lúnasa or Lammas, the early harvest festival of northwestern Europe, on the first of the month. Although the beginning of the harvest season is a reminder that the days are starting to shorten, the powers of light are still strong: the Lychnapsia or Lamp-Lighting is held at mid-month in honor of Isis, and Vulcan, god of forges and fire, is honored now as well. The birthday of Pallas Athena, the resolutely virgin warrior who stands outside the cycles of love and fertility, is also celebrated in August, during the ancient festival of the Panathenaea. And at the end of the month comes the holiday of Nike, or Victoria, the goddess of victory.

AUGUST 1: LÚNASA

Lúnasa (the modern Irish spelling of both the holiday and the month of August) honors the great pan-Celtic god known in Ireland as Lugh Ildánach (All-Skilled), and it also marks the very first stages of the harvest in northwestern Europe. These two facets of the holiday are intimately related: Lugh is, according to the Irish tradition, the god who makes this harvest possible, for he slays the chthonic god who holds the gods of fertility in bondage, and secures for his people the secrets of agriculture.

Although Lugh was once believed to be a sun god, this view is now regarded as likely incorrect; instead, he seems to be closer to a Celtic version of Mercury, a god of oaths and cleverness and many talents. He's known in Wales as Llew Llaw Gyffes, and on the Continent as Lugus. Many inscriptions to him have survived in Spain, and the city of Lyon in France is named after him.

As is the case with all Celtic holidays, there is a dearth of appropriate ancient material. There are, however, some medieval accounts of Lugh that we can turn to, as well as some later poems both for Lugh and for other harvest gods and goddesses.

The Birth and Naming of Llew

Anonymous (from the *Mabinogion*) (twelfth–thirteenth centuries CE),
translated by Charlotte Guest; modernized by B. Nolan

This excerpt from the Fourth Branch of the Mabinogion *(the medieval Welsh narrative cycle that contains the literary remnants of British mythology) tells how Llew was born and got his name, which means something like "Bright-haired (or Lion-maned) Skillful Hand." It begins at the court of King Math, who asks his nephew Gwydion to help him find a virgin assistant, for Math has a taboo that requires him to rest his feet in the lap of a virgin when he is not at war. Gwydion suggests his sister Arianrhod ("Silver Wheel," originally probably a moon goddess), with interesting results.*

A cordwainer is a shoemaker (as opposed to a cobbler, who is a shoe-mender).

"Lord," said Gwydion the son of Don, "...seek Arianrod, the daughter of Don, your niece...."

And they brought her unto him. "Ha, damsel," said [Math], "are you a maiden?" "I know not, lord, other than that I am." Then he took up his magic wand, and bent it. "Step over this," said he, "and I shall know if you are maiden." Then stepped she over the magic wand, and there appeared forthwith a fine chubby yellow-haired boy. And at the crying out of the boy, she went towards the door. And thereupon some small form was seen; but before any one could get a second glimpse of it, Gwydion had taken it, and had flung a scarf of velvet around it and hidden it. Now the place where he hid it was the bottom of a chest at the foot of his bed.

As Gwydion lay one morning on his bed awake, he heard a cry in the chest at his feet.... Then he arose in haste, and opened the chest: and when he opened it, he beheld an infant boy stretching out his arms from the folds of the scarf, and casting it aside. And he took up the boy in his arms, and carried him to a place where he knew there was a woman that could nurse him. And he agreed with the woman that she should take charge of the boy.

And one day Gwydion... went to the Castle of Arianrod, having the boy with him; and when he came into the Court, Arianrod arose to meet him, and greeted him and bade him welcome. "Heaven prosper you," said he. "Who is the boy that follows you?" she asked. "This youth, he is your son," he answered. "Alas," said she, "what has come unto you that you should shame me thus? Why do you seek my dishonor, and retain it so long as this?" "Unless you suffer dishonor greater than that of my bringing up such a boy as this, small will be your disgrace." "What is the name of the boy?" said she. "Verily," he replied, "he has not yet a name." "Well," she said, "I lay this destiny upon him, that he shall never have a name until he receives one from me." "Heaven bears me witness," answered he, "that you are a wicked woman. But the boy shall have a name how displeasing soever it may be to you. As for you, that which afflicts you is that you are no longer called a damsel." And thereupon he went forth in wrath. . . .

And the next day he arose and took the boy with him, and went to walk on the seashore. . . . And there he saw some sedges and seaweed, and he turned them into a boat. And out of dry sticks and sedges he made some Cordovan leather . . . and he colored it in such a manner that no one ever saw leather more beautiful than it. Then he made a sail to the boat, and he and the boy went in it to the port of the castle of Arianrod. And he began forming shoes and stitching them, until he was observed from the castle. And when he knew that they of the castle were observing him, he disguised his aspect, and put another semblance upon himself, and upon the boy, so that they might not be known. "What men are those in yonder boat?" said Arianrod. "They are cordwainers," answered they. "Go and see what kind of leather they have, and what kind of work they can do."

So they came unto them. And when they came he was coloring some Cordovan leather, and gilding it. And the messengers came and told her this. "Well," said she, "take the measure of my foot, and desire the cordwainer to make shoes for me." So he made the shoes for her, yet not according to the measure, but larger. The shoes then were brought unto her, and behold they were too large. "These are too large," said she, "but he shall receive their value. Let him also make some that are smaller than they." Then he made her others that were much smaller than her foot, and sent them unto her. "Tell him that these will not go on my feet," said she. And they told him this. "Verily," said he, "I will not make her any shoes, unless I see her foot." And this was told unto her. "Truly," she answered, "I will go unto him."

So she went down to the boat, and when she came there, he was shaping shoes and the boy stitching them. "Ah, lady," said he, "good day to you." "Heaven prosper you," said she.

"I marvel that you cannot manage to make shoe according to a measure." "I could not," he replied, "but now I shall be able."

Thereupon behold a wren stood upon the deck of the boat, and the boy shot at it, and hit it in the leg between the sinew and the bone. Then she smiled. "Verily," said she, "with a steady hand did the lion aim at it." "Heaven reward you not, but now has he got a name. And a good enough name it is. Llew Llaw Gyffes be he called henceforth."

FROM "THE COMING OF LUGH"

Ella Young (1867–1956)

This story from the Celtic Revival in Ireland retells the Irish story of Lugh's coming to the fortress of the gods at the royal hill of Tara (the "dun of Nuada"). Lugh is initially denied entry; only when he is revealed as the Ildánach, the All-Skilled, is he welcomed into the hall to join the rest of the Tuatha Dé Danann, the Irish gods—many of whom, such as Dian Cecht the healer and Luchtae the carpenter, are mentioned here.

Nuada was at the time the king of the gods. A dun is an ancient stone-fort settlement.

[Lugh] put his shining armor from him and wrapped himself in a dark cloak and went on foot to the dun of Nuada. He struck the brazen door, and the Guardian of the Door spoke to him from within.

"What do you seek?"

"My way into the dun."

"No one enters here who has not his craft. What can you do?"

"I have the craft of a Carpenter."

"We have a carpenter within; he is Luchtae, son of Luchaid."

"I have the craft of a Smith."

"We have a smith within, Colum of the three new ways of working."

"I have the craft of a Champion."

"We have a champion within; he is Ogma himself."

"I have the craft of a Harper."

"We have a harper within, even Abhcan, son of Bicelmos; the Men of the Three Gods chose him in the faery hills."

"I have the craft of a Poet and Historian."

"We have a poet and historian within, even En, son of Ethaman."

"I have the craft of a Wizard."

"We have many wizards and magicians within."

"I have the craft of a Physician"

"We have a physician within, even Dian Cecht."

"I have the craft of a Cupbearer."

"We have nine cupbearers within."

"I have the craft of a Brazier."

"We have a brazier within, even Credne Cerd."

"Go hence and ask your king if he has within any one man who can do all these things. If he has, I will not seek to enter."

The Guardian of the Door hurried in to Nuada.

"O King," he said, "the most wonderful youth in the world is waiting outside your door to-night! He seeks admittance as the Ildana, the Master of Every Craft."

"Let him come in," said King Nuada.

Lugh came into the dun. Ogma, the Champion, took a good look at him. He thought him young and slender, and was minded to test him. He stooped and lifted the Great Stone that was before the seat of the King. It was flat and round, and four score yoke of oxen could not move it. Ogma cast it through the open door so that it crossed the fosse which was round the dun. That was his challenge to the Ildana.

"It is a good champion-cast," said Lugh. "I will better it."

He went outside. He lifted the Stone and cast it back not through the door, but through the strong wall of the dun so that it fell in the place where it had lain before Ogma lifted it.

"Your cast is better than mine!" said Ogma. "Sit in the seat of the champion with your face to the King."

Lugh drew his hand over the wall; it became whole as before. He sat in the champion-seat.

"Let chess be brought," said the King.

They played, and Lugh won all the games. ...

"Truly you are the Ildana," said Nuada. "I would fain hear music of your making, but I have no harp to offer you."

"I see a kingly harp within reach of your hand," said Lugh.

"That is the harp of the Dagda. No one can bring music from that harp but himself. When he plays on it, the four Seasons Spring, Summer, Autumn, and Winter pass over the earth."

"I will play on it," said Lugh.

The harp was given to him.

Lugh played the music of joy, and outside the dun the birds began to sing as though it were morning and wonderful crimson flowers sprang through the grass flowers that trembled with delight and swayed and touched each other with a delicate faery ringing as of silver bells. Inside the dun a subtle sweetness of laughter filled the hearts of every one: it seemed to them that they had never known gladness till that night.

Lugh played the music of sorrow. The wind moaned outside, and where the grass and flowers had been there was a dark sea of moving waters. The De Danaans within the dun bowed their heads on their hands and wept, and they had never wept for any grief.

Lugh played the music of peace, and outside there fell silently a strange snow. Flake by flake it settled on the earth and changed to starry dew. Flake by flake the quiet of the Land of the Silver Fleece settled in the hearts and minds of Nuada and his people: they closed their eyes and slept, each in his seat.

Lugh put the harp from him and stole out of the dun. The snow was still falling outside. It settled on his dark cloak and shone like silver scales; it settled on the thick curls of his hair and shone like jewelled fire; it filled the night about him with white radiance. He went back to his companions.

The sun had risen in the sky when the De Danaans awoke in Nuada's dun. They were light-hearted and joyous and it seemed to them that they had dreamed overnight a strange, beautiful dream.

FROM *THE SECOND BATTLE OF MOYTURA*

Anonymous (ca. ninth century BCE), translated by Whitley Stokes

The medieval manuscript from which this selection is taken, Cath Dédenach Maige Tuired *or* The Second Battle of Moytura, *is one of the earliest written sources of Irish mythology we have. In this excerpt, Lugh and the Tuatha Dé Dannan enter into battle against the Fomorians, the chthonic gods of Ireland, who had enslaved the Tuatha Dé Danann and treated them cruelly. After Lugh slays their king, his grandfather Balor, he secures the promise of an eternally good harvest from Bres, one of the Fomorians, in exchange for sparing his life.*

A brehon was an advocate or judge in ancient Ireland. A glaive is a spear, and kine are cows.

The hosts uttered a great shout as they entered the battle. Then they came together and each of them began to smite the other.

Many beautiful men fell there in the stall of death. Great the slaughter and the grave-lying that was there! Pride and shame were there side by side. There was anger and indignation.... Harsh, moreover, was the thunder that was there throughout the battle, the shouting of the warriors and the clashing of the shields, the flashing and whistling of the glaives and the ivory-hilted swords, the rattling and jingling of the quivers, the sound and winging of the darts and the javelins, and the crashing of the weapons!

... Lugh and Balor of the Piercing Eye met in the battle. An evil eye had Balor. That eye was never opened save only on a battle-field. Four men used to lift up the lid of the eye with a (polished) handle which passed through its lid. If an army looked at that eye, though they were many thousands in number they could not resist a few warriors. Hence had it that poisonous power.... Then he and Lugh met.

"Lift up mine eyelid, my lad," says Balor, "that I may see the babbler who is conversing with me."

The lid is raised from Balor's eye. Then Lugh cast a sling-stone at him, which carried the eye through his head. And so it was his own army that looked at it. And it fell on the host of the Fomorians, and thrice nine of them died beside it....

Thereafter the battle became a rout, and the Fomorians were beaten to the sea.

Thereafter Lugh and his comrades found Bres son of Elathu unguarded. He said: "It is better to give me quarter than to slay me"

"What then will follow from that?" says Lugh.

"If I be spared," says Bres, "the kine of Erin will always be in milk."

"I will set this forth to our wise men," says Lugh.

Hence Lugh went to Maeltne Mór-brethach, and said to him: "Shall Bres have quarter for giving constant milk to the kine of Erin?"

"He shall not have quarter," said Maeltne; "he has no power over their age or their (offspring) though he can milk them so long as they are alive."

Lugh said to Bres: "That does not save thee: thou hast no power over their age and their (offspring) though thou canst milk them."

"'Is there aught else that will save thee, O Bres?" says Lugh.

"There is in sooth. Tell your brehon that for sparing me the men of Ireland shall reap a harvest in every quarter of the year."

Said Lugh to Maeltne: "Shall Bres be spared for giving the men of Ireland a harvest of corn every quarter?"

"This has suited us," said Maeltne: "the spring for ploughing and sowing, and the beginning of summer for the end of the strength of corn, and the beginning of autumn for the end of the ripeness of corn and for reaping it. Winter for consuming it."

"That does not rescue thee," said Lugh to Bres.

"Less than that rescues thee," saith Lugh.

"What?" says Bres.

"How shall the men of Ireland plough? How shall they sow? How shall they reap? After making known these three things thou wilt be spared."

"Tell them' says Bres 'that their ploughing be on a Tuesday, their casting seed into the field be on a Tuesday, their reaping on a Tuesday."

So through that stratagem Bres was let go free.

FATE
Francis Ledwidge (1887–1917)

The Irish poet Ledwidge here recalls the battle between Lugh and Balor—and the terror that the dark god Balor can still hold for modern humans.

Lugh made a stir in the air
With his sword of cries,
And fairies thro' hidden ways
Came from the skies,
And their spells withered up the fair
And vanquished the wise.

And old lame Balor came down
With his gorgon eye
Hidden behind its lid,
Old, withered and dry.
He looked on the wattle town,
And the town passed by.

These things I know in my dreams,
The crying sword of Lugh,
And Balor's ancient eye
Searching me through,
Withering up my songs
And my pipe yet new.

LUGHNASADH DANCE
Gwydion Pendderwen (1946–1982)

This song, originally from the LP Songs for the Old Religion, *works equally well as a poem. Tailtiu was the foster-mother of Lugh, and Balor is a chthonic Irish god who threatens the gods of fertility and light, and by extension humankind as well. Balor has a single eye that will kill anything that it looks upon; Lugh took out the eye with his slingshot during the Second Battle of Moytura. Balor's eye did fly out of his body according to the recorded legend, but the idea that it became the sun seems to be a bit of hyperbole on the part of Gwydion. Lugh is often named as the father of Sétanta/Cúchulainn, the Irish Achilles, but Cúchulainn's mother is always named as Deichtine, the sister of the King of Ulster. However, given that all these characters are legendary, it may be that Gwydion could have made a case for Deichtine as an incarnation of Ériu or Erin—that is, Ireland herself. In the following, italicized text represents the chorus.*

Lugh the light of summer bright, clothed all in green;
Tailtiu, his mother true, rise up and be seen.

At your festival sound the horn, calling the people again,
Child of barleycorn, newly summer-born, ripening like the grain.

Lugh grew tall from spring to fall and sought to find a wife,
But Balor came and made his claim and swore to take his life.

At your festival sound the horn, calling the people again,
Child of barleycorn, newly summer-born, ripening like the grain.

The two did fight from morn 'till night, when Lugh did strike him one.
And Balor's eye flew in the sky and there became the sun.

At your festival sound the horn, calling the people again,
Child of barleycorn, newly summer-born, ripening like the grain.

Lugh he sped and made his bed with Erinn in the north,
And there they lay for many a day and soon a child came forth.

At your festival sound the horn, calling the people again,
Child of barleycorn, newly summer-born, ripening like the grain.

The child grew tall from spring to fall, Sétanta was his name,
And then at length by honor's strength Cúchulainn he became.

At your festival sound the horn, calling the people again,
Child of barleycorn, newly summer-born, ripening like the grain.

From "The Shadow House of Lugh"

Ethna Carbery (1864–1902)

This poem, from the Celtic Revival, imagines the house of Lugh after his triumph.

Dream-fair, beside dream waters, it stands alone:
A winging thought of Lugh made its cornerstone:
A desire of his heart raised its walls on high,
And set its crystal windows to flaunt the sky.

Its doors of the white bronze are many and bright,
With wondrous carven pillars for his Love's delight,
And its roof of the blue wings, the speckled red,
Is a flaming arc of beauty above her head.

Like a mountain through mist Lugh towers high,
The fiery-forked lightning is the glance of his eye,
His countenance is noble as the Sun-god's face–
The proudest chieftain he of a proud Dedanaan race.

He bides there in peace now his wars are all done–
He gave his hand to Balor when the death-gate was won,
And for the strife-scarred heroes who wander in the shade,
His door lieth open, and the rich feast is laid.

Lammas

Leanne Daharja Veitch

These lyrics from the Australian choral composer's Wheel of the Year *cycle celebrate Lammas or "Loaf-Mass"—the English holiday of the first fruits of harvest, also held on the first of August—as the beginning of the end of summer.*

Bring the crops in against the weather:
Wheat and barley and hops and hay.
Working, harvesting in together—
Celebrating Lammas today.

Night draws nearer, and wind blows colder:
Wheat and barley and hops and hay.
Gather in as the days grow shorter,
Celebrating Lammas today.

Cull the last of the Summer's bounty:
Wheat and barley and hops and hay.
Welcome in Autumn's golden beauty—
Celebrating Lammas today.

Bid farewell to the days of Summer:
Wheat and barley and hops and hay.
Calling in the cool rains of Winter,
Celebrating Lammas today.

FROM "TO THE GODS"

Adam Oehlenschläger (1779–1850), translated by Rune Bjørnsen

Frey, brother of Freya, is the Norse god associated with good harvest. Gullinbursti is his golden-haired boar, who sometimes pulls the god's chariot.

Frey! golden fruitful!
Lord of plenty!
You, that gave grain to the Earth
Shaken from your Gullinbursti.
Give me a modest meal,
While my song in the forest sounds.

FROM "FOR THE VANADÍS"

Gudrun of Mimirsbrunnr (twenty-first century)

Here Freya's gold neck-ring or necklace, Brisingamen, gives the goddess the epithet Brisingamen-Bearer.

Hail to the Jeweled Lady
on Lammas morning
whose flesh is her treasure,
and worth all the greatest treasure,
all that gold can buy.

O Freya Brisingamen-Bearer,
help me to know my own worth
for I am dull and shrunken with years of downcast eyes
and I have forgotten the mystery of the proud glance.

JOHN BARLEYCORN

Traditional English / Scottish, collected by Robert Burns; spelling standardized

There are literally hundreds of versions of this great Scots/English ballad, which recounts the life, maiming, death, and resurrection of the spirit of the grain, personified as "John Barleycorn." Because the resurrection takes the form of beer or spirits, alcohol was once referred to as "John Barleycorn" as well. The ballad itself is not ancient, but it does reflect the enduring Pagan tradition of the Dying God of vegetation, which survived in rural folk traditions long after the ascent of Christianity.

This version of the Barleycorn ballad was collected by the great Scots poet Robert Burns. There are also many recordings of the song, from folk versions by Steeleye Span and Fairport Convention to Traffic's rock- and jazz-influenced "John Barleycorn Must Die."

There were three kings into the east,
Three kings both great and high,
And they have sworn a solemn oath
John Barleycorn should die.

They took a plough and ploughed him down,
Put clods upon his head,
And they have sworn a solemn oath
John Barleycorn was dead.

But the cheerful Spring came kindly on
And showers began to fall;
John Barleycorn got up again,
And sore surprised them all.

The sultry suns of Summer came,
And he grew thick and strong:
His head well arm'd with pointed spears,
That no one should him wrong.

The sober Autumn entered mild,
When he grew wan and pale;
His bending joints and drooping head
Showed he began to fail.

His color sickened more and more,
He faded into age;
And then his enemies began
To show their deadly rage.

They've taken a weapon, long and sharp,
And cut him by the knee;
They tied him fast upon a cart,
Like a rogue for forgerie.

They laid him down upon his back,
And cudgelled him full sore.
They hung him up before the storm,
And turned him o'er and o'er.

They filled up a darksome pit
With water to the brim,
They heaved in John Barleycorn-
There, let him sink or swim!

They laid him upon the floor,
To work him farther woe;
And still, as signs of life appeared,
They tossed him to and fro.

They wasted o'er a scorching flame
The marrow of his bones;
But a miller used him worst of all,
For he crushed him between two stones.

And they have taken his very hero blood
And drank it round and round;
And still the more and more they drank,
Their joy did more abound.

John Barleycorn was a hero bold,
Of noble enterprise;
For if you do but taste his blood,
'Twill make your courage rise.

'Twill make a man forget his woe;
'Twill heighten all his joy:
'Twill make the widow's heart to sing,
Though the tear were in her eye.

Then let us toast John Barleycorn,
Each man a glass in hand;
And may his great posterity
Ne'er fail in old Scotland!

AUGUST 12: THE LAMP-LIGHTING

The worship of the great goddess Isis was born in Egypt, but by the middle of the first century BCE her devotion had spread to Greece; soon afterward, she began to be honored in Rome as well. Conservative Romans initially resisted her arrival, fearing that Egyptian gods constituted a threat to traditional Roman religion, but this feeling soon faded away: by the first centuries CE, there were many temples to Isis throughout the empire.

The *Lychnapsia*, which means "the lamp-lighting," was originally an Egyptian festival in honor of Isis, but it had become Romanized by the first centuries CE. It commemorates the goddess' birthday, which her devotees celebrated by lighting lamps in her temples and in their homes—a beautiful festival of lights in the waning days of summer.

INVOCATION OF ISIS
Apuleius (ca. 124–ca. 170 CE), translated by Andrew Lang

Andrew Lang was a nineteenth-century folklorist, anthropologist, and spiritualist who is best known today for his color-coded collections of fairy tales: The Green Fairy Book, The Red Fairy Book, *etc. This is his translation of the invocation to Isis from the ancient Roman novel* The Golden Ass.

Here, in the tradition of Roman syncretism, Isis is equated with many other goddesses, as Apuleius calls upon her "by all the names men know you by."

Thou that art sandalled on immortal feet
With leaves of palm, the prize of Victory;
Thou that art crowned with snakes and blossoms sweet,
Queen of the silver dews and shadowy sky,
I pray thee by all names men name thee by!
Demeter, come, and leave the yellow wheat!
Or Aphrodite, let thy lovers sigh!
Or Dian, from thine Asian temple fleet!

Or, yet more dread, divine Persephone
From worlds of wailing spectres, ah, draw near;
Approach, Selene, from thy subject sea;
Come, Artemis, and this night spare the deer:
By all thy names and rites I summon thee;
By all thy rites and names, Our Lady, hear!

FROM "TANNHAUSER"

Aleister Crowley (1875–1947)

Isis am I, and from my life are fed
    All stars and suns, all moons that wax and wane,
Create and uncreate, living and dead,
    The Mystery of Pain.
I am the Mother, I the silent Sea,
    The Earth, its travail, its fertility.
Life, death, love, hatred, light, darkness, return to me—
    To Me!

FROM *COMMENTARIES ON PLATO'S "TIMAEUS"*

Proclus Lycaeus (412–485 CE), translated by B. Nolan

These are the words that were supposed to be inscribed underneath a statue of Isis at Sais, an ancient Egyptian cultic center. They were much commented on in antiquity, and gave rise to the title of Helena Blavatsky's famous nineteenth-century esoteric work, Isis Unveiled.

I am Isis. I am all that has been, all that is, all that shall be; no mortal man has ever me unveiled. The fruit of my womb is the sun.

FROM "ISIS"

Frances L. Mace (1836–1899)

This seems to be a meditation at the feet of the veiled statue of Isis in Sais.

Low at her feet I watch and dream;
She will not lift her veil;
I dimly see a brow sublime
And features grand and pale,
And feel a mighty heart replies
To all my rapture or my sighs.

She is so near her breathing falls
On my attentive ear,
She is so far the twilight stars
Shine through her mantle clear
As silent as the grave may be,
And yet the soul of melody.

The lotus trembling on her brow
Exhales divine perfume;
The mystic splendor of her smile
Pervades my narrow gloom.
The dearth of solitary hours
She answers with a thousand flowers.

Oppressed by haunting, hindering cares
My heart rebels at fate;
She stoops to me, and lo! I share
Her own imperial state.
I glide beyond my prison bars
And walk with her the path of stars.

"I AM THE STAR" FROM *MOON MAGIC*

Dion Fortune (1890–1946)

The ceremonial magician and novelist Dion Fortune (Violet Mary Firth) published this invocation of the Great Goddess, whom she identified with Isis, in her magical novel Moon Magic.

I am the star that rises from the sea,
The twilight sea.
I bring men dreams that rule their destiny.
I bring the moon-tides to the souls of men;
The tides that flow and ebb and flow again;
These are my secret, these belong to me.

I am the eternal Woman, I am she—
The tides of all men's souls belong to me.
The tides that flow and ebb and flow again;
The secret, silent tides that govern men;
These are my secret, these belong to me.

Out of my hands he takes his destiny.
Touch of my hands bestows serenity—
These are the moon-tides, these belong to me.
Isis in heaven, on earth, Persephone;
Diana of the Moon, and Hecate.
Veiled Isis, and Aphrodite from the sea,
All these am I and they are seen in me.

HYMN TO ISIS FROM HER TEMPLE AT PHILAE III

Anonymous (ca. 690 BCE), translated by Louis V. Žabkar

Philae, near the First Cataract of the Nile, was the site of a large temple complex dedicated to Isis and Osiris. The Ennead are a (variable) grouping of the nine foremost deities of ancient Egypt, somewhat similar to the idea of the Olympian twelve in Greece. Isis and Osiris are among their number.

O Isis, the Great, God's mother, Lady of Philae,
God's Wife, God's Adorer, and God's Hand,

God's mother and Great Royal Spouse,
Adornment and Lady of the Ornaments of the Palace.

Lady and desire of the Green Fields,
Nursling who fills the palace with her beauty,
Fragrance of the palace, mistress of joy,
Who completes her course in the Divine Place.

Rain-cloud that makes green the fields when it descends,
Maiden, sweet of love, Lady of Upper and Lower Egypt,
Who issues orders among the divine Ennead,
According to whose command one rules.

Princess, great of praise, lady of charm,
Whose face enjoys the trickling of fresh myrrh.

From "Forces of Things"

Victor Hugo (1802–1885)

French novelist Victor Hugo, author of The Hunchback of Notre-Dame *and* Les Misérables, *here equates Isis with Nature herself.*

Nature, veiled Isis, sits at our door,
Unknowable grandmother with kindly gaze,
Ancient like Cybele and fresh like Iris,
That which we do here on earth passes before your face;
All ugliness is effaced by your radiance....

Hymn to Isis II

Isidorus (ca. 100 BCE), translated by Vera F. Vanderlip

In this prayer, inscribed on the gates of a temple in the Fayum region of Egypt, Isis is equated with the goddess of Good Luck (Agathē Tychē) and Renenūtet, goddess of harvest, known in Greek as Hermouthis. Agathos Daimon is the spirit of the vineyards and fields of grain; here he seems to be equated with Sokonopis, a crocodile god. Anchoēs seems to be another name for Horus.

Hail, Agathē Tychē, greatly renowned Isis, mightiest
Hermouthis, in you every city rejoices;
O Discoverer of Life and Cereal food wherein all

mortals delight because of your blessings.

All who pray to you to assist their commerce,

prosper in their piety forever;

All who are bound in mortal illnesses in the grip of death,

if they but pray to you, quickly attain your renewal of Life.

How truly the Agathos Daimon, mighty Sokonopis,

dwells as your temple-mate, that goodly Bestower of wealth,

Creator of both earth and the starry heaven,

and of all rivers, and very swift streams;

and Anchoës your Son, who inhabits the height of heaven,

is the rising Sun who shows forth the light.

All indeed who wish to beget offspring,

if they but pray to you, attain fruitfulness.

Persuading the gold-flowing Nile, you lead it in season

over the land of Egypt as a blessing for men.

Then all vegetation flourishes and you apportion to all

whom you favor, a life of unspeakable blessings.

Remembering your gifts, men to whom you have granted wealth

and great blessings which you give them to possess all their lives,

All duly set aside for you one tenth of these blessings

rejoicing each year at the time of your Festival.

Joyful after your festival, they return home

reverently and are filled with the sense of blessedness that comes only from you.

Grant a share of your gifts also to me, Lady Hermouthis,

Your suppliant, happiness and especially the blessing of children.

"ISIS SPEAKS" FROM *THE GOLDEN ASS*

Apuleius (ca. 124–ca. 170), translated by Harold Edgeworth Butler

In this excerpt from the ancient Roman novel, Isis responds to the prayers of her devotee, reminding him that she is the incarnation of all goddesses.

Phrygians were, roughly, people who hail from what is now Turkey, and they worshipped Cybele, the Mother of the Gods, at Pessinus, a town now called Ballhisar. Minerva, or Athena, is here called "Cecropian" because Cecropia is an old name for the Acropolis, site of her shrine at Athens. Cyprians are denizens of Cyprus, whose city Paphos is said to be where Aphrodite came ashore after her birth from the sea. "Stygian" means "of the Styx," the river of the Underworld. Bellona is a Roman war-goddess, and "the Rhamnusian" is the goddess Nemesis, who punishes arrogance and wrongdoing.

I am come, moved by thy supplication, I, nature's mother, mistress of all the elements, the first-begotten offspring of the ages, of deities mightiest, queen of the dead, first of heaven's denizens, in whose aspect are blent the aspects of all gods and goddesses. With my rod I rule the shining heights of heaven, the health-giving breezes of the sea, the mournful silence of the underworld. The whole earth worships my godhead, one and individual, under many a changing shape, with varied rites and by many diverse names. There the Phrygians, first-born of men, call me the mother of the gods that dwells at Pessinus; there the Athenians, sprung from the soil they till, know me as Cecropian Minerva; there the wave-beaten Cyprians style me Venus of Paphos; the archer Cretans, Diana of the hunter's net; the Sicilians, with their threefold speech, Stygian Proserpine; the Eleusinians, the ancient goddess Ceres. Others call me Juno, others Bellona, others Hecate, others the Rhamnusian, but those on whom shine the first rays of the sun-god as each day he springs to new birth, the Arii and the Ethiopians, and the Egyptians mighty in ancient lore, honor me with my peculiar rites and call me by my true name, Isis the Queen. I am come in pity for thy woes. I am come propitious and strong to aid.

FROM "THE THUNDER, PERFECT MIND"

Anonymous (before 350 CE), translated by Anne McGuire

The extraordinary poem from which this excerpt comes, the subject of much scholarly debate, is part of the Nag Hammadi, a cache of early Gnostic and Christian texts discovered in Egypt in 1945. The speaker is clearly a goddess, who promises everlasting life to her followers; although she is never named, it seems to me reasonable to consider her a manifestation of Isis, the foremost goddess of Egypt, particularly since she says that her "image is multiple in Egypt." This hymn is not, however, part of traditional Isiac worship.

I was sent from the Power
And I have come to those who think upon me.
And I was found among those who seek after me.

Look at me, you who think upon me;
And you hearers, hear me!

You who are waiting for me, take me to yourselves.
And do not pursue me from your vision.
And do not make your sound hate me, nor your hearing.
Do not be ignorant of me at any place or any time.
Be on guard!
Do not be ignorant of me.

For I am the first and the last.
I am the honored and the scorned,
I am the harlot and the holy one.
I am the wife and the virgin.
I am the m[oth]er and the daughter.
I am the members of my mother.

I am the barren one and the one with many children.
I am she whose marriage is multiple, and I have not taken a husband.
I am the midwife and she who does not give birth.
I am the comforting of my labor pains.

I am the bride and the bridegroom.
It is my husband who begot me.
I am the mother of my father and the sister of my husband.
And he is my offspring.
I am the servant of him who prepared me and I am the lord of my offspring.
But he is the one who be[got me] before time on a day of birth and he is my offspring in time, and my power is from him.
I am the staff of his power in his youth and he is the rod of my old age.
And whatever he wills happens to me.

I am the incomprehensible silence and the much-remembered thought.
I am the voice of many sounds and the utterance (logos) of many forms.
I am the utterance of my name.

Why, you who hate me, do you love me
And hate those who love me?
You who deny me, confess me,
And you who confess me, deny me.

You who speak the truth about me, tell lies about me,

And you who have told lies about me, speak the truth about me.

You who know me, become ignorant of me; and may those who have been ignorant of me come to know me.

For I am knowledge and ignorance.

I am shame and boldness.

I am unashamed, I am ashamed.

I am strength and I am fear.

I am war and peace.

Give heed to me.

I am the disgraced and the exalted one.

Give heed to my poverty and my wealth.

Do not be haughty to me when I am discarded upon the earth,

And you will find me among [those] that are to come.

And do not look upon me on the garbage-heap and go and leave me discarded.

And you will find me in the kingdoms.

And do not look upon me when I am discarded among those who are disgraced and in the least places,

And then laugh at me.

And do not cast me down among those who are slain in severity.

But as for me, I am merciful and I am cruel.

Be on guard!

Do not hate my obedience,

And do not love my self-control in my weakness.

Do not forsake me,

And do not be afraid of my power.

Why then do you despise my fear

And curse my pride?

I am she who exists in all fears and boldness in trembling.

I am she who is weak, and I am well in pleasure of place.

I am foolish and I am wise.

Why have you hated me in your counsels?

(Is it) because I shall be silent among those who are silent,

And I shall appear and speak?

Why then have you hated me, you Greeks?

Because I am a non-Greek among non-Greeks?

For I am the Wisdom of Greeks

And the Gnosis of non-Greeks.

I am judgment for Greeks and non-Greeks.

I am the one whose image is multiple in Egypt.

And the one who has no image among non-Greeks.

I am she who has been hated everywhere and who has been loved everywhere.

I am she who is called Life and you have called Death.

I am she who is called Law and you have called Lawlessness.

I am the one you have pursued, and I am the one you have restrained.

I am the one you have scattered and you have gathered me together.

Before me you have been ashamed and you have been unashamed with me.

I am she who observes no festival and I am she whose festivals are many. ...

Behold, then, his utterances and all the writings that have been completed.

Give heed, then, listeners, and you also, angels,

And those who have been sent,

And you spirits who have arisen from the dead.

For I am the one who alone exists,

And I have no one who will judge me.

For many are the sweet forms that exist in numerous sins

And unrestrained acts and disgraceful passions, and temporal pleasures,

Which are restrained until they become sober

And run up to their place of rest.

And they will find me there,

And they will live and they will not die again.

PRAYER TO ISIS

Christina Walshe (1888–1959)

This beautiful prayer was set to music by English composer Rutland Boughton.

O Isis, Mother of God, to thee I pray!

Forget not thy daughters here upon the earth.

Forgive them, for they have turned away from thee—

They who labor, suffer, and weep—

How much thou only knowest!—

Have forgotten that they are the daughters of Isis,

For they think they are the daughters and wives of men.

O come, Isis, and in thy majesty

Make thy throne in the hearts of women.

Teach them their right to honor,

And their queenship 'spite of suffering.

In thy glorious motherhood stoop down

And raise their hearts to dwell with thee in proud and passionate joy.

O Isis, Mother of God, hear my prayer!

MID-AUGUST: ATHENA'S BIRTHDAY

The gray-eyed goddess Pallas Athena (the Roman Minerva), deity of wisdom, war, and artisanal skill, is celebrated every August, the time when she is supposed to have been born, fully formed and dressed in armor, from the head of Zeus. In Athens, her eponymous city, her holiday was called the Panathenaea; it was held at a time that corresponds more or less to our August 13. On this day an elaborate procession would make its way to the Parthenon, her great temple on the Acropolis, laden with gifts for the goddess, and, after offerings were presented to her, a great feast would be held. Once every four years the festival became the Greater Panathenaea, and included athletic games and contests of poetry and music. In antiquity the Panathenaic Games rivaled the better-known Olympic Games for attendance and prestige, and were believed to be much older.

It isn't necessary to have a full-blown procession or athletic contest to worship Athena, however. Any of the following hymns would work as a tribute to the goddess in honor of her sacred day.

HYMN TO ATHENA

Percy Bysshe Shelley (1792–1822)

"Tritogenia" means "goddess born from the head" (Athena was born from the head of Zeus). The Aegis, which both Zeus and Athena bear, is a shield or breastplate sporting the head of Medusa. The sun is the son of Hyperion referred to here.

I sing the glorious Power with azure eyes,
Athenian Pallas! timeless, chaste, and wise,
Tritogenia, town-preserving Maid,
Revered and mighty; from his awful head
Whom Jove brought forth, in warlike armor dressed,
Golden, all radiant! wonder strange possessed
The everlasting Gods that Shape to see,
Shaking a javelin keen, impetuously
Rush from the crest of Aegis-bearing Jove;
Fearfully Heaven was shaken, and did move
Beneath the might of the Cerulean-eyed;
Earth dreadfully resounded, far and wide;
And, lifted from its depths, the sea swelled high
In purple billows, the tide suddenly
Stood still, and great Hyperion's son long time
Checked his swift steeds, till, where she stood sublime,
Pallas from her immortal shoulders threw
The arms divine; wise Jove rejoiced to view.
Child of the Aegis-bearer, hail to thee,
Nor thine nor others' praise shall unremembered be.

PALLAS ATHENA

Madeline Vaughn Abbott and Bertha Haven Putnam (1893?)

Athena is a natural symbol of women's education. This little hymn in her honor was written in the late nineteenth century at an American women's college.

Pallas Athena, goddess
Of learning and might,

We have come to you
To worship your divinity.
Hear us, hear us.

Bless us, we ask.
Grant us wisdom.
Let us be with you forever.
Hear us, blessed goddess.
Hear us, hear us.

Bless now our lanterns,
Let them always shine brightly,
Lighting our paths,
Lighting up the darkness.
Hear us, hear us.

FROM "THE BATH OF PALLAS"

Callimachus (ca. 310/305–ca. 240 BCE),
translated by A. W. Mair and G. R. Mair, modernized by B. Nolan

"The Phrygian" here is Paris, prince of Troy, who famously judged a beauty contest between Hera, Athena, and Aphrodite on Mount Ida in Turkey (near the Simois River), with catastrophic results. Argos is a city in Greece that has been continuously inhabited for about seven thousand years, and Inakhos is the name of a nearby river, now called the Panitsa. "Pelasgians" and the "daughters of Pelasgus" refer to the native inhabitants of Greece.

Pallas is an epithet of Athena, which means "to brandish." Athena's strong association with cities is highlighted here: she is both the Sacker of Cities (as she was at Troy) and the Keeper of Cities, depending on how well-disposed she is toward the inhabitants. "Her own tree" refers to the olive, whose oil is the only cosmetic Athena loves.

All you that are companions of the Bath of Pallas, come forth, come forth! I heard but now the snorting of the sacred steeds, and the goddess is ready to go. Haste now, O fair-haired daughters of Pelasgus, haste! Never did Athena wash her mighty arms before she drove the dust from the flanks of her horses—not even when, her armor all defiled with filth, she returned from the battle of the lawless Giants; but first she loosed from the care her horses' necks, and in the springs of Oceanus washed the flecks of sweat and from their mouths that champed the bit cleansed the clotted foam.

O come … and bring not, companions of the Bath, for Pallas perfume nor alabasters (for Athena loves not mixed unguents), neither bring you a mirror. Always her face is fair, and, even when the Phrygian judged the strife on Ida, the great goddess looked not … into the transparent eddy of Simois. … But Pallas, after running twice sixty double courses … took and skillfully anointed her with simple unguents, the birth of her own tree. And, O maidens, the red blush arose on her, as the color of the morning rose or seed of pomegranate. Wherefore now also bring only the manly olive oil, wherewith Castor and wherewith Heracles anoint themselves. And bring her a comb all of gold, that she may comb her hair, when she hath anointed her glossy tresses.

Come forth, Athena, Sacker of Cities, golden-helmeted, who rejoices in the din of horse and shield. Today, water-carriers, dip not your pitchers—today, O Argos, drink from the fountains and not from the river. … For, mingling his waters with gold and with flowers, Inakhos will come from his pastoral hills, bringing fair water for the Bath of Athena. But beware, O Pelasgian, lest even unwittingly you behold the Queen. Whoso shall behold Pallas, Keeper of Cities, naked, shall look on Argos for this the last time. Lady Athena, do come forth. …

[T]hat word is fulfilled over which Pallas bows; since to Athena only among his daughters has Zeus granted that she should win all things that belong to her sire, O companions of the Bath, and no mother bore that goddess, but the head of Zeus. The head of Zeus bows not in falsehood, and in falsehood his daughter has no part.

Now comes Athena in very deed. … Hail, goddess. … Hail when you drive forth your steeds, and home again may you drive them with joy. …

FROM THE ORPHIC HYMN TO ATHENA

Anonymous (ca. 200 CE), translated by B. Nolan

Renowned Pallas, born only of great Zeus, blessed, magnanimous goddess, brave in combat, your name is honored everywhere, you are known but still unknowable. You climb mountains and cross crevasses, and your heart rejoices in the woodlands. You love the weapons of war, and you pierce human spirits with madness, frenzy. Furious maiden, Gorgon-slayer, refusing the bed of desire but blessed mother of all art, berserker, you make the evil insane and the good wise. You are female and male, mother of war, many-formed dragoness, potent and illustrious, Giant-killer, Horse-driver, queenly Tritogenia, you deliver us from evil, both in the day and in the watches of the night.

FROM "PALLAS-ATHENA"

Arlita Dodge (1916)

There is a great deal to ponder in this curious little poem, published in a New York literary magazine during World War I. Is the author hoping that a mass conversion of Christians to the worship of the goddess will take place at some future date, or suggesting that Christians might want to worship Athena alongside Jesus, or just hoping that some of the goddess's archetypal attributes might come to be adopted by the Christian world? It is not entirely clear—but what is clear is that this is an impassioned plea for peace, prudence (as symbolized by the olive, Athena's gift to humankind), and a reawakening of the goddess.

The Parthenon is Athena's ancient temple in Athens. The chiton *is a Greek tunic.*

The Greeks who, mid the twilight grey
    That filled the stately Parthenon,
Stole in with outstretched hands to pray
To her who guarded them, are gone.
    Their golden chitons haunt no more
The pillars were her shadow fell,
    And yet she stands there—evermore
Athena guards the citadel!

Daughter of Zeus, beyond the sea,
    They need thee now; stretch out the hand
That touched with immortality
    The glories of a lyric land,
And lend them vision; through their tears
    Let them descry thy olive-tree;
Let peace pour down the swinging years
    And Christian nations worship thee!

From *The Eumenides*

Aeschylus (ca. 525–455 BCE),
translated by Gilbert Murray, modernized by B. Nolan

A prayer for deliverance. Lake Tritonis was the name of an ancient lake sometimes supposed to have been in Libya, though Tunisia has also been suggested as a possible site. In some stories Athena was born near the lake, or taken there immediately after her birth from her father's head.

Once more I pray the Lady of this place,
Athena, to my aid. Let her but come
Myself, my … people and my home
Shall without war be hers, hers true of heart
And changeless. Therefore, wherever you are,
In some far wilderness of Libyan earth,
By those Tritonid waters of your birth;
Girded for deeds or veiled on your throne. …
Guiding the storm, like some bold Lord of War,
Oh, hear! A goddess hears though afar
Bring me deliverance in this my hour!

Excerpts from Proclus's Hymn to Athena

Proclus Lycaeus (ca. 412–485 CE), translated by B. Nolan

The Pagan philosopher Proclus was particularly devoted to the goddess Athena, his great patron. When her statue was removed from the Parthenon (her temple in Athens) by Christians who wished to make her temple into a church, Proclus dreamt that the goddess came to him and asked to stay at his house. He welcomed her in the knowledge that, even though her official temples were gone, her worship would live on in the homes of the faithful.

Athena fought with the Olympian gods against the Titans, or Giants. The Acropolis in Athens is both the site of the Parthenon and the place where Athena gave the olive tree to humankind during a competition with Poseidon for the naming of the city. Athena won the competition, although Poseidon showed his displeasure with the children of Cecrops (the Athenians), as noted below.

Hear me, daughter of Zeus of the Aegis! You sprang forth from the bright head of the Father, shield-bearing Amazon, mighty daughter of a mighty father, golden-helmeted, armed with your spear, Pallas Tritogenia. Oh Lady, listen kindly to my prayer; do not let my words go out unanswered into the aether. You opened the holy gates of wisdom, you vanquished the giants, born of earth, who fought against the gods, and you protected your unassailable virginity by leaving the lustful Smith. You saved the whole heart of the dismembered Bacchus when he was butchered by the Titans, bringing it safely to the Father so that, in accordance with his divine will, Dionysus would be born again from Semele and the divine fire. ... You make beautiful each aspect of human life with your many skills, for you fill humans with the desire to create all crafts. You won the high Acropolis, an outward sign of the great height of your divinity. You love the nourishing earth, Mother of scholarship; and you competed with your uncle and insured that Athens would have your name, when you created the olive-tree for all time. ... O hear me, with your radiant, holy face, and grant me, in all my soul's travels in this world, a safe haven, and the illumination of your sacred stories, and wisdom, and love. Fill my heart with such strength that it draws me up from the material world toward heaven, the world of the gods. And if in life I make a terrible mistake due to my own folly or bad impulses, please forgive me, savior of mortals, kindly goddess; since I am yours, please keep me from the dreadful punishments meted out to the guilty. And please grant me health and keep disease and pain at bay, by your divine hand. ... I ask you from the bottom of my heart, Lady, please hear me!

FROM "ATHENA"

Henry E. Clay (1910)

Athena once famously grabbed the Greek hero Achilles by the hair, preventing him from killing King Agamemnon in a blind rage. She greatly favored Ulysses, the Greek king renowned for his cleverness.

Hail Wisdom! Stately blue-eyed maid
Of Grecian story, still arrayed
In virgin robes; nor yet afraid
To don the helmet and the shield,
And grasp the shining spear, and wield
With heroes on life's battle-field,
Some rash Achilles to restrain,
To urge the laggards o'er the plain,
Or guide Ulysses home again. ...

Forsake her not, for surely she
Shall blessings bring, and gain with thee
The Palace of the Pure and Free.

"STERN GODDESS" FROM THE *THEBAID*

Papinius Statius (ca. 45–ca. 96 CE), translated by B. Nolan

Athena wears the Gorgon head—the head of Medusa, which turns men to stone.

Stern goddess, glory and wisdom of your mighty father, you are great in war, you wear upon your cheeks the fierce splendor of your terrible helmet, where the blood-spattered Gorgon shines with rage … look graciously on my offering. … As always, in war and peace I will give you the many first-fruits of the work.

FROM "APOLLO"

Eugene Lee-Hamilton (1845–1907)

Hark, never cease
The pure chaste hymns to hail the mighty child
Of the cleft brows of Zeus, all undefiled;
Armed friend of peace
From whose strong breastplate streams transcendent light,
Whose spear makes dim the meteors of the night;
Pure Patroness of plenty and increase,
Mistress of sunny cities walled and white!

FROM *THE KNIGHTS*

Aristophanes (ca. 446–ca. 386 BCE), anonymous translation (1912),
modernized by B. Nolan

Oh! Pallas, guardian of Athens, you, who reign over the most pious city, the most powerful, the richest in warriors and in poets, hasten to my call, bringing in your train our faithful ally in all our expeditions and combats, Victory, who smiles on our choruses and fights with us against our rivals. Oh! goddess! manifest yourself to our sight. …

FROM "ATHENA"

Juanita Tramana (1916)

The Parthenon, Athena's temple in Athens, was and is one of the wonders of the world. After the ascent of Christianty it became a church, and later a mosque, and then finally a munitions dump for the Ottoman Empire, when it was severely damaged by fire. Still, enough of its glory survived to make it one of the foremost tourist sites of the world, and an enduring bone of contention between the governments of Greece and Great Britain, where large sections of the frieze and other sculptures ended up. But, as this poem reminds us, all the glory of the Parthenon is as nothing beside the splendor of the goddess it housed.

Hail, Athena! Proud daughter of a noble race divine!
Enthroned upon thy sacred hill whose splendor once did shine
On all the world around. Unrivalled on that lovely throne,
Thy beauty dimmed the luster of the glorious Parthenon....

FROM *THE WOMEN AT THE THESMOPHORIA*
Aristophanes (ca. 446–ca. 386 BCE),
anonymous translation (1912), modernized by B. Nolan

Aristophanes's comedy The Women at the Thesmophoria *is a brilliant parody of contemporary Athenian society, the playwright Euripides, and misogyny in general. The Thesmophoria was an ancient Greek festival in honor of Demeter, but in the play Athena is invoked, as well.*

Oh! Pallas, who are fond of dances, hasten hither at my call. Oh! chaste virgin, the protectress of Athens, I call you in accordance with the sacred rites, you, whose evident protection we adore and who keeps the keys of our city in your hands. Do you appear, you whose just hatred has overturned our tyrants. The womenfolk are calling you; hasten hither at their bidding along with Peace....

STANZAS FROM "ATHENE"
Robert Brown (1878)

A rollicking ballad in honor of the goddess, who was sometimes associated with the aether in antiquity. Dight means "clothed," in this case in armor.

From the vault of the sky, from the deeps on high
    I have sprung in harness dight;
A strength and a will both swift and still
    As the comets and stars of the night.
A luminous track through the darkness black,
    I illumine the human mind;

As the starry eyes, serene and wise,
    I steadily shine on the blind;
The spirit of wisdom, the spirit of truth
    In me may a mortal find.

At morn I am heard in the song of the bird,
    At noon in the trumpet's tone;
And the hum of the bee, and the roll of the sea,
    And the echoes are all mine own:
Calm speech is mine, and the song divine,
    And the air of my Father's heaven;
I am Queen of the Sky beneath and on high
    As far as the planets seven;
The spirit of freshness, the spirit of youth
    I give, for to me they were given.

I am old, I am young, I can sing, I have sung,
    I can wander o'er earth and o'er sea;
I have taught, I shall teach, and no language or speech
    But will breathe of my echoes and me;
The Olympian height, and the depths of the night,
    And whatever has been, or shall be,
I have known from of old and my bards have foretold
    Heaven's working, and heaven's decree;
The spirit of knowledge, the spirit of peace,
    Both now and eternally.

AUGUST 23: VULCANALIA

Vulcan, the lame Roman god of fire, volcanoes, and the forge, is the equivalent of the Greek Hephaistos. In Rome he was honored with bonfires in late August, perhaps because it is the hottest time of the year. Despite the great regard with which smiths were traditionally held in early Indo-European societies, Vulcan is not too well-known today (although he did lend his name to the fiery volcano). Nevertheless, as the god of all metalworking and metallurgy, he is the author of much of civilization.

HOMERIC HYMN TO HEPHAESTOS

Anonymous (ca. 700–500 BCE), translated by Hugh G. Evelyn-White

Sing, clear-voiced Muse, of Hephaestus famed for inventions. With bright-eyed Athena he taught men glorious crafts throughout the world, men who before used to dwell in caves in the mountains like wild beasts. But now that they have learned crafts through Hephaestus the famed worker, easily they live a peaceful life in their own houses the whole year round.

Be gracious, Hephaestus, and grant me success and prosperity!

FROM "ON VULCAN"

Nicholas Billingsley (1658)

Lemnos is an island in the Aegean Sea. Etna is a volcano, and so a fitting worksop for a divine smith; Lipara or Lipari is an Aeolian island with a number of small volcanoes. Brontes, Pyrachmon, and Steropes are all Cyclopes (the plural of Cyclops), and assistants of Vulcan. The invading giants are the Titans.

The sooty god of Jove and Juno sprung,
For his deformity from heaven flung,
Fell down into the Island Lemnos, with
The fall grew lame; made of the gods the smith:
There sets up trade. On sulphry Etna's top,
And Lipara sometimes he sets up shop;
Where, with the one-eyed monstrous Cyclopes,
Brontes, Pyrachmon and huge Steropes,
Jove's thunder-armor for the gods he made
Against those giants which would heaven invade:
To him the lion, terriblest of beasts
Was consecrated; in his honor feasts,
And sacrifices, celebrated were. . . .

ORPHIC HYMN TO HEPHAESTOS

Anonymous (ca. 200 CE) , translated by B. Nolan

Indomitable Hephaestos, mighty, great-hearted spirit, glittering one, shimmering one, great god who illuminates the lives of mortals, strong-handed lord who lives in your works, great craftsman of the cosmos, perfect element, highest, all-consuming, all-taming, all-commanding—you are the sun, the moon, the stars, and the sky, all the pure lights: these things are the parts of you seen by the world. You may be found in every nation, every city, every home; and you reside in the bodies of humans, mighty giver of a multitude of blessings. Hear me, holy one, as I call you to this sacred libation, please come gently to the rites of welcome, tame the savage anger of wild fire, even as nature burns in our own bodies.

HEPHAESTUS

Sir William Watson (1858–1935)

It is impossible to overstate the importance of the gifts of Hephaestus—bronze and, later, iron—to humankind; civilization would not have been possible without them. Here Hephaestus, as god of volcanoes, becomes a fashioner of the literal world as well.

Etna is a volcano in Sicily.

The Subduer of Iron, the Lord of fierce Flame,
Amid mortals he tarried—the God that was lame;
And divine though his lineage, and heavenly his birth,
Full deep were his tangles with cavernous Earth,
When far in Mount Etna's hot heart he abode,
Where fearsome and splendid his furnaces glowed.

"Whatsoever is mighty," he cried out in glee,
"Twixt Hammer and Anvil is fashioned by me."
And abysses volcanian up-thundered their joy,
For he smote like the Powers that create and destroy;
The Pow'rs that sublimely the fuel have hurled
On the fires of the forges where shaped is the world.

AUGUST 24: THE DAY OF VICTORY

Although she is mostly remembered today for having had her name co-opted by a soulless multinational corporation, Nike, the goddess of victory (or Victoria as she was known to the Romans), was an important goddess in the ancient world. Nike (say knee-KAY, not NIGH-kee) had a temple in Athens, where this festival was celebrated, and there was also an altar to Victoria, her Roman equivalent, in the Roman Senate until 357 CE, when it was removed by the Emperor Constantius (although it was briefly restored by the Pagan Emperor Julian and continued to be hauled in and out of the Senate before its final removal by the Christians). As Victoria, she was perhaps the most emotive symbol of what the Roman state understood itself to be—strong, just, and triumphant—and, since the founders of America very self-consciously modeled themselves on the ancient Romans, Victoria's image can now be found on public buildings in cities throughout the United States, including in Washington, New York, Baltimore, and San Francisco.

But Nike is much more than a goddess of conquest and empire. She fights for justice (even if the humans who invoke her often don't) and was the charioteer of Zeus in the final battle against the Titans. She is often shown next to Zeus and Athena, or authority and wisdom, respectively.

ORPHIC HYMN TO VICTORY

Anonymous (ca. 200 CE), translated by B. Nolan

I call upon mighty Nike, besought by mortals, she who alone can free us from the violence of contention, she who alone can grant sweet triumph to those she favors. You judge the contests, the deeds of honor, and grant the prize of the laurel crown. Queen of all, you grant noble fame born of strife, which burgeons in the festivals of peace, held in honor of your glory. So come, longed-for goddess with the shining eyes, come kindly and grant glory to our worthy works.

FROM "ODE 11"

Bacchylides (ca. 518–ca. 451 BCE), translated by Diane Arnson Svarlien

Styx is the goddess of the river that flows through the Underworld.

Victory, giver of sweet gifts…in golden Olympus, standing beside Zeus, you judge the achievement of excellence for immortals and mortals alike. Be gracious, daughter of Styx with her long hair, the upright judge.

SEPTEMBER

Autumn comes in with September, a month balanced, like the equinox itself, between opposites. The month starts off with a great feast in honor of Jove or Zeus, king of the gods. Then, as the nights lengthen, it's time to remember the most famous festival of the ancient Graeco-Roman world: the Greater Eleusinian Mysteries, a celebration of the two goddesses, Demeter and Persephone. The Mysteries are but one of a series of holidays honoring the earth goddesses, and here, at the height of the harvest, they may be joined by counterparts such as Gaia, Hertha, and Physis, in a great celebration of the Earth herself. Still, this fertility festival comes with a sobering coda: it is the definitive end of the season of light and growth.

SEPTEMBER 13: THE FEAST OF JOVE, PART I

Jove or Jupiter, the Roman equivalent of the Greek Zeus, is the king of the gods and Lord of Thunder. As husband, father, son, and brother, this ancient sky god creates and oversees relationships within the family of the gods; as the god who freed his Olympian brothers and sisters from eternal imprisonment in the body of their murderous father, he is acknowledged as their leader. In keeping with his royal status, he was given a spectacular ritual feast in his temple at Rome every September (which, after the ceremonies were over, would be eaten by the priests and distributed to the poor). A second, smaller feast was celebrated in his honor in November.

Today would be a good day to make a donation to a soup kitchen or throw a party in honor of Zeus, but the following collection of poems and prayers will allow you to fete the god with words as well as food.

HOMERIC HYMN TO ZEUS

Anonymous (ca. 700–500 BCE), translated by Hugh G. Evelyn-White

Themis is the goddess of justice and divine law; her name is closely related to the Sanskrit word dharma. *Zeus is the son of the Titan Cronos.*

I will sing of Zeus, chiefest among the gods and greatest, all-seeing, the lord of all, the ful-filler who whispers words of wisdom to Themis as she sits leaning towards him.

Be gracious, all-seeing Son of Cronos, most excellent and great!

"ZEUS FILLS THE HEAVENS" FROM *PHAENOMENA*

Aratus of Soli (ca. 310–240 BCE), translated by G. R. Mair, modernized by B. Nolan

From an ancient astronomical text comes this paean to Zeus. The Elder Race refers to the Titans, ancestors of the Olympian gods.

From Zeus let us begin; him do we mortals never leave unnamed; full of Zeus are all the streets and all the market-places of men; full is the sea and the havens thereof; always we all have need of Zeus. For we are also his offspring; and he in his kindness unto mortals gives favorable signs and wakens the people to work, reminding them of livelihood. He tells what time the soil is best for the labor of the ox and for the mattock, and what time the seasons are favorable both for the planting of trees and for casting all manner of seeds. For himself it was who set the signs in heaven, and marked out the constellations, and for the year devised what stars chiefly should give to men right signs of the seasons, to the end that all things might grow unfailingly. Wherefore him do men ever worship first and last. Hail, O Father, mighty marvel, mighty blessing unto men. Hail to you and to the Elder Race! Hail, ye Muses, right kindly, every one!

ORPHIC HYMN TO ZEUS OF THE LIGHTNING

Anonymous (ca. 200 CE?), translated by B. Nolan

I invoke great Zeus, holy, resounding, illustrious, airy, burning, you who move in fire, bursting in the air as lightning, you who raise your terrifying voice in the flight of clouds, terrible, vengeful, unstoppable, divine Zeus of lightning, source of all things, most power-ful Lord, please grant my life a happy ending.

THE HYMN OF THE KOURETES

Anonymous (before 200 CE), translated by Gilbert Murray, modernized by B. Nolan

This hymn comes from an inscription that was discovered in 1904 at the sanctuary of the Dictaean Zeus on Crete. Dicte or Dikte was the mountain where Zeus was hidden from his murderous father, Cronos or Kronos, and secretly raised—but it could also be anywhere the worship of Zeus is kept alive in the face of adversity.

Kouros is here used as a title of Zeus; a kouros is the personification of idealized youth. So Zeus here is not the bearded father figure, but the young warrior who overthrew his murderous father.

Themis is the goddess of justice; the Daimones are spirits following in Zeus's train. Io is a religious cry of greeting and exultation.

Io, Kouros most Great, I give thee hail, Kronian, Lord of all that is wet and gleaming, you are come at the head of thy Daimones. To Dikte for the Year, Oh, march, and rejoice in the dance and song,

That we make to you with harps and pipes mingled together, and sing as we come to a stand at your well-fenced altar.

Io, Kouros most Great, I give thee hail, Kronian, Lord of all that is wet and gleaming, you are come at the head of thy Daimones. To Dikte for the Year, Oh, march, and rejoice in the dance and song,

For here the shielded Nurturers [Kouretes] took you, a child immortal, from Rhea, and with noise of beating feet hid you away.

Io, Kouros most Great, I give thee hail, Kronian, Lord of all that is wet and gleaming, you are come at the head of thy Daimones. To Dikte for the Year, Oh, march, and rejoice in the dance and song,

And the Horai began to be fruitful … and all wild living things were held about by wealth-loving Peace.

Io, Kouros most Great, I give thee hail, Kronian, Lord of all that is wet and gleaming, you are come at the head of thy Daimones. To Dikte for the Year, Oh, march, and rejoice in the dance and song,

To us also leap for full jars, and leap for fleecy flocks, and leap for fields of fruit, and for hives to bring increase.

Io, Kouros most Great, I give thee hail, Kronian, Lord of all that is wet and gleaming, you are come at the head of thy Daimones. To Dikte for the Year, Oh, march, and rejoice in the dance and song,

Leap for our Cities, and leap for our sea-borne ships, and leap for our young citizens and for goodly Themis.

ZEUS IS THE FIRST

Orphic fragment (before 300 CE), translated by Isaac Preston Cory

This Orphic fragment written in honor of a bisexual (in the sense of two-sexed), horned Zeus honors him as lord of everything that is. The opening is clearly reminiscent of the Revelation of St. John ("I am the Alpha and the Omega, the first and the last …") but since the dating of both works is debatable, it is impossible to say which came first. A daemon is a spirit.

Zeus is the first. Zeus the thunderer, is the last.
Zeus is the head. Zeus is the middle, and by Zeus all things were fabricated.
Zeus is male, Immortal Zeus is female.
Zeus is the foundation of the earth and of the starry heaven.
Zeus is the breath of all things. Zeus is the rushing of indefatigable fire.
Zeus is the root of the sea: He is the Sun and Moon.
Zeus is the king; He is the author of universal life;
One Power, one Dæmon, the mighty prince of all things:
One kingly frame, in which this universe revolves,
Fire and water, earth and ether, night and day,
And Metis (Counsel) the primeval father, and all-delightful Eros (Love).
All these things are United in the vast body of Zeus.
Would you behold his head and his fair face,
It is the resplendent heaven, round which his golden locks
Of glittering stars are beautifully exalted in the air.
On each side are the two golden taurine horns,
The risings and settings, the tracks of the celestial gods;
His eyes the sun and the Opposing moon;
His unfallacious Mind the royal incorruptible Ether.

ZEUS AND DESTINY

Cleanthes of Assos (ca. 300 BCE), translated by Sir John Lubbock

Inarguable common sense from a Stoic philosopher.

Lead me, O Zeus, and thou O Destiny,
The way that I am bid by you to go:
To follow I am ready. If I choose not,
I make myself a wretch, and still must follow.

TO JOVE THE BENEFICENT

Anonymous (1827)

O Thou, that holdest in thy spacious hands
     The destinies of men! whose eye surveys
Their various actions! Thou, whose temple stands
     Above all temples! Thou, whom all men praise!
     Of good the author! Thou, whose wisdom sways
The universe! all bounteous! grant to me
     Tranquillity, and health, and length of days;
Good will towards all, and reverence unto Thee;
Allowance for man's failings, of my own
     The knowledge; and the power to conquer all
Those evil things to which we are too prone
     Malice, hate, envy—all that ill we call.
To me a blameless life, Great Spirit! grant,
Nor burdened with much care, nor harrowed by much want.

FROM *ALCIBIADES II*

Plato (ca. 428–348 BCE), translated by B. Nolan

The famous expression "Be careful what you ask for; you might get it" is encapsulated here, in an excerpt from one of the famous dialogues of Socrates.

Lord Zeus, grant us what is good, whether or not we pray for it,
But what is bad, even if we beg you for it, keep it far from us.

EVENSONG

Robert Herrick (1591–1674)

This is a lovely Renaissance reminder to pray, which is itself a prayer. A matin *is a morning prayer, the daytime counterpart of evensong.*

Begin with Jove; then is the work half done,
And runs most smoothly when 'tis well begun.
Jove's is the first and last: the morn's his due,
The midst is thine; but Jove's the evening too;
As sure a matin does to him belong,
So sure he lays claim to the evensong.

FATHER ZEUS

Archilochus (680–645 BCE), translated by B. Nolan

O Zeus, father Zeus, the might of Heaven is yours. You keep account of the actions of men, both the wicked and the good, and even the wickedness and righteousness of animals.

ORPHIC HYMN TO ZEUS

Anonymous (ca. 200 CE?), translated by B. Nolan

Zeus is "Cronian" because he is the son of Cronos.

Renowned Zeus, undying god, we bow before you in prayer and testimony of salvation. Great king, you bring to light divine works: blessed goddess Mother Earth, the mountains resounding with winds, the sea and the starry fields of heaven arrayed in the sky. Cronian Zeus, indomitable, sceptered king, raining down thunder, ferocious All-Father, beginning and end of everything, Earthshaker, increaser, purifier, you who make the world tremble, Lord of Thunder and Lightning, O Zeus the Sower, hear me, shapeshifter! Grant us unvarying health and deathless peace, and wonderful prosperity free from sin.

LATE SEPTEMBER: THE AUTUMNAL EQUINOX AND THE GREATER ELEUSINIAN MYSTERIES

Autumn brings with it the memory of the Greater Eleusinian Mysteries, the ancient rites held in honor of the earth goddess Demeter and her daughter Persephone. These Mysteries were renowned throughout the classical Pagan world, and men and women from all walks of life came to the Greek town of Eleusis to be initiated into them. The Mysteries were old even in antiquity (there is reason to believe that they dated to about 1500 BCE), and it's impossible to overstate the awe they inspired in the ancient world. (Consider that the Roman Emperor Nero, then the most powerful person in the classical world, after having provided evidence of his insensibility to religion, law, and social norms by murdering his mother, voluntarily withdrew from the Mysteries when the high priest called for anyone with familial blood on his hands to leave the holy precinct.)

But although we know that the Mysteries were held in high regard, that they honored the goddesses of the earth, and that they provided their initiates with a transcendent experience designed to free them from the fear of death, we do not know what actually happened inside the initiation hall. Before the would-be initiates entered they all swore strict vows of secrecy, and those vows seem to have been kept with exemplary rigor. Theories about what took place abound, but the truth is that, in our current state of knowledge, we have little in the way of hard facts.

But if the practice of the Mysteries is beyond us, we do know that the death and renewal of plant life and the nourishing power of the earth were at their core. We also know that they were celebrated at about the time of the autumnal equinox, in late September or early October, although whether or not they were directly linked to the equinox is an open question. But, in keeping with the spirit of the Mysteries, we can pause at the time of equal day and equal night to honor the goddesses of the earth, without whom none of us would exist, and to remember that spring will follow on the heels of the coming winter.

HOMERIC HYMN TO EARTH, MOTHER OF US ALL

Anonymous (ca. 700–500 BCE), translated by Hugh G. Evelyn-White

I will sing of well-founded Earth, mother of all, eldest of all beings. She feeds all creatures that are in the world, all that go upon the goodly land, and all that are in the paths of the seas, and all that fly: all these are fed of her store. Through you, O queen, men are blessed in their children and blessed in their harvests, and to you it belongs to give means of life to mortal men and to take it away. Happy is the man whom you delight to honor! He has all things abundantly: his fruitful land is laden with corn, his pastures are covered with cattle, and his house is filled with good things. Such men rule orderly in their cities of fair women: great riches and wealth follow them: their sons exult with ever-fresh delight, and their daughters in flower-laden bands play and skip merrily over the soft flowers of the field. Thus is it with those whom you honor O holy goddess, bountiful spirit.

Hail, Mother of the gods, wife of starry Heaven; freely bestow upon me for this my song substance that cheers the heart! And now I will remember you and another song also.

ORPHIC HYMN TO GAIA

Anonymous (ca. 200 CE?), translated by B. Nolan

Gaia is the primordial Greek goddess of the earth.

O goddess Gaia, mother of gods and humankind, nurturer of all, giver of all, nurse of all, destroyer of all, in summer you burst with fruit and flowers, green and fertile. Changeable maiden, foundation of the never-ending cosmos, you give birth to the many types of food. Never-ending, very-honored, you keep a rich storehouse and you rejoice in the green plants and gentle breezes, O goddess garlanded with countless flowers. You rejoice in rain, as around you the finely-wrought panoply of the stars revolves and eternal Nature. O Blessed Queen, may you prosper the delicious fruits, and may you graciously grant us happy seasons.

"O GENTLE CREATRESS" FROM THE *THEBAID*

Papinius Statius (ca. 45–ca. 96 CE), adapted from an anonymous translation of 1767

In this hymn to the earth the "Promethean arts" refer to fire and cooking, and the stones of Pyrrha are humankind. "The finny race" are fish; "cars" here means "chariots."

O gentle Creatress—of the Gods above,
Humans beneath—from whose endless love

The woods are clad with greeness, rivers flow
And animals with life's warm current glow,
Hail, fairest part of the material world,
From whom arose the stones by Pyrrha hurled,
Promethean arts, and food for humankind,
Improved by change, with various arts refined.
Old Ocean rests sustained on your embrace,
Your wide extent contains the finny race,
The feathered kind, and beasts in their lairs.
Round you, the prop of worlds, in empty air
Sublimely poised the swift machine of heaven,
And the bright cars by Sun and Luna driven,
Whose lights alternate gild the star-paved Pole
In motion annual and daily do roll.

FROM "HYMN TO NATURE"

Edgar Lee Masters (1868–1950)

Nature is one idea, one spirit.
To learn that she is the many in the one
Is to be at peace with the peace of wisdom.
For though she changes eternally, and is never at rest
She is steadfast with changeless laws.
Everywhere you will stand in the presence of her thought,
Feeling it as the air from a revolving wheel,
Or as the tingling current of a dynamo.
The breadth and depth of her thought will show you
That man's thought is from her, traveling as a ripple
Upon a rivulet from the currents of a sea.
For man is in her, and she is in man,
Whom she has brought forth with all creatures.
But above all out of her sacred womb
Is the miracle, the spirit of man, which is herself,
Given the eyes of herself with which to see her,
And flamed with her fire with which to obey her.
She has told neither man nor beasts whence they came.

Nor whither they go;—

But at her bidding they follow her path,

Enveloped in darkness by her,

Yet urged by her to seek the light,

And made obedient to her,

Though they rebel against her.

ORPHIC HYMN TO NATURE

Anonymous (ca. 200 CE?), translated by Asphodel P. Long and D. Scott

O Nature, mother goddess of all, artificer mother,

celestial, venerated, goddess of richness, sovereign,

all-subduer, untamed, steering, lighting all,

almighty, nursing mother of all,

Undecaying, first born, legendary, enabling us,

Born of the night, all-wise, light-bringing, powerful in restraint

The track of your feet is whirling and silent motion

O sacred one, cosmic mother of the Gods,

unending one, bringing all to completion, common to all, but belonging to yourself alone

self-fathered, yet without a father, beloved, gladsome, great,

flowerlike, garlanded, beloved, accessible and wise,

leader, accomplisher, life giving, all nourishing maiden,

self-sufficient, justice, combining in yourself all the Graces, presiding

Goddess of earth, air and sea,

bitter to the worthless, sweet to those who honor you,

all-wise, all-giving guardian queen of all,

Bringing food, freely endowing us with ripening plenty,

Thou, father, mother of all, with us as nourisher and nurse,

swift birth giver, blessed one, rich in seed, begetter of the seasons,

Creator of all, shaper, source of all richness, sea goddess,

everlasting, setting in motion, all wise, full of care,

Never failing, you whirl with quick force.

All flowing, circular in motion, shape shifting,

on your fair throne, you are honored, alone you perfect your design,

Loud thundering you sit above the rulers,

Fearless, all subduer, you are destiny fiery goddess of fate

You deathless, are everlasting life and know the future.

You are the all and you alone create.

But Goddess we pray you in good season lead us to peace, health and increase of prosperity.

FROM "A LITANY TO EARTH"

Antonius Musa (first cen. CE), translated by J. Wight Duff
and Arnold M. Duff, modernized by B. Nolan

Goddess revered, O Earth, of all nature Mother, engendering all things and re-engendering them from the same womb, because you only supply each species with living force, you divine controller of sky and sea and of all things, through you is nature hushed and lays hold on sleep, and you likewise renew the day and banish night. You cover Pluto's shades and chaos immeasurable: winds, rains and tempests you detain, and, at your will, let loose, and so convulse the sea, banishing sunshine, stirring gales to fury, and likewise, when you will, you speed forth the joyous day. You bestow life's nourishment with never-failing faithfulness, and, when our breath has gone, in you we find our refuge: so, whatsoever you bestow, all falls back to you. Deservedly are you called Mighty Mother of Gods, since in dutiful service you have surpassed the divinities of heaven, and you are that true parent of living species and of gods, without which nothing is ripened or can be born. You are the Mighty Being and queen of divinities, O Goddess. You, divine one, I adore and your godhead I invoke: graciously vouchsafe me this which I ask of you, and with due fealty, Goddess, I will repay thee thanks. Give ear to me, I pray, and favor my undertakings; this which I seek of you, Goddess, vouchsafe to me willingly.

POMONA

Anonymous (1870)

Pomona, the Roman goddess of fruit, orchards, and gardens, is another deity who is not too well-known today, although she has given her name to cities, ships, and a college (not to mention several brand names of fruit-related products). But autumn, when her fruit is harvested, is a good time to remember this goddess, whose husband, Vertumnus, is the shape-shifting god of seasons.

She comes, all laden with the teeming wealth
Of harvest yet unreaped. Her golden hair
Braided with scarlet poppies, flowing waves
In sunny ripples o'er her shoulders bright,

As holding Earth in her embrace, she moves
On in triumphal progress.
      She is crowned,
Crowned with the mellow russet apple globes,
Red-streaked with scarlet veins, her brown hands stored
With purple plums, whereon the ash bloom sits
Unbrushed by envious fingers. In her lap
Nestles the queenly peach, her crimson down
Coy-mingling with the amber apricot,
And the rich treasures of the bending vine,
Blue-black and white, in beaded clusters, add
Their glories to the store.
      King Autumn bows,
Wheat-crowned, his ruddy head, at the approach
Of this his smiling spouse, as blithe he pours
At her fair feet brown rustling filberts ripe,
Medlars, and hazel-nuts, and all his share,
To swell her marriage portion. Thus they crown
With mutual gifts the bride-feast of the year!

POMONA

Clinton Scollard (1891)

Here the goddess helps the fruit ripen in the night. Samarcand or Samarkand is a city in Uzbekistan.

At noon of night the goddess, silver-stoled,
Came with light foot across the moonlit land,
And breezes soft as blow o'er Samarcand
Stirred her free hair that glinted like clear gold;
Sweet were her smiling lips, as when of old
Vertumnus wooed her on the grassy strand
Of some swift Tuscan river overspanned
By sunny skies that knew no breath of cold.

So when the door of dawn grew aureate,
And broken was the dim night's peaceful hush

By harvesters uprisen to greet the morn,
They knew Pomona had passed by in state,
For on the apples was a rosier blush,
And on the grapes a richer luster born.

FROM "POMONA"

George Bancroft Griffith (1841–1909), modernized by B. Nolan

Queen of garden and fruit-tree, hail!
Your kisses, fresh as the daisy's bloom,
Give blossom and bud, strength and perfume;
And your breath vigor to leaf and bough:
All graces unite to you endow!

FROM "HERTHA"

Algernon Charles Swinburne (1837–1909)

Hertha, or Nerthus, was a Germanic fertility goddess, whom Swinburne exalts as the universal Goddess from whom all life springs. Here she is associated with Yggdrasil, the great world tree of Norse belief.

I am that which began;
    Out of me the years roll;
  Out of me God and man;
    I am equal and whole;
God changes, and man, and the form of them bodily; I am the soul.

  Before ever land was,
    Before ever the sea,
  Or soft hair of the grass,
    Or fair limbs of the tree,
Or the fresh-coloured fruit of my branches, I was, and thy soul was in me.

  First life on my sources
    First drifted and swam;
  Out of me are the forces
    That save it or damn;
Out of me man and woman, and wild-beast and bird; before God was, I am.

I the grain and the furrow,
  The plough-cloven clod
And the ploughshare drawn thorough,
  The germ and the sod,
The deed and the doer, the seed and the sower, the dust which is God.

What is here, dost thou know it?
  What was, hast thou known?
Prophet nor poet
  Nor tripod nor throne
Nor spirit nor flesh can make answer, but only thy mother alone.

I am in thee to save thee,
  As my soul in thee saith;
Give thou as I gave thee,
  Thy life-blood and breath,
Green leaves of thy labor, white flowers of thy thought, and red fruit of thy death.

The tree many-rooted
  That swells to the sky
With frondage red-fruited,
  The life-tree am I;
In the buds of your lives is the sap of my leaves: ye shall live and not die.

My own blood is what stanches
  The wounds in my bark;
Stars caught in my branches
  Make day of the dark,
And are worshipped as suns till the sunrise shall tread out their fires as a spark.

I bid you but be;
  I have need not of prayer;
I have need of you free
  As your mouths of mine air;
That my heart may be greater within me, beholding the fruits of me fair.

O my sons, O too dutiful
   Toward Gods not of me,
 Was not I enough beautiful?
     Was it hard to be free?
For behold, I am with you, am in you and of you; look forth now and see.

HERTHA

Nora Chesson (1871–1906)

Another ode to the goddess Hertha.

I am the spirit of all that lives,
Labors and loses and forgives.
My breath's the wind among the reeds;
I'm wounded when a birch-tree bleeds.
I am the clay nest 'neath the eaves
And the young life wherewith it brims.
The silver minnow where it swims
Under a roof of lily-leaves
Beats with my pulses; from my eyes
The violet gathered amethyst.
I am the rose of winter skies,
The moonlight conquering the mist.

I am the bird the falcon strikes;
My strength is in the kestrel's wing,
My cruelty is in the shrikes.
My pity bids the dock-leaves grow
Large, that a little child may know
Where he shall heal the nettle's sting.
I am the snowdrop and the snow,
Dead amber, and the living fit—
The corn-sheaf and the harvester.

My craft is breathed into the fox
When, a red cub, he snarls and plays

With his red vixen. Yea, I am
The wolf, the hunter, and the lamb;
I am the slayer and the slain,
The thought new-shapen in the brain.
I am the ageless strength of rocks,
The weakness that is all a grace,
Being the weakness of a flower.

The secret on the dead man's face
Written in his last living hour,
The endless trouble of the seas
That fret and struggle with the shore,
Strive and are striven with evermore—
The changeless beauty that they wear
Through all their changes—all of these
Are mine. The brazen streets of hell
I know, and heaven's gold ways as well.
Mortality, eternity,
Change, death, and life are mine—are me.

FROM "DEMETER"

Eleanor Deane Hill (1918)

Dim through the trees
Comes one whose footfalls do no injury,
Unbent, the grass quivers beneath her feet;
And sooth, for her delight,
Abroad in the young night,
The flowers, in worship meet,
Shake all their censers sweet;
The trees their mistress know,
And deck themselves to show
Worship and fealty.
Demeter, homing from her daily toil,
Loved of, and loving husbandmen, for whom

Her robe is full of gifts, fragrant of soil;
Giver of crops and quickener of bloom,
Hers is the sacred Wheat,
Hallowed because of man's necessity.
A thousand altars smoke to her. …

CERES

Charlotte Thurston (1907)

Here the plants of the earth praise the Roman goddess Ceres, who is often depicted in a chariot pulled by dragons.

A voice from the burnished orchard,
　　A breeze from the yellowing grain,
From the uplands of New England,
　　From the vast Dakotan plain;
A whisper from purpling vineyard,
　　A rustle where brown nuts cling:
Hark, hark, where the soft earth-voices
　　The song of the harvest sing:

"Hail, hail to you, Mother Ceres!
　　We sprang at your beckoning hand;
We gladden the hearts of mortals,
　　Great Mother, at your command.
You knocked at our realm of darkness;
　　At the flash of your torch we came;
You wrapped us in rain and sunbeam;
　　You wrapped us in gold and flame."

"Right well have you wrought, my children,
　　Enthralled in my charmed spell;
Ablaze in your harvest glory,
　　I leave you to man. Farewell."
The gleam of a torch; faint echoes
　　Of the queenly voice out ring;
The scarlet glint of a poppy,
　　The rush of a dragon's wing.

DEMETER

Elizabeth Coatsworth (1893–1986)

Demeter reminds a group of reapers (apparently annoyed at the space taken up by inedible flowers) that, as vital as are the necessities, beauty is also important for life.

And hearing the complaints of the reapers,
    The Lady straightened her back above the sheaves,
    Wiping the sweat from her eyes,
    Towering like a golden pillar among them.
"Fools," she said,
    Are you not content with receiving the gift of grain
    That you must grudge the flowers to Persephone?"
    And then in their silence she spoke again:
    "You are blind with greed," said she;
    "Is the wheat enough? Is it enough to live?
    Do you need nothing to fill your hearts?
    You forget," said Demeter," it is the songs you sing for joy
    of the flowers
    That strengthen your arms for the swing of the heavy
    scythes."

FROM "APOLLO"

Eugene Lee-Hamilton (1845–1907)

A wain is a wagon or cart.

The harvest-hymns
Rise from the fields, where, in the setting sun,
The reapers stretch by sheaves of golden dun
Their weary limbs;
While many a sunburnt lad or maiden weaves
With every corn-flower that the sickle leaves

Demeter's harvest-crowns, or binds and trims
For the Great Mother her allotted sheaves.

The whole west glows
Like a vast sea of rosy molten ore
Where, here and there, great tracks of pearly shore
Or gleaming rows
Of crimson reefs and isles of amber blaze;
And through the whole a mighty fan of rays
Spreads as the sun approaches earth and throws
A farewell glance before he goes his ways.

A rich warm scent
Of summer ripeness fills the fertile plain;
The ox, unyoked, kneels chewing near the wain;
In one sound blent
The voices of the insect-swarms that fill
Each furrow, indefatigably trill
And chirp and hum; until the bright day spent,
Invokes the dusk to make the lone fields still.

FROM "FOR THE VANADÍS"

Gudrun of Mimirsbrunnr (twenty-first century)

Here Freya, Norse goddess of fertility, is reaping a harvest of another kind: the noble dead.

Hail to the Warrior Woman
on the Equinox morning,
white-armored, choosing the slain
by her own glorious criteria,
harbor to the defenders of beauty.
O Freya who rides with Valkyries,
give me strength to defend all that I love
for I am dull and frightened with years of defeat
and I have forgotten the mystery of shieldmates in love.

FROM "AN ELEUSINIAN CHANT"

John Warren, Baron de Tabley (1835–1895)

Warren here imagines what the Eleusinian experience might have been like, drawing on an ancient source that reported—with what veracity, no one knows—that a stalk of wheat was held aloft by a priest at the culmination of the Mysteries; the wheat presumably symbolized the fact that, although the wheat dies during winter, it will rise again. "She" is, of course, the goddess Demeter.

… For she sits, she sits in the inward shrine
In a garden gown and a wheaten crown.
Stand apart! ye non-elect.
Ere our mysteries begin.
He only keeps his soul erect,
Who is clean from soil of sin.
As the garment, which ye wear.
Let your mind be pure as snow;
To those who love and those who dare
The mighty mother is not slow
To bring illumination near.
To melt the veil, unwrap the night
And flood upon the eye and ear
The sights of dread and sounds of might.
Ye alone shall gaze in fear
Whose eyes are ready for the sigh;
Ye alone shall trembling hear
Whose minds can fathom depth and height;
And ye alone shall peep and peer
To astral circle, crystal sphere,
Till the deaf man shall hear
And the blind man gain light.

And lo, our mystic service ends
With symbol of the thrice-ploughed field,
A fearful weird that sign portends,
A root immortal, when the seed
Of awful harvests blends

A fallow ripe with mystic deed.
Extinguish now all light;
Pray fervently each one.
Ye have known a strange delight,
Ye are wise in love of might;
Ye see beyond the sight
Of a world of fleeting night.
Our mysteries are done.

OCTOBER

October opens with the second annual festival in honor of Mars, and then continues with another celebration of the Two Goddesses: the ancient Greek festival of the Thesmophoria. This mixture of the great war god and the famous goddesses of agriculture may seem incongruous, but in parts of the ancient world the agricultural season coincided with campaigning season; so Mars is a planter as well as a warrior, and a reaper of both grain and men. Here in the waning days of the year, it's time to send off the spirits of vitality and fertility with a joyous last hurrah to tide them over until we meet again in the coming year.

OCTOBER 15: OCTOBER MARS

During the ides of October, the ancient Romans held horse races and offered up a sacrifice to Mars in an unusual rite that may have pre-dated the founding of Rome itself. Nowadays we can offer prayers, candles, and cakes to the war gods Mars and Ares in order to calm the fertile but fierce gods' turbulence as we enter into the season of winter.

FROM *ANELIDA AND ARCITE*
Geoffrey Chaucer (1343–1400), translated by B. Nolan

Geoffrey Chaucer is the most famous English-language poet of the Middle Ages, best known for his Canterbury Tales.

Bellona is a Roman war goddess, and Pallas is an epithet of Athena, who is sometimes a goddess of war, among other things. Thrace *refers to a rather ambiguous area in southeast Europe.*

You fierce god of arms, Mars the red
That in the frosty country called Thrace

Within your grisly temple full of dread
Honored are as patron of that place
With your Bellona and Pallas full of grace;
Be present and my song continue and lead,
At my beginning thus to you I plead.

"ARES" FROM *THE SUPPLIANTS*

Aeschylus (ca. 525–ca.455 BCE), translated by Herbert Weir Smyth

A prayer for peace, to the Greek god of war.

Therefore let there fly forth from our overshadowed lips a prayer of gratitude. Never may pestilence empty this city of its men nor strife stain the soil of the land with the blood of slain inhabitants. But may the flower of its youth be unplucked, and may Ares, the partner of Aphrodite's bed, he who makes havoc of men, not shear off their bloom.

HOMERIC HYMN TO ARES

Anonymous (ca. 100–500 CE), translated by Hugh G. Evelyn-White

This hymn is believed to have been written much later than all the other Homeric hymns—possibly as late as the early Middle Ages.

Ares, exceeding in strength, chariot-rider, golden-helmed, doughty in heart, shield-bearer, Savior of cities, harnessed in bronze, strong of arm, unwearying, mighty with the spear, O defence of Olympus, father of warlike Victory, ally of Themis, stern governor of the rebellious, leader of righteous men, sceptred king of manliness, who whirl your fiery sphere among the planets in their sevenfold courses through the aether wherein your blazing steeds ever bear you above the third firmament of heaven; hear me, helper of men, giver of dauntless youth! Shed down a kindly ray from above upon my life, and strength of war, that I may be able to drive away bitter cowardice from my head and crush down the deceitful impulses of my soul. Restrain also the keen fury of my heart which provokes me to tread the ways of blood-curdling strife. Rather, O blessed one, give me boldness to abide within the harmless laws of peace, avoiding strife and hatred and the violent fiends of death.

FROM "ARES, GOD OF WAR"

Herbert Asquith (1881–1947)

Herbert Asquith, who fought in the first World War, acknowledges the power and the freedom that Ares may bring—and nevertheless prays that he will sleep in the arms of Aphrodite. An anodyne *is a palliative drug; it can be a sleep agent, or a painkiller.*

When all the guns have fired their last salute,
And the tongues of all the world are mute,
And life is dearer than to right a wrong,
Then may he weary of his burning wine,
And rest forever in the arms divine
Of Aphrodite passionate and pale—
But Hark! He comes! Hail, Ares! Lord of Thunder, Hail!

He rides above the ocean and the snow,
His trail is on the curtain of the skies:
Brighter than dawn, his young eternal eyes
Shine in the eyes of Valor far below:
Now Mammon hides beneath his trembling halls,
While Honor marches singing into war;
On strange forgotten hearts a radiance falls,
As ever nearer, burning from afar,
The sword of Ares gleams above the morning star.

The other gods are weaker; thou alone
Dost break the king and bend the emperor's knee:
Lower than unto Christ they bow to thee,
Lord of the slave, and guardian of the free,
Steel-hearted Ares, shaker of the throne;
Young god of battle, restless lover, hail!
For, once a man has seen thine eyes aflame,
And mounted on the horses of the gale,

Death is a nothing, life an empty name:
Arise and lead us ere our blood be tame,
O lord of thunder, Ares of the crimson mail!'

———

Sleep, Ares, Sleep! For, once the dice are thrown,
Empires to thee are leaves upon the air!
Ere all the homes go smoking to the skies,
And men are swept upon the battle-blast,
Ere all the tears are wept from women's eyes,
O Queen of Love, hold now the Lover fast,
And let him taste eternal anodyne at last!

FROM "THE LIGHT OF STARS"

Henry Wadsworth Longfellow (1807–1882)

In this poem the planet Mars takes on the attributes of the deity with which it has been intimately associated for millennia. It is a paean to the spirit of fortitude and endurance the warrior god embodies.

There is no light in earth or heaven
    But the cold light of stars;
And the first watch of night is given
    To the red planet Mars.

Is it the tender star of love?
    The star of love and dreams?
O no! from that blue tent above,
    A hero's armor gleams.

And earnest thoughts within me rise,
    When I behold afar,
Suspended in the evening skies,
    The shield of that red star.

O star of strength! I see thee stand
 And smile upon my pain;
Thou beckonest with thy mailèd hand,
 And I am strong again.

The star of the unconquered will,
 He rises in my breast,
Serene, and resolute, and still,
 And calm, and self-possessed.

And thou, too, whosoe'er thou art,
 That readest this brief psalm,
As one by one thy hopes depart,
 Be resolute and calm.

O fear not in a world like this,
 And thou shalt know erelong,
Know how sublime a thing it is
 To suffer and be strong.

LATE OCTOBER: THESMOPHORIA

From the hypermasculinity of Mars we come to the entirely feminine: the Thesmophoria, a women's festival observed throughout ancient Greece in honor of Demeter and Persephone. Although we have more information about this celebration than we do about the Eleusinian Mysteries, we don't have an enormous amount; Greek writers tended to be male, and men were not allowed to attend or observe the Thesmophoria. We do know that decorated baskets were carried in a ritual procession, that there was a day of fasting, and also that there was a day when obscene jokes were told, to remind worshippers of how Demeter, worn out with long searching for her lost daughter, was able to laugh again when her angry friend exposed herself to the goddess. But there's no question that the heart of the festival is the celebration of the deities who preside over the agricultural cycle of the year, and so here's a collection of appropriately autumnal poetry to honor the Two Goddesses.

FROM *PROSERPINE*

Mary Shelley (1797–1851)

Mary Shelley was the feminist author of Frankenstein, *and the wife of the poet Percy Shelley.*

"Car" here means "chariot." Tartarus is the abyss of the Underworld, the Lethe is the river of forgetfulness, and Elysium is paradise. Enna is the locality in Sicily where Persephone was said to have been abducted.

Thy fate, sweet Proserpine, is sealed by Jove,
When Enna is starred by flowers, and the sun
Shoots his hot rays straight on the gladsome land,
When Summer reigns, then thou shalt live on Earth,
And tread these plains, or sporting with your nymphs,
Or at your Mother's side, in peaceful joy.
But when hard frost congeals the bare, black ground,
The trees have lost their leaves, and painted birds
Wailing for food sail through the piercing air;
Then you descend to deepest night and reign
Great Queen of Tartarus, 'mid shadows dire,
Offspring of Hell,—or in the silent groves
Of fair Elysium through which Lethe runs,
The sleepy river; where the windless air
Is never struck by flight or song of bird,

But all is calm and clear, bestowing rest,
After the toil of life, to wretched men,
Whom thus the Gods reward for sufferings
Gods cannot know; a throng of empty shades!
The endless circle of the year will bring
Joy in its turn, and separation sad;
Six months to light and Earth,—six months to Hell.

Farewell, sweet child, Queen of the nether world,
There shine as chaste Diana's silver car
Islanded in the deep circumfluous night.
Giver of fruits! for such thou shalt be styled,

Sweet Prophetess of Summer, coming forth
From the slant shadow of the wintry earth,
In thy car drawn by snowy-breasted swallows!
Another kiss, and then again farewell!
Winter in losing thee has lost its all,
And will be doubly bare, and hoar, and drear,
Its bleak winds whistling o'er the cold pinched ground
Which neither flower or grass will decorate.

FROM "THE APPEASEMENT OF DEMETER"
George Meredith (1828–1909)

In this excerpt Nobel Prize nominee George Meredith imagines that moment that Demeter, in the midst of a starving world that she has devastated in revenge for her daughter's abduction and rape, is finally able to laugh again. Meredith, as a Victorian, was unable to deal directly with the Greek tradition that held that Demeter laughed when her companion Baubo, a bawdy old woman, exposed her genitalia to the goddess. He did, however, understand that sexuality had to be at the root of the release of tension, and so he imagined Demeter watching two horses attempting to mate. The outcome, however, is the same: the laughter of the goddess will renew the earth after the desolation of winter.

Iambe is an alternative name for Baubo, the jokester who made Demeter laugh; it is from her name that we derive the English word "iambic."

She laughed: since our first harvesting heard none
Like thunder of the song of heart: her face,
The dreadful darkness, shook to mounted sun,
And peal on peal across the hills held chase.
She laughed herself to water; laughed to fire;
Laughed the torrential laugh of dam and sire
Full of the marrowy race.
Her laughter, Gods! was flesh on skeleton.

The valley people huddled, broke, afraid,
Assured, and taking lightning in the veins,
They puffed, they leaped, linked hands, together swayed,
Unwitting happiness till golden rains

Of tears in laughter, laughter weeping, smote
Knowledge of milky mercy from that throat
Pouring to heal their pains:
And one bold youth set mouth at a shy maid.

Iambe clapped to see the kindly lusts
Inspire the valley people, still on seas,
Like poplar-tops relieved from stress of gusts,
With rapture in their wonderment; but these,
Low homage being rendered, ran to plough,
Fed by the laugh, as by the mother cow
Calves at the teats they tease:
Soon drove they through the yielding furrow-crusts.

Uprose the blade in green, the leaf in red,
The tree of water and the tree of wood:
And soon among the branches overhead
Gave beauty juicy issue sweet for food.
O Laughter! beauty plumped and love had birth.
Laughter! O thou reviver of sick Earth!
Good for the spirit, good
For body, thou! to both art wine and bread!

DEPARTURE OF PROSERPINE

Francis Ledwidge (1887–1917)

In this poem, the goddess Proserpine reflects on the fact that "the gods' way" is sometimes hard, even for the gods.

Old mother Earth for me already grieves,
Her morns wake weeping and her noons are dim,
Silence has left her woods, and all the leaves
Dance in the windy shadows on the rim
Of the dull lake thro' which I soon shall pass
To my dark bridal bed
Down in the hollow chambers of the dead.
Will not the thunder hide me if I call,

Wrapt in the corner of some distant star
The gods have never known?
Alas! alas!
My voice has left with the last wing, my fall
Shall crush the flowery fields with gloom, as far
As swallows fly.
Would I might die
And in a solitude of roses lie
As the last bud's outblown.
Then nevermore Demeter would be heard
Wail in the blowing rain, but every shower
Would come bound up with rainbows to the birds
Wrapt in a dusty wing, and the dry flower
Hanging a shrivelled lip.
This weary change from light to darkness fills
My heart with twilight, and my brightest day
Dawns over thunder and in thunder spills
Its urn of gladness
With a sadness
Through which the slow dews drip
And the bat goes over on a thorny wing.
Is it a dream that once I used to sing
From Ægean shores across her rocky isles,
Making the bells of Babylon to ring
Over the wiles
That lifted me from darkness to the Spring?
And the King
Seeing his wine in blossom on the tree
Danced with the queen a merry roundelay,
And all the blue circumference of the day
Was loud with flying song.——
—But let me pass along:
What brooks it the unfree to thus delay?
No secret turning leads from the gods' way.

From "Demeter"

HD (1886–1961)

In this excerpt from HD's strange and beautiful poem, Demeter demands not sacrifice or artifice, but remembrance: "keep me before you, after you, with you."

Delphi is the site of Apollo's famous oracle.

I

Men, fires, feasts,
steps of temple, fore-stone, lintel,
step of white altar, fire and after-fire,
slaughter before,
fragment of burnt meat,
deep mystery, grapple of mind to reach
the tense thought,
power and wealth, purpose and prayer alike,
(men, fires, feasts, temple steps)—useless.

Useless to me who plant
wide feet on a mighty plinth,
useless to me who sit,
wide of shoulder, great of thigh,
heavy in gold, to press
gold back against solid back
of the marble seat:
useless the dragons wrought on the arms,
useless the poppy-buds and the gold inset
of the spray of wheat.

Ah they have wrought me heavy
and great of limb—
she is slender of waist,
slight of breast, made of many fashions;
they have set her small feet
on many a plinth;
she they have known,

she they have spoken with,
she they have smiled upon,
she they have caught
and flattered with praise and gifts.

But useless the flattery
of the mighty power
they have granted me:
for I will not stay in her breast
the great of limb,
though perfect the shell they have
fashioned me, these men!

Do I sit in the market place—
do I smile, does a noble brow
bend like the brow of Zeus—
am I a spouse, his or any,
am I a woman, or goddess or queen,
to be met by a god with a smile—and left?

II

Do you ask for a scroll,
parchment, oracle, prophecy, precedent;
do you ask for tablets marked with thought
or words cut deep on the marble surface,
do you seek measured utterance or the mystic trance?

Sleep on the stones of Delphi—
dare the ledges of Pallas
but keep me foremost,
keep me before you, after you, with you,
never forget when you start
for the Delphic precipice,
never forget when you seek Pallas
and meet in thought
yourself drawn out from yourself

like the holy serpent,
never forget
in thought or mysterious trance—
I am greatest and least.

TO THE DEMETER OF CNIDOS
(WRITTEN IN THE BRITISH MUSEUM)

Edna Worthley Underwood (1873–1961)

Gazing at a famous statue of Demeter, American poet Underwood longs for the majestic calm of the goddess.

Lone waters where the ships vex not the sea,
Dim lakes at twilight where the lilies sleep
And blacken with their whiteness deep on deep,
Are not serene as is the brow of thee.
Some far-off sun of peace I can not see
Shines still upon thy cheek and chin which keep
A shadowed splendor where I fain would steep
My soul in sunsets of serenity.

Great Mother, on thy throne of tragic calm
Which shakes me as the sunlight shakes the star,
Just once, Great Mother, ere for aye I cease,
Upon my futile heart let fall this balm
Grant me to glimpse within some gate ajar
The pearl-pale sunrise of thy pagan peace.

FROM "DEMETER"

Callimachus (ca. 310/305–ca. 240 BCE),
adapted from the translation by Alexander Mair

This hymn seems to have been written especially for the Thesmophoria, since both the sacred basket (whose contents are unknown) and the fast mentioned in the first paragraph are elements of the festival.

This poem recounts how Erysichthon, son of Triopas, king of Thessaly, was punished for cutting down the trees in Demeter's sanctuary at Dotium in order to build himself a house. Because he refused to stop even when the goddess asked him to, she cursed him with an insatiable hunger that nonetheless did not keep him from losing weight—a powerful parable of the consequences of greed and environmental destruction.

The Triopidae were a powerful clan in Thessaly, from whom Erysichthon was descended; Mimas is a giant, the son of Gaia, who is buried on an island off the coast of Naples. Dotium is part of the Thessalian plain in Greece, and Pelasgians are Greeks. Mimas is a mountain in Ionia. Hesperus is the Evening Star, and Deo is another name for Demeter. Triptolemus is the milk-son of Demeter. "She that is heavy and she that stretches her hand to Eileithyia and she that is in pain" refers to pregnant or laboring women.

As the Basket comes, greet it, women, saying "Demeter, greatly hail! Lady of much bounty, of many measures of corn." As the Basket comes, from the ground shall you behold it, you uninitiated, and gaze not from the roof or from aloft—child nor wife nor maid hath shed her hair—neither then nor when we spit from parched mouths fasting. Hesperus from the clouds marks the time of its coming: Hesperus, who alone persuaded Demeter to drink, when she pursued the unknown tracks of her stolen daughter.

No, let us not speak of that which brought the tear to Deo! Better to tell how she gave cities pleasing ordinances; better to tell how she was the first to cut straw and holy sheaves of corn-ears and put in oxen to tread them, what time Triptolemus was taught the good craft; better to tell—a warning to men that they avoid transgression—how (she made the son of Triopas hateful and pitiful) to see.

…In holy Dotium dwelt the Pelasgians and unto you they made a fair grove abounding in trees; hardly would an arrow have passed through them. Therein was pine, and therein were mighty elms, and therein were pear-trees, and therein were fair sweet-apples; and from the ditches gushed up water as it were of amber. And the goddess loved the place to madness, even as Eleusis, as Triopum, as Enna.

But when their favoring fortune became angry with the Triopidae, then the worse counsel took hold of Erysichthon. He hastened with twenty attendants, all in their prime, all men-giants able to lift a whole city, arming them both with double axes and with hatchets, and they rushed shameless into the grove of Demeter. Now there was a poplar, a great tree reaching to the sky, and thereby the nymphs were wont to sport at noontide. This poplar was smitten first and cried a woeful cry to the others. Demeter marked that her holy tree was in pain, and she was angered and said: "Who cuts down my fair tree?" Straightway she likened her to Nicippe, whom the city had appointed to be her public priestess, and in her hand she grasped her fillets and her poppy, and from her shoulder hung her key. And [Nicippe] spoke to soothe the wicked and shameless man and said: "My child, who cuts down the trees which are dedicated to the gods, stay, my child, child of your parents' many prayers, cease and turn back your attendants, lest the lady Demeter be angered, whose holy place you make desolate."

But with a look more fierce than that wherewith a lioness looks on the hunter on the hills of Tmarus—a lioness with new-born cubs, whose eye they say is of all most terrible—he said: "Vie back, lest I fix my great axe in thy flesh! These trees shall make my tight dwelling wherein evermore I shall hold pleasing banquets enough for my companions." So spoke the youth and Nemesis recorded his evil speech. And Demeter was angered beyond telling and put on her goddess shape. Her steps touched the earth, but her head reached unto Olympus. And they, half-dead when they beheld the lady goddess, rushed suddenly away, leaving the bronze axes in the trees. And she left the others alone—for they followed by constraint beneath their master's hand—but she answered their angry king: "Yes, build your house, dog that you are, where you shall hold festival; for frequent banquets shall be yours hereafter." So much she said and devised evil things for Erysichthon.

Straightway she sent on him a cruel and evil hunger—a burning hunger and a strong—and he was tormented by a grievous disease. Wretched man, as much as he ate, so much did he desire again. Twenty prepared the banquet for him, and twelve drew wine. For whatsoever things vex Demeter, vex also Dionysus; for Dionysus shares the anger of Demeter. His parents for shame sent him not to common feast or banquet, and all manner of excuse was devised.

… And even as the snow upon Mimas, as a wax doll in the sun, yea, even more than these he wasted to the very sinews: only sinews and bones had the poor man left. His mother wept, and greatly groaned his two sisters, and the breast that suckled him and the ten handmaidens over and over.

So long as there were stores in the house of Triopas, only the chambers of the house were aware of the evil thing; but when his teeth dried up the rich house, then the king's son sat at the crossways, begging for crusts and the cast-out refuse of the feast. O Demeter, never may that man be my friend who is hateful to you, nor ever may he share party-wall with me; ill neighbours I abhor.

Sing, maidens and mothers, say with them: "Demeter, greatly hail! Lady of much bounty, of many measures of corn." And as the four white-haired horses convey the Basket, so unto us will the great goddess of wide dominion come bringing white spring and white harvest and winter and autumn, and keep us to another year. And as unsandalled and with hair unbound we walk the city, so shall we have foot and head unharmed for ever. And as the van-bearers bear vans full of gold, so may we get gold unstinted. Far as the City Chambers let the uninitiated follow, but the initiated even unto the very shrine of the goddess—as many as are under sixty years. But she that is heavy and she that stretches her hand to Eileithyia and she that is in pain—sufficient it is that they go so far as their knees are able. And to them Deo shall give all things to overflowing, even as if they came unto her temple.

Hail, goddess, and save this people in harmony and in prosperity, and in the fields bring us all pleasant things! Feed our kine, bring us flocks, bring us the corn-ear, bring us harvest! And nurse peace, that he who sows may also reap. Be gracious, O thrice-prayed for, great Queen of goddesses!

FROM "DEMETER"

Eleanor Deane Hill (1918)

Even in the midst of autumn we should remember that spring will come again.

Not less those meads were loved, when autumn's yield
Of berried fruits for the birds' harvesting
Wilted beneath the breath from the cold star,
And drifts of leaves along the grass did fling,
After their mad and whirling dance, a shield
To guard the soil from the investing cold,
And give the plants security, there deep
In Earth's warm heart, till presently they hear
Demeter call them from their lifting sleep
To cheer the world with the old tale fresh told.
So as Demeter trod the herbage sweet

The flowers bent themselves her steps to greet,
And flung their incense rare
To please her nostrils, into the cool air;
Fresher than frankincense or musk,
Their odors filled the gathering dusk,
And lightened was her day-long toil
By the thank-offering of the soil;
And in her heart,
She blessed them severally, apart.

PERSEPHONE

Frederic Manning (1882–1935)

Australian poet Frederic Manning here mourns the temporary absence of the goddess. A garth *is a garden or yard.*

Yea, she hath passed hereby, and blessed the sheaves,
And the great garths, and stacks, and quiet farms,
And all the tawny, and the crimson leaves.
Yea, she hath passed with poppies in her arms,
Under the star of dusk, through stealing mist,
And blessed the earth, and gone, while no man wist.

With slow, reluctant feet, and weary eyes,
And eye-lids heavy with the coming sleep,
With small breasts lifted up in stress of sighs,
She passed, as shadows pass, among the sheep;
While the earth dreamed, and only I was ware
Of that faint fragrance blown from her soft hair.

The land lay steeped in peace of silent dreams;
There was no sound amid the sacred boughs.
Nor any mournful music in her streams:
Only I saw the shadow on her brows,
Only I knew her for the yearly slain,
And wept, and weep until she come again.

FROM *DEMETER, A MASK*

Robert Bridges (1844–1930)

While fighting to recover her abducted daughter, Demeter explains the source of her overwhelming power—and why even Zeus will have to come to terms with her, eventually.

Robert Bridges was Britain's Poet Laureate from 1913 to 1930.

> The universal life dwells first in the Earth,
> The stones and soil; therefrom the plants and trees
> Exhale their being; and on them the brutes
> Feeding elaborate their sentient life,
> And from these twain mankind; and in mankind
> A spirit lastly is form'd of subtler sort
> Whereon the high gods live, sustain'd thereby,
> And feeding on it, as plants on the soil,
> Or animals on plants. Now see! I hold,
> As well ye know, one whole link of this chain:
> If I should kill the plants, must not man perish?
> And if he perish, then the gods must die.

STROPHE FROM "THE SEARCH AFTER PROSERPINA"

Aubrey de Vere (1814–1902)

Here the Irish poet Aubrey de Vere imagines Proserpina's return, with her engaging in the traditional Anglo-Celtic custom of maying, i.e., celebrating May Day by gathering flowers and dancing.

Sicily was the traditional setting of Persephone's abduction.

> Proserpina once more
>   Will come to us a-Maying;
> Sicilian meadows o'er
>   Low-singing and light-playing.
> The wintry durance past,
> Delight will come at last:
>   Proserpina will come to us—
>   Will come to us a-Maying.

NOVEMBER

November starts with what is arguably the most important holiday of the year for many modern Pagans: Samhain, the old Hiberno-British New Year, the ancestor of our modern Hallowe'en. This month of lengthening darkness ends the harvest season, which is reflected not only in Samhain—the last celebration of the harvest season that begins at Lúnasa—but also in the Isia, a Roman Egyptian celebration honoring the goddess Isis's mourning for her dead husband, Osiris, god of fertility and agriculture. Then, as the temperatures begin to plummet and winter walks the land, the month closes with another feast in honor of Jove, the eternal sky god.

NOVEMBER 1: SAMHAIN

From time immemorial, the insular Pagan Celts celebrated their new year at this time, a tradition that persisted for several centuries after the coming of Christianity. (Continental Celts, on the other hand, celebrated their new year in the spring.) This festival is the direct ancestor of both the secular Hallowe'en and the Christian All Saints' Day and All Souls' Day. *Samhain* is the Irish and Scots Gaelic name for both this New Year's festival and the month of November.

Samhain marks the traditional end of the harvest, when the last of the crops would be brought in and stored for the coming winter. Because it marked the end of the growing season, Samhain's connection with the dead, especially dead ancestors, has always been strong. It has long been regarded as a time when the dead might return to visit the living, and, therefore, a time when prophecy and magic might flourish.

No literature about Samhain has survived from Celtic antiquity, but there are some medieval and later works that are appropriate to the season, dealing as they do with the underworld or otherworld. And because of the holiday's strong association with death and magic, it seems perfectly reasonable to honor magic and Underworld deities from other traditions on this day, too.

SAMHAIN

Leanne Daharja Veitch (2004)

From the modern Australian choral work Wheel of the Year *comes this tribute to the holiday. It reflects Australian flora with the inclusion of eucalyptus as an herb of remembrance.*

Eucalyptus, rosemary,
Burning brightly for remembrance:
Burning bright for purity
On this night when we remember. ...

Once again, Shadow's Eve.
Light the candle at the window.
Set a light to guide them home
Through the darkness of the night.

Contemplate our visions,
Dreaming of times long gone:
Dreaming of our loved ones
Who have passed across our lives. ...

Eucalyptus, rosemary,
Burning brightly for remembrance
Burning bright for purity
On this night when we recall.

SONG OF THE APPLE TREES

William Sharp (1855–1905)

Avalon is the Otherworld of the British and Breton Celts, a legendary island of apple trees and happiness where, according to some legendary accounts, the soul goes when the body dies—or, as in the famous case of King Arthur, where heroes can go to avoid death.

"Thrid" is an archaic word meaning "threaded."

Song of Apple-trees, honeysweet and murmurous,
Where the swallows flash and shimmer as they thrid the foamwhite maze,
Breaths of far-off Avalon are blown to us, come down to us,
Avalon of the Heart's Desire, Avalon of the Hidden Ways!
Song of Apple-blossom, when the myriad leaves are gleaming
Like undersides of small green waves in foam of shallow seas,
One may dream of Avalon, lie dreaming, dreaming, dreaming,
Till wandering through dim vales of dusk the stars hang in the trees.
Song of Apple-trees, honeysweet and murmurous,
When the night-wind fills the branches with a sound of muffled oars,
Breaths of far-off Avalon are blown to us, come down to us,
Avalon of the Heart's Desire, Avalon of the Hidden Shores.

FROM "THE SPOILS OF ANNWN"

"Taliesin" (probably ca. 900 CE), version by B. Nolan

No one is certain just how old this curious Welsh poem from The Book of Taliesin *is (although it certainly pre-dates its early-thirteenth-century manuscript), nor what its true significance may be. However, it clearly describes a trip to the Otherworld, undertaken by King Arthur and a band of warriors, from which—not surprisingly—very few men returned. In* The White Goddess *Robert Graves suggests that it refers to the reincarnation of heroes, and that the seven who returned from the raid are in fact humans who have died and been reborn; Scottish poet and musician Robin Williamson suggests that the various castles the men visit represent "stations of the soul on its journey after death." In spite of all the uncertainty that surrounds the poem, however, it is one of the very few premodern connections we have with the ancient Celtic Otherworld—and it is also beautiful for its own sake.*

Translating this poem is full of pitfalls, as a great deal of the language is obscure and editorial decisions have to be made; different translators have come to very different conclusions. In this version I have tried to take into account the many different translations of this poem and the body of scholarship that surrounds it, but I do not claim that my choices have been the correct ones. I have tried to make them coherent as far as possible, but that is all I can promise.

Annwn is the Welsh name for the otherworld; its etymology suggests that it is an underworld as well. The "pearl-encrusted cauldron" is almost certainly the prototype of the Holy Grail. Gwydion is the Welsh god of magic and eloquence, and a trickster, who in the Mabinogion fell afoul of Pwyll and Pryderi, god-kings in their own right. The names of the castles are open to much interpretation, while a number of the other references—such as Cwy—are unidentifiable.

Praise to the Lord, the ruler of the realm, the king
Whose power extends to the ends of the earth.

Gwydion was trapped in the Castle Barrow,
Through the curse of Pwyll and Pryderi.
No one before him had entered into that prison;
A faithful servant, he was bound
With a chain of silver water.
And before the plunder of the dead
Most bitterly he sang.
And we bards shall invoke him
Until the end of the world.
Three times the fill of the ship Prydwen we entered.
None rose again from the Castle of the Grave,
But only seven.

Songs were sung in my honor, my praise
Rang through the four-corned castle, four times turning,
My poetry was born inside the cauldron
Kindled by the breath of the nine maidens,
The pearl-encrusted, dark-bordered cauldron
Of the Lord of Annwn, which will boil
Not the coward's food, nor the liar's.
The flaming sword of light was lifted to it
And left in Lleminawc's hand.
The lamps were burning at the gates of hell
When we went with Arthur, a brilliant quest,

None returned from the Castle of Delirium
But only seven.

Songs were sung in my honor, my praise
Rang through the four-cornered castle
On the Island of the Strong Door,
Where running water mingles with sparkling jet
And wine glitters in the cups of the company.
Three times the fill of the ship we set sail,
But none came back again from the Castle of Rigor
But only seven.

I have little praise for those little scribblers
Who beyond the Glass Castle saw not
The courage of Arthur. There were
Six thousand men on their ramparts;
It was difficult to speak with their watchman.
Three times the fill of the ship we went with Arthur.
None rose up from the Castle of Dangers
But only seven.

I have little praise for the little men who let their shield-straps slacken.
They do not know the day of our creation, nor whether
Cwy was born at noon. Who caused him to refuse
To go to the meadows of Dewy? They do not know the brindled ox,
Or his wide headband, or the one hundred and forty links upon his collar.
When we went with Arthur—sorrowful memory—
None returned from the Castle of God
But only seven.

I have little praise for little men
Whose wills are as slack as their shields,
They don't know the day the ruler was created
What hour of the day the owner was born,
Or what animal is their silver-headed creature.
When we went with Arthur, agonizing the fight,
None rose up from the Castle of the Prison
But only seven.

FAERY SONG

William Sharp (1855–1905)

The "lordly ones" are the Tuatha Dé Danann, the gods of the island Celts; here they are portrayed, as was common in the nineteenth century, as ethereal beings possessed of a supernatural pallor. This is an excerpt from English composer Rutland Boughton's fairy tale opera The Immortal Hour.

How beautiful they are, the lordly ones
Who dwell in the hills, in the hollow hills.
They have faces like flowers
And their breath is a wind
That blows over summer meadows
Filled with dewy clover.
Their limbs are more white than shafts of moonshine,
They are more fleet than the March wind,
They laugh and are glad and are terrible
When their lances shake and glitter
Ev'ry green reed quivers.
How beautiful they are,
How beautiful,
The lordly ones in the hollow hills.

FROM "I-BREASIL"

Ethna Carbery (1864–1902)

I-Breasil or Hy-Brasil is another legendary Otherworldly island—from Ireland, this time.

There is a way I am fain to go—
To the mystical land where all are young,
Where the silver branches have buds of snow
And every leaf is a singing tongue.

It lies beyond the night and day,
Over shadowy hill, and moorland wide,
And whoso enters casts care away,
And wistful longings unsatisfied.

A blossom of fire is each beauteous bird,
Scarlet and gold on melodious wings.
And never so haunting a strain was heard
From royal harp in the Hall of Kings.

The sacred trees stand in rainbow dew,
Apple and ash and the twisted thorn,
Quicken and holly and dusky yew,
Ancient ere ever gray Time was born.

The oak spreads mighty beneath the sun
In a wonderful dazzle of moonlight green—
O would I might hasten from tasks undone,
And journey whither no grief hath been!

THE WASHER OF THE FORD

William Sharp (1855–1905)

On a darker note: the Washer at (or of) the Ford, a traditional supernatural figure in Gaelic-speaking regions, is a form of the Morrígan, the Great Queen, Irish goddess of death and war, and inexorable fate. Here she is cast rather in the mold of the Hindu goddess Kali, as a divine destroyer and liberator combined.

There is a lonely stream afar in a lone
    dim land:
It hath white dust for shore it has, white bones
    bestrew the strand:
The only thing that liveth there is a naked
    leaping sword;
But I, who a seer am, have seen the whirling hand
     Of the Washer of the Ford.

A shadowy shape of cloud and mist, of gloom
    and dusk, she stands,
     The Washer of the Ford:
She laughs, at times, and strews the dust
    through the hollow of her hands.

She counts the sins of all men there, and
    slays the red-stained horde—
The ghosts of all the sins of men must know
    the whirling sword
      Of the Washer of the Ford.

She stoops and laughs when in the dust she
    sees a writhing limb:
"Go back into the ford," she says, "and
    hither and thither swim;
Then I shall wash you white as snow, and
    shall take you by the hand,
And slay you here in the silence with this
    my whirling brand,
And trample you into the dust of this white
    windless sand"—

This is the laughing word
Of the Washer of the Ford
Along that silent strand.

"ODIN'S RUNE SONG" FROM THE *HÁVAMÁL*

Medieval Icelandic (ca. 1270), translated by Henry Bellows, modernized by B. Nolan

Here is a medieval description of how Odin, the king of the Norse gods, sacrificed himself to himself, and thereby obtained the knowledge of writing. Like the Spoils of Annwn, *it is full of riddling passages, but the overarching message is clear: knowledge can only be attained through sacrifice.*

*   Bolthern is a jötunn or giant, while Bestla is the mother of Odin. Othrörir is the name of a vessel containing the mead of poetry.*

*   Samhain was not celebrated as such in Norse lands, but the association of magic, death, and the Otherworld is in keeping with the holiday.*

I [know] that I hung on the windy tree,
Hung there for nights full nine;
With the spear I was wounded, and offered I was
To Odin, myself to myself,
On the tree that none may ever know
What root beneath it runs.

None made me happy with loaf or horn,
And there below I looked;
I took up the runes, shrieking I took them,
And forthwith back I fell.

Nine mighty songs I got from the son
Of Bolthern, Bestla's father;
And a drink I got from the goodly mead
Poured out from Othrörir.

Then began I to thrive, and wisdom to get,
I grew and well I was;
Each word led me to another word,
Each deed to another deed.

Runes shalt thou find, and fateful signs,
That the king of singers colored,
And the mighty gods have made;
Full strong the signs, full mighty the signs
That the ruler of gods doth write.

Odin for the gods, Dain for the elves,
And Dvalin for the dwarfs,
Alsvith for giants and all mankind,
And some myself I wrote.

Knowest how one shall write, knowest how one shall rede?
Knowest how one shall tint, knowest how one makes trial?
Knowest how one shall ask, knowest how one shall offer?
Knowest how one shall send, knowest how one shall sacrifice?

Better no prayer than too big an offering,
By thy getting measure thy gift;
Better is none than too big a sacrifice,
So Thund of old wrote ere man's race began,
Where he rose on high when home he came.

FROM "BALDER DEAD"

Matthew Arnold (1822–1888)

An account of life after death in Valhalla, from the Norse tradition. The Nornies are the Norns, the three Fates; Midgard is Middle-Earth, our world; and Bifrost is the rainbow bridge between the worlds of the gods and mortals. Heimdall or Heimdallr is the guardian of the rainbow.

Forth from the east, up the ascent of heaven,
Day drove his courser with the shining mane;
And in Valhalla, from his gable-perch,
The golden-crested cock began to crow.
Hereafter, in the blackest dead of night,
With shrill and dismal cries that bird shall crow,
Warning the gods that foes draw nigh to heaven;
But now he crew at dawn, a cheerful note,
To wake the gods and heroes to their tasks.
And all the gods and all the heroes woke.
And from their beds the heroes rose, and donned
Their arms, and led their horses from the stall,
And mounted them, and in Valhalla's court
Were ranged; and then the daily fray began.
And all day long they there are hacked and hewn
'Mid dust, and groans, and limbs lopped off, and blood;
But all at night return to Odin's hall
Woundless and fresh: such lot is theirs in heaven.
And the Valkyries on their steeds went forth
Toward earth and fights of men; and at their side
Skulda, the youngest of the Nornies, rode;
And over Bifrost, where is Heimdall's watch,
Past Midgard fortress, down to earth they came;
There through some battle-field, where men fall fast,
Their horses fetlock-deep in blood, they ride,
And pick the bravest warriors out for death,
Whom they bring back with them at night to heaven,
To glad the gods, and feast in Odin's hall.

FROM "ODIN'S RAVENS' SONG"

Seventeenth-century Icelandic, translated by Benjamin Thorpe

In this prophetic poem, all the orders of the immortals have a function in the running of the world—as do humans: to endure. The Allfather is Odin, the Alfar are often translated as "Elves" or "Elfs," the Vanir are one of the two Norse tribes of gods, the Nornir are the three Fates, the Thursar or Jötnar are giants, and the Valkyriur or Valkyries are the supernatural shield-maidens of Thor.

Allfather works,
the Alfar discern,
the Vanir know,
the Nornir indicate,
the Ividia brings forth,
men endure,
the Thursar await,
the Valkyriur long.

FROM "FOR THE VANADÍS"

Gudrun of Mimirsbrunnr (ca. 2015)

Seid or seiðr is a type of Norse magic strongly associated with the goddess Freya, as well as Odin.

Hail to the Mistress of Seid
on Hallows' morning,
mysterious and seductive through the gauze
of her own wisdom, glowing confident
in the ways of women's magic.
O Freya wreathed in veils of smoke,
open my eyes to possibility
for I am dull and blind with years of illusion
and I have forgotten the mystery of the candle's flame.

From "Hymn to Persephone"

Craig Arnold (1967–2009)

American poet Craig Arnold refers to Persephone by her ancient title Koré, *or maiden.*

Help me remember this: how once, when the dead were locked
out of the ground, and wandered, sleepless and sun-blinded,
she was the one who took them each by the hand and helped them
lay their bodies back in the dark sweet decay
gladly, as onto a lover's bed. They called her Koré,
the Maiden, a dark queen with a crown of blood-colored poppies,
whose fingers lift the cool coins from a dead girl's eyelids,
whose breath in a man's mouth releases him from memory.

From "Hymn to Proserpine"

Algernon Charles Swinburne (1837–1909)

Here Swinburne celebrates Properine, Queen of the Underworld, as the greatest of all goddesses, because she grants humans rest.

I have lived long enough, having seen one thing, that love hath an end;
Goddess and maiden and queen, be near me now and befriend.
Thou art more than the day or the morrow, the seasons that laugh or that weep;
For these give joy and sorrow; but thou, Proserpina, sleep.
Sweet is the treading of wine, and sweet the feet of the dove;
But a goodlier gift is thine than foam of the grapes or love.

"O Mighty Hermes" from *The Libation-Bearers*

Aeschylus (ca. 525–ca. 455 BCE), translated by E. D. A. Morshead

The play from which this excerpt is taken won first prize at the Dionysia competition in 458 BCE. Here the heroine Electra invokes Hermes before she attempts to contact the spirits of her dead ancestors.

O mighty Hermes, warder of the shades,
Herald of upper and of under world,
Proclaim and usher down my prayer's appeal
Unto the gods below, they that with eyes

Watchful behold these halls, my sire's of old—
And unto Earth, the mother of all things,
And foster-nurse, and womb that takes their seed.

ORPHIC HYMN TO THANATOS

Anonymous (ca. 200 CE?), translated by B. Nolan

Hear me, O Death, whose kingdom is without limit and who has sway over everything that lives. Long ago you determined the sacred length of our time. Your sleep severs the soul from the body, breaks the bonds of nature, lets the living rest forever. Everyone knows you, but some you are cruel to: those who are cut when the bud is in full bloom—in the end this is your decision, alone, and you will not heed tears or prayers. But still, O holy one, I beg you, with prayers and oaths, to grant us long lives, for old age is a great prize for mortals.

NOVEMBER 3: THE ISIA

The Isia, a festival in honor of the goddess Isis, began to be celebrated in Rome during the early empire. The exact date or dates of the festival are not entirely clear, but it was held sometime in late October/early November; the third of November may have been the culmination of the celebration. It is likely that it was a celebration of the death of the god Osiris and his resurrection by his sister-wife Isis. Not much else is known about the holiday (which may have originally been celebrated at the Winter Solstice and may have shifted over time as the Egyptian calendar did), but it is an excellent time, as we draw on toward the end of the old year and the birth of the new, to remember the goddess who grants rebirth.

FELLOWSHIP OF ISIS PRAYER

Olivia Robertson (twentieth century)

The Fellowship of Isis, an influential society dedicated to the worship of the goddess, was founded in Ireland in 1976 by the late priestess Olivia Robertson and others. Their poetic liturgies are beautiful invocations of the goddess.

Divine Isis, Goddess of Ten Thousand names, I invoke your Grace. The Gods above adore You, the Gods below do homage to You: You set the orb of heaven spinning above the poles,

You give light to the sun, You govern the universe. At Your voice, the spirits of earth rejoice, the elements obey. At Your nod the winds blow, clouds drop wholesome rain upon the earth, seeds quicken, buds swell. Birds that fly through the air, beasts that prowl on the mountain, serpents that lurk in the dust, all these tremble in single awe of You. Come to our temple, O Goddess: dwell in our shrine: make our hearth Your altar: our hearts Your home.

The Cyme Inscription

Anonymous (ca. 100 BCE), translated by Frederick C. Grant

Cyme, where this inscription was found, is a city on the coast of modern-day Turkey. This hymn describes a syncretic Isis, who is at once both Egyptian and Greek, as well as the source of all civilization and the mitigator of human barbarism (note the very chilling line "I made with my brother Osiris an end to the eating of men").

Bubastis was a city sacred to the cat goddess Bast, who is equated with Isis here. Kronos is the Greek Titan, father of Zeus.

I am Isis, the mistress of every land, and I was taught by Hermes, and with Hermes I devised letters, both the sacred and the demotic, that all things might not be written with the same letter.

I gave and ordained laws for human beings, which no one is able to change.

I am eldest daughter of Kronos.

I am wife and sister of King Osiris.

I am she who finds fruit for humans.

I am mother of King Horus.

I am she that rises in the Dog Star.

I am she that is called goddess by women.

For me was the city of Bubastis built.

I divided the earth from the heaven.

I showed the paths of the stars.

I ordered the course of the sun and the moon.

I made strong the right.

I brought together woman and man.

I appointed to women to bring their infants to birth in the tenth month.

I ordained that parents should be loved by children.

I laid punishment upon those disposed without natural affection toward their parents.

I made with my brother Osiris an end to the eating of men.

I revealed mysteries unto human beings.

I taught humans to honor images of the gods.

I consecrated the precincts of the gods.

I broke down the governments of tyrants.

I made an end to murders.

I compelled women to be loved by men.

I made the right to stronger than gold and silver.

I ordained that the true should be thought good.

I devised marriage contracts.

I assigned to Greeks and barbarians their languages.

I made the beautiful and the shameful to be distinguished by nature.

I ordained that nothing should be more feared than an oath.

I have delivered the plotter of evil against other humans into the hands of the one he plotted against.

I established penalties for those who practice injustice.

I decreed mercy to suppliants.

I protect righteous guards.

With me the right prevails.

I am the Queen of rivers and winds and sea.

No one is held in honor without my knowing it.

I am the Queen of war.

I am the Queen of the thunderbolt.

I stir up the sea and I calm it.

I am in the rays of the sun.

I inspect the courses of the sun.

Whatever I please, this too shall come to an end.

With me everything is reasonable.

I set free those in bonds.

I am the Queen of seamanship.

I make the navigable unnavigable when it pleases me.

I created walls of cities.

I am called the Lawgiver.

I brought up islands out of the depths into the light.

I am the Queen of rainstorms.

I overcome Fate.

Fate hearkens to me.

Hail, O Egypt, that nourished me!

"PRAYER TO ISIS" FROM *THE GOLDEN ASS*

Apuleius (ca. 124–ca. 170 CE), translated by Harold Edgeworth Butler,
modernized by B. Nolan

An invocation of Isis in all of her many forms, from a novel in which her divine intercession saves the protagonist.

Queen of heaven, whether you are Ceres, the kindly mother from whom in the beginning spring the fruits of earth, who, rejoicing to have found your daughter, took from men their bestial provender of old-world acorns and showed them a sweeter food, and now honor exceedingly the soil of Eleusis; or whether you are Venus the heavenly one, who at the first beginning of thing united the diversity of the sexes in the power of Love that is born of you, and, after you had brought to birth the race of man that shall endure from generation to generation, are now honored in your island shrine of Paphos; or whether you are Phoebus's sister, who with gentle healing brings relief to women in travail and has reared such multitudes, and now are worshipped in the most glorious fanes of Ephesus; or whether you are Proserpine, to whom men render shuddering reverence with howls by night, you whose threefold visage awes the wild rages of the goblin-dead and holds fast the gates of hell, who wander in many a diverse grove and are propitiated with varied rites; you that with your tender feminine light do illume the walls of all cities and with your moist fires do nurture the springing seeds, and dispense your beams that shift and change with the changes of the sun; by whatever name, by whatever rite, in whatever semblance man may invoke you, now aid me in my utter woe, restore my shattered fortunes and give pause and peace to the cruel calamities that I have endured.

TEARS OF ISIS

Frances L. Mace (1836–1899)

The story of Horus's childhood injury and Isis's distress is a standard part of Egyptian accounts of the goddess, but Frances Mace has added to it here, making Isis's tears a source of healing for humankind.

When Isis, by true mother love oppressed,
Held wounded Horus to her goddess breast,
Each tear that touched the sympathetic earth
To some rich, aromatic herb gave birth.

Such healing sprang from her celestial pain,

Mortals no longer seek relief in vain,

For oft as spring awakes the slumbering years,

In wood and meadow blossom Isis' tears.

O Goddess of the starry lotus bloom!

Thou didst foreshadow many a lonely doom;

Thy sorrow by divinest alchemy

Could comfort others, who could comfort thee?

"LAMENT FOR OSIRIS" FROM *CLEOPATRA*

Andrew Lang (1844–1912)

Although this poem was written by Andrew Lang, it comes from a novel by H. Rider Haggard. Amenti is a name for the Egyptian underworld.

Sing we Osiris dead,
   Lament the fallen head:
The light has left the world, the world is gray.
   Athwart the starry skies
   The web of darkness flies,
And Isis weeps Osiris passed away.
   Your tears, ye stars, ye fires, ye rivers, shed,
   Weep, children of the Nile, weep for your lord is dead!

Softly we tread, our measured footsteps falling
   Within the sanctuary sevenfold;
Soft on the dead that liveth are we calling:
   "Return, Osiris, from thy Kingdom cold!
   Return to them that worship thee of old."

Within the court divine
   The sevenfold sacred shrine
We pass, while echoes of the temple walls
   Repeat the long lament
   The sound of sorrow sent
Far up within the imperishable halls,

Where, each in other's arms, the sisters weep,
Isis and Nephthys, o'er his unawaking sleep.

Softly we tread, our measured footsteps falling
    Within the sanctuary sevenfold;
Soft on the dead that liveth are we calling:
    "Return, Osiris, from thy kingdom cold!
    Return to them that worship thee of old."

O dweller in the west,
    Lover and lordliest,
Thy love, thy sister Isis, calls thee home!
    Come from thy chamber dun
    Thou master of the sun,
Thy shadowy chamber far below the foam!
    With weary wings and spent
    Through all the firmament,
Through all the horror-haunted ways of hell,
    I seek thee near and far,
    From star to wandering star,
Free with the dead that in Amenti dwell.
    I search the height, the deep, the lands, the skies,
    Rise from the dead and live, our lord Osiris, rise!
Softly we tread, our measured footsteps falling
    Within the sanctuary sevenfold;
Soft on the dead that liveth are we calling:
    "Return, Osiris, from thy kingdom cold!
    Return to them that worship thee of old."

LAMENT OF ISIS

Helen Bantock (1868–1961)

From the Bantocks' song cycle Songs of Egypt *comes this beautiful lament for Osiris.*

Gone is my love, my lord,
Gone is my beautiful one.
Lonely by land and sea,

Still am I wand'ring on,
Searching the earth, the wave,
Seeking his hidden grave.

Heaven and earth are dim,
The hours are long in their flight.
Dreary the sun by day,
Dreary the moon by night,
Watching while others sleep,
Weary I wake and weep.

To the great gods I cry,
They will not answer my prayer,
Gone is my love, my lord,
I am alone with despair.
Gone is my lovely one,
I am alone, I am alone.

AT THE FEET OF ISIS

Anonymous (early twentieth century)

This anonymous poem was published in The Oxford Book of English Mystical Verse *in 1924. A* guerdon *is a reward.*

Her feet are set in darkness—at Her feet
We kneel, for She is Mother of us all—
A mighty Mother, with all love replete;
We, groping 'midst the shadow's dusky pall,
Ask not to see the upper vision bright,
Enough for us Her feet shine clear—all virgin white.

Her wings are tipped with golden light, but we
Ken but the shadow at Her pinions' base—
We kneel before Her feet, we cannot see
The glory that illuminates Her face,
For he who t'wards the vision gazeth up
Finds first the stricken breast—the sacrificial cup!

Her feet gleam in the darkness—at Her feet
We lay the price of those twin pearls of Heav'n—
All that man hath—an offering incomplete
Is his who yet his best would leave ungiv'n;
And as She stoops Her guerdon to bestow,
His life's blood in Her cup, outstretched there, needs must flow!

Her wings are in the shadow—Lo! they cast
That shadow e'en o'er Heav'n's own light, we cry,
For in the darkness, terrible and vast,
She spreads the wing to which the soul must hie;
But, to that shelter led, our upward gaze
Beholds Her pinions formed of Light's celestial rays!

Her feet are in the darkness, but Her face
Is in high Heav'n—all Truth inhabits there;
All Knowledge and all Peace, and perfect grace,
And in the wonder of Her joy they share
Who, blindly clinging to Her feet erstwhile,
Obtained the priceless gift—the vision of Her smile.

FROM "HYMN TO ISIS FROM HER TEMPLE AT PHILAE VI"

Pharaoh Userkare-meramun (ca. 690 BCE), translated by Louis V. Žabkar

An Egyptian ruler wrote (or had written) this hymn in honor of Isis. Re or Ra is the sun god, and his barque is the sun itself. The ka is a layer of the human soul, and Heh is the god of infinity.

Philae, which comprised two large islands in the Nile (since flooded for the construction of the Aswan Dam) was a major cult center of Isis during the Pharaonic and Ptolemaic eras. During the latter, worshippers from Egypt, Greece, and Nubia made regular pilgrimages to the complex to worship the goddess.

Come to the Palace, you who makes gods and men live,
You to whose ka Heh stretches himself up,
Whom Re has raised upon his head,
Who shines as the diadem upon his forehead.

You are the one who rises and dispels darkness,
Shining when traversing the primeval ocean,

The Brilliant One in the celestial waters
Travelling in the barque of Re.

Rest in the great, august Palace;
Come to the Palace of the Feasts at the time of solemn offerings;
O Golden One, Re, possessor of the Two Lands, will never be far from you,
So that the Noble One may circle the realm of the dead in the company of her brother
Osiris.

FROM *THE GOLDEN ASS*

Apuleius (ca. 124–ca. 170 CE),
translated by Frederick C. Grant, modernized by B. Nolan

Apuleius wrote in Latin but was born in Algeria, and was a member of the people now called the Berbers. His bawdy novel of magic and adventure, The Golden Ass, *is well worth reading.*

O holy and eternal guardian of the human race, who always cherishes mortals and blesses them, you care for the woes of miserable men with a sweet mother's love. Neither day nor night, nor any moment of time, ever passes by without your blessings, but always on land and sea you watch over men; you drive away from them the tempests of life and stretch out over them your saving right hand, wherewith you unweave even the inextricable skein of the Fates; the tempests of Fortune you assuage and you restrain the baleful motions of the stars. You the gods above adore, you the gods below worship. It is you that whirl the sphere of heaven, that give light to the sun, that govern the universe and trample down Tartarus. To you the stars respond, for you the seasons return, in you the gods rejoice, and the elements serve you. At your nod the winds blow, the clouds nourish (the earth), the seeds sprout, and the buds swell. Before your majesty the birds tremble as they flit to and fro in the sky, and the beasts as they roam the mountains, the serpents hiding in the ground, and the monsters swimming in the deep. But my skill is too slight to tell your praise, my wealth too slender to make you due offerings of sacrifice. Nor has my voice that rich eloquence to say what I feel would suffice for your majesty—no, not even had I a thousand mouths, a thousand tongues, and could continue forever with unwearied speech! Therefore the only thing one can do, if one is devout but otherwise a pauper, that I will strive to do. Your face divine and your most holy deity—these I will hide away deep within my heart; your image I shall treasure forever!

SIRIUS

Archibald Lampman (1861–1899)

Archibald Lampman was a Canadian poet who often wrote on Pagan themes. Here he imagines him-
self at the temple of Hathor in Denderah, worshipping her by the light of Sirius, her star. Hathor, a
goddess of love, fertility, and cattle, was sometimes identified with Isis.

The old night waned, and all the purple dawn
Grew pale with green and opal. The wide earth
Lay darkling and strange and silent as at birth,
Save for a single far-off brightness drawn
Of water gray as steel. The silver bow
Of broad Orion still pursued the night,
And farther down, amid the gathering light,
A great star leaped and smouldered. Standing so,
I dreamed myself in Denderah by the Nile;
Beyond the hall of columns and the crowd
And the vast pylons, I beheld afar
The goddess gleam, and saw the morning smile,
And lifting both my hands, I cried aloud
In joy to Hathor, smitten by her star!

FROM *ISIS*

Philippe Quinault (1635–1688)

Isis, Isis, turn your eyes on us
See the ardor of our zeal.
The celestial court calls to you,
Everyone reveres you in these halls
Isis, Isis is immortal
Isis will shine in these halls.
Isis partakes, with the Gods,
Of eternal glory.

HYMN TO ISIS III

Isidorus (ca. 100 CE), translated by Vera Fredericka Vanderlip

The Egyptian priest Isidorus led a desperate, doomed revolt against the Roman rule of Egypt. Hermouthis is a harvest goddess, and Agathe Tyche was the Greek goddess of fortune; Deo is an epithet of Demeter; Leto is the mother of Artemis and Apollo; and Nanaia or Nane is an Armenian goddess. Thiouis *means "only one" or "unique."*

O wealth-giver, Queen of the gods, Hermouthis, Lady
Omnipotent Agathe Tyche, greatly renowned Isis,
Deo, highest Discoverer of all life,
Manifold miracles were Your care that you might bring
Livelihood to mankind and morality to all;
(and) You taught customs that justice might in some measure prevail;
You gave skills that men's life might be comfortable,
And You discovered the blossoms that produce edible vegetation.
Because of You heaven and the whole earth have their being;
And the gusts of the winds and the sun with its sweet light.
By Your power the channels of Nile are filled, every one,
At the harvest season and its most turbulent water is poured
On the whole land that produce may be unfailing.
All mortals who live on the boundless earth,
Thracians, Greeks and Barbarians,
Express Your fair Name, a Name greatly honored among all, (but)
Each (speaks) in his own language, in his own land.
The Syrians call You: Astarte, Artemis, Nanaia,
The Lycian tribes call You: Leto, the Lady,
The Thracians also name You as Mother of the gods,
And the Greeks (call You) Hera of the Great Throne, Aphrodite,
Hestia the goodly, Rheia and Demeter.
But the Egyptians call You 'Thiouis' (because they know) that You, being
One, are all
Other goddesses invoked by the races of men.
Mighty One, I shall not cease to sing of Your great Power,
Deathless Savior, many-named, mightiest Isis,

Saving from war, cities and all their citizens:

Men, their wives, possessions, and children.

As many as are bound fast in prison, in the power of death,

As many as are in pain through long, anguished, sleepless nights,

All who are wanderers in a foreign land,

And as many as sail on the Great Sea in winter

When men may be destroyed and their ships wrecked and sunk. ...

All (these) are saved if they pray that You be present to help.

Hear my prayers, O One whose Name has great Power;

Prove Yourself merciful to me and free me from all distress.

NOVEMBER 13: THE FEAST OF JOVE, PART II

It's time for another banquet to fete the Father of the Gods! In mid-November comes the second part of the Roman feast of the god Jove, also known as Jupiter or Zeus, the first part of which is celebrated in September. A smaller feast would traditionally be held on this day.

FROM *ISIS*

Philippe Quinault (1635–1688), translated by B. Nolan

This excerpt from Jean-Baptiste Lully's opera describes the descent of Jupiter to Earth.

The powerful god who throws down thunder

Decided, scepter in hand, to come down

From heaven to the earth

To hunt the evils that torment humans.

May the earth carefully respond to this honor,

With echoes resounding in these charming places,

Announcing that, today, for the happiness of the world,

Jupiter descends.

ORPHIC HYMN TO DAEMON

Anonymous (ca. 200 CE), translated by B. Nolan

A daemon is not a demon, per se, but just a neutral term for a spirit. Here it refers to the Great Spirit, Zeus.

I call to the Great Spirit, the terrible and kindly Lord Zeus, Father of All, who gives life to humankind. Great Zeus, wanderer, avenger, Emperor of All, whose appearance brings wealth when you come, full of abundance, into a house: you refresh mortals weary from labor, for you hold the keys of mortal happiness and misery. O holy one, o pure one, drive away fear, which destroys all who live throughout the world. Please grant a goodly, noble end to my life.

FROM "HYMN TO ZEUS"
Callimachus (ca. 310/305–ca. 240 BCE),
adapted from the translation by A. W. Mair and G. R. Mair

Callimachus was a Libyan librarian at the famous Library of Alexandria in Egypt. Here he prays to Zeus as the lord of governance and giver of peace and prosperity. Rheia or Rhea is the mother of Zeus, and Adrasteia is the nymph who took care of him after he was born. The Curetes or Korybantes were the warlike attendants of Cybele; they hid Zeus from his father Cronus, who had sworn to kill him. Parrhasia is a region in Arcadia, in Greece.

At libations to Zeus what else should rather be sung than the god himself, mighty for ever, king for evermore … dealer of justice to the sons of Heaven?

In Parrhasia it was that Rheia bore you, where was a hill sheltered with thickest brush. Thence is the place holy … Adrasteia laid you to rest in a cradle of gold, and you did suck the rich teat of the she-goat Amaltheia, and thereto eat the sweet honey-comb. … And lustily round you danced the Curetes a war-dance, beating their armor, that Cronus might hear with his ears the din of the shield, but not your infant noise.

Fairly did you wax, O heavenly Zeus, and fairly were you nurtured, and swiftly did grow to manhood, and speedily came the down upon your cheek. But, while yet a child, you devised all the deeds of perfect stature. Therefore your kindred, though an earlier generation, grudged not that you should have heaven for your appointed habitation. … You were made sovereign of the gods not by casting of lots but by the deeds of your hands, your might and that strength which you have set beside your throne. … And you chose that which is most excellent among men—not you the skilled in ships, nor the wielder of the shield, nor the minstrel: these did you straightway renounce to lesser gods, other cares to others. But you chose the rulers of cities themselves, beneath whose hand is the lord of the soil, the skilled in spearmanship, the oarsman, yes, all things that are: what is there that is not under the ruler's sway? Thus smiths, we say, belong to Hephaestus; to Ares, warriors; to Artemis of the Tunic, huntsmen; to Phoebus they that know well the strains of the lyre. But from Zeus come kings; for nothing is diviner than the kings of Zeus. So you chose them for your own lot, and gave them cities to guard. And you seated yourself in the high places of the cities, watching who rule their people with crooked judgements, and who rule otherwise. And you have bestowed upon them wealth and prosperity abundantly; unto all, but not in equal measure....

Hail! greatly hail! most high Son of Cronus, giver of good things, giver of safety. Your works who could sing? There has not been, there shall not be, who shall sing the works of Zeus. Hail! Father, hail again! And grant us goodness and prosperity. Without goodness wealth cannot bless men, nor goodness without prosperity. Give us goodness and weal.

FROM *MNEMOSYNE*
Moero (late fourth–early third cen. BCE), translated by B. Nolan

Moero was a Byzantine poet. Little of her work has survived, but in this fragment from a much longer work (sadly, mostly lost) she recounts how Zeus was protected by birds while in hiding from his murderous father, Cronos. Mnemosyne is the muse of memory.

King Zeus grew up in Crete, hidden from all the holy gods, far from his father. He grew to strength in the sacred cave, nursed by the doves who brought him ambrosia from Ocean's gentle streams, while a great eagle, ceaselessly drawing nectar out of a rock, carried the drink in its beak to wise Zeus. And having triumphed over his father, Cronos, all-knowing Zeus granted the eagle immortality and brought him to live in heaven. Nor did he forget to honor the tremulous doves, whom he made messengers of the changing seasons.

FROM "THE ELEUSINIAN FESTIVAL"
Friedrich von Schiller (1759–1805), anonymous translator, modernized by B. Nolan

Father Zeus, who reign over all
That in airy mansions dwell,
Let a sign from you now fall
That you love this offering well!
And from the unhappy crowd
That, as yet, has never known thee,
Take away the eye's dark cloud,
Showing them their deity!

HYMN TO ZEUS

Cleanthes of Assos (ca. 300 BCE),
adapted from the translation by Frederick C. Grant

Boxer and Stoic philosopher Cleanthes wrote this hymn to Zeus as Lord of the Universe and Upholder of Justice.

Most glorious of immortals, Zeus
The many-named, almighty evermore,
Nature's great Sovereign, ruling all by law,
Hail to you! On you 'tis meet and right

That mortals everywhere should call.
From you was our begetting; ours alone
Of all that live and move upon the earth
The lot to bear God's likeness.
You will I ever chant, your power praise!

For you this whole vast cosmos, wheeling round
The earth, obeys, and where you lead
It follows, ruled willingly by you.
In your unconquerable hands you hold fast,
Ready prepared, that two-timed flaming blast,
The ever-living thunderbolt:
Nature's own stroke brings all things to their end.
By it you guide aright the sense instinct
Which spreads through all things, mingled even
With stars in heaven, the great and small—
You who are King supreme for evermore!

Naught upon earth is wrought in your despite, O God.
Nor in the ethereal sphere aloft which ever winds
About its pole, nor in the sea—save only what
The wicked work, in their strange madness,
Yet even so, you know to make the crooked straight.
Prune all excess, give order to the orderless,
For unto you the unloved still is lovely—
And thus in one all things are harmonized,

The evil with the good, that so one Word
Should be in all things everlastingly.

One Word—which evermore the wicked flee!
Ill-fated, hungering to possess the good,
They have no vision of God's universal law,
Nor will they hear, though if obedient in mind
They might obtain a noble life, true wealth.
Instead they rush unthinking after ill:
Some with a shameless zeal for fame,
Others pursuing gain, disorderly;
Still others folly, or pleasures of the flesh.
[But evils are their lot] and other times
Bring other harvests, all unsought—
For all their great desire, its opposite!

But, Zeus, you giver of every gift,
Who dwell within the dark clouds, wielding still
The flashing stroke of lightning, save, we pray,
Your children from this boundless misery.
Scatter, O Father, the darkness from their souls,
Grant them to find true understanding
On which relying you justly rule all—
While we, thus honored, in turn will honor you,
Hymning your works forever, as is meet
For mortals while no greater right
Belongs even to the gods than evermore
Justly to praise the universal law!

FROM "HYMN TO ZEUS"

Francis Ledwidge (1887–1917)

From Irish poet Francis Ledwidge, a prayer for Zeus to bring peace to a soul in pain. Cars, *here, means "chariots."*

God, whose kindly hand doth sow
The rainbow showers on hill and lawn,

To make the young sweet grasses grow
And fill the udder of the fawn.
Whose light is life of leaf and flower,
And all the colors of the birds.
Whose song goes on from hour to hour
Upon the river's liquid words.
Reach out a golden beam of thine
And touch her pain. Your finger-tips
Do make the violets' blue eclipse
Like milk upon a daisy shine.

God, who lights the little stars,
And overnight the white dew spills.
Whose hand doth move the season's cars
And clouds that mock our pointed hills.
Whose bounty fills the cow-trod wold,
And fills with bread the warm brown sod.
Who brings us sleep, where we grow old
'Til sleep and age together nod.

Reach out a beam and touch the pain
A heart has oozed thro' all the years.
Your pity dries the morning's tears
And fills the world with joy again!

ORPHIC HYMN TO RHEA

Anonymous (ca. 200 CE?), translated by B. Nolan

Rhea the Titan is the mother of Zeus and an ancient mother goddess; the Milky Way was thought to have been created from her breast milk. She is often equated with the goddess Cybele, which is why she is described as being pulled in a lion-drawn chariot.

Famous Rhea, daughter of multiform Protogonos, whose sacred chariot is pulled by the bull-slaying lions, O ecstatic maiden, you dance to the beat of drums and clash of cymbals, O mother of Zeus, Lord of Olympus, Bearer of the Aegis. Famed and honored, holy consort of Cronos, you love the mountains and the ritual cries of mortals. First Queen, indomitable, you rejoice in the shouts of conflict; steadfast truth-teller, savior, Mother of gods and men, you are born from the earth and the endless sky, the sea, and the winds. Ethereal, ever-moving, come, holy queen, kindly redeemer, please bring peace and wealth, banishing death and contagion to the ends of the earth.

FROM "ZEUS"

John Warren, Lord de Tabley (1835–1895)

In this poem, Zeus is imagined as very far removed from the concerns of mortals or of Earth—but awesome nonetheless.

Who hath revealed his name,
Father of clouds, eternal, king of death,
Who, ere the mountains came,
Or gentle winds drew breath,
Sat in the morning light and had no care,
Great and austerely fair,
For ages and for ages, till at last
Creation ripened fast,
And at his feet the infant world began.
Under his throne the dew and spice of morn
And little wells arose,
The glory of the leaves, and newly bom
The wonder of the rose.

DECEMBER

The dark nights of December are full of celebratory lights. The last month of the year is packed full of Pagan holidays, from the festival of Faunus, the Roman Pan at the beginning of the month to Mithra's birthday at the end. December is full of reasons to celebrate, but at the heart of the holiday season is the Winter Solstice—the time when light is reborn in the world, an eternal promise of brighter days to come.

DECEMBER 5: THE COUNTRY FAUNALIA

The Country Faunalia was a Roman holiday, but, as a rural festival, it probably wasn't celebrated in Rome itself. It was a time when farmers and villagers would pause after their fall labors to honor Faunus (or Pan), the protector of their flocks. At the beginning of the winter holiday season, we too can stop for a moment to make an offering to the goat-foot god, whose protection helps keep the Wheel of the Year turning.

FROM "THE SHEPHERD'S HOLIDAY"

Ben Jonson (1572–1637)

Thus, thus begin, the yearly rites
    Are due to Pan on these bright nights;
    His morn now riseth and invites
    To sports, to dances, and delights:
    All envious and profane, away!
    This is the shepherds' holiday.

ORPHIC HYMN TO PAN

Anonymous (ca. 200 CE?), translated by Patrick Dunn

Echo is a nymph who can only repeat the last words spoken to her; Pan fell in love with her, although it is not clear whether or not she ever returned his affection.

I call mighty Pan, the god of shepherds
and the whole universe together; sky
and sea, the all-regal earth, and deathless
fire: for these are the limbs of Pan himself.
Come, blessed, spinning, cavorting, enthroned
with the Seasons, goat-limbed, Bacchic, frenzy
of gods' inspiration under the stars.
You strike cosmic harmony with playful
song. You, the aider of imagination
and bringer of terrible images
to mortal fears, delighting in shepherds
and herdsmen among the fountains. Sharp-eyed
hunter, the lover of Echo, you dance
with the nymphs. All-growing god, the father
of all, many-named daimon, the ruler
of the cosmos, increaser, light-bringer,
fruitful Paian, cave-haunting god, heavy
with wrath, truly the horned Zeus, for through you
the boundless plain of earth lies firm, but
deeply flowing waters of the tireless
seas yield, and ocean, surrounding the earth
with waters, and the air that we share
nourishment, the spark of life, the eye
of most nimble fire high above: For these
holy things stand apart by your command;
you change the natures of all by your wise
will, nourishing the human race throughout

the boundless world. So come blessed one, frenzied
with divine inspiration to this most
holy libation: give life a good end
and send out Pan's passion to the earth's ends.

FROM "PAN-WORSHIP"
Eleanor Farjeon (1881–1965)

God of Nature,
Thrice hailing thee by name with boisterous lungs
I will thrill thee back from the dead ages, thus:
Pan! Pan! O Pan! bring back thy reign again
Upon the earth! ...

PAN
Ralph Waldo Emerson (1803–1882)

This piece is not for the faint of heart: Emerson honors Pan as the animating force behind human existence but warns that our human lives are fleeting music.

O what are heroes, prophets, men,
But pipes through which the breath of Pan doth blow
A momentary music. Being's tide
Swells hitherward, and myriads of forms
Live, robed with beauty, painted by the sun;
Their dust, pervaded by the nerves of God,
Throbs with an overmastering energy
Knowing and doing. Ebbs the tide, they lie
White hollow shells upon the desert shore,
But not the less the eternal wave rolls on
To animate new millions, and exhale
Races and planets, its enchanted foam.

HYMN TO PAN

John Fletcher (1579–1625)

While we think of Pan as a god closely linked to the act of sex, in this selection from the Jacobean play The Faithful Shepherdess *he is also given control over the other side of sexuality: chastity.*

Sing his praises that doth keep
    Our flocks from harm.
Pan, the father of our sheep;
    And arm in arm
Tread we softly in a round,
Whilst the hollow neighbouring ground
Fills the music with her sound.

Pan, O great god Pan, to thee
    Thus do we sing!
Thou who keep'st us chaste and free
    As the young spring:
Ever be thy honor spoke
From that place the morn is broke
To that place day doth unyoke!

FROM "TO FAUNUS"

Horace (65–8 BCE), translated by Thomas Irwin

The Roman poet Horace mentions the December Faunalia in this ode; Horace was noted for his fondness for Faunus, the Roman Pan. In this loose translation, kine *are cows and* hinds *are farm laborers.*

Oh, Faunus, lover of the flying nymphs,
Tread lightly round the sunny fields that close
My little farm, and o'er thy shoulder cast,
Departing, one propitious glance upon
My orchard's branchy gloom
And nursery of vines. . . .

And when in northern air the winter star
For thy light footstep marks a silver path,
The straw-thatched cottage shall keep holiday,
And through cool grassy meadows roam its folk,
Mid oxen free from toil
And ruminating kine:

And when in warmest fold the sheep are penned,
The blue smoke drifts along the hamlet roofs,
And woodlands strew the ground with rural leaves,
To thee the jocund hinds shall sing, and beat
The Autumn-wearied earth
In triple-rounding dance.

"HYMN TO PAN" FROM *ENDYMION*

John Keats (1795–1821)

In this excerpt from his long poem Endymion, *Keats combines Pan the god of shepherds with Pan the Great All. Here a group of worshippers, gathered before his temple on Mount Lykaion (Mount Lycean) in Arcadia, Greece, the ancient center of his cult, offer up a prayer to Pan as the merry rustic god who saves lambs from hunting eagles, keeps diseases away from farms, and teases the nymphs by throwing seashells into their rooms—but also to Pan as "a symbol of immensity;/A firmament reflected in a sea;/An element filling the space between;/An unknown."*

Dryope is the mother of Pan, and Syrinx is the nymph he loved with an unrequited passion. A paean is a hymn of praise.

O Thou, whose mighty palace roof doth hang
From jagged trunks, and overshadoweth
Eternal whispers, glooms, the birth, life, death
Of unseen flowers in heavy peacefulness;
Who lov'st to see the hamadryads dress
Their ruffled locks where meeting hazels darken;
And through whole solemn hours dost sit, and hearken
The dreary melody of bedded reeds—
In desolate places, where dank moisture breeds

The pipy hemlock to strange overgrowth;
Bethinking thee, how melancholy loth
Thou wast to lose fair Syrinx—do thou now,
By thy love's milky brow!
By all the trembling mazes that she ran,
Hear us, great Pan!

　　O thou, for whose soul-soothing quiet, turtles
Passion their voices cooingly 'mong myrtles,
What time thou wanderest at eventide
Through sunny meadows, that outskirt the side
Of thine enmossed realms: O thou, to whom
Broad leaved fig trees even now foredoom
Their ripen'd fruitage; yellow girted bees
Their golden honeycombs; our village leas
Their fairest-blossom'd beans and poppied corn;
The chuckling linnet its five young unborn,
To sing for thee; low creeping strawberries
Their summer coolness; pent up butterflies
Their freckled wings; yea, the fresh budding yea
All its completions—be quickly near,
By every wind that nods the mountain pine,
O forester divine!

　　Thou, to whom every fawn and satyr flies
For willing service; whether to surprise
The squatted hare while in half sleeping fit;
Or upward ragged precipices flit
To save poor lambkins from the eagle's maw;
Or by mysterious enticement draw
Bewildered shepherds to their path again;
Or to tread breathless round the frothy main,
And gather up all fancifullest shells
For thee to tumble into Naiads' cells,
And, being hidden, laugh at their out-peeping;

Or to delight thee with fantastic leaping,
The while they pelt each other on the crown
With silvery oak apples, and fir cones brown—
By all the echoes that about thee ring,
Hear us, O satyr king!

O Hearkener to the loud clapping shears,
While ever and anon to his shorn peers
A ram goes bleating: Winder of the horn,
When snouted wild-boars routing tender corn
Anger our huntsman: Breather round our farms,
To keep off mildews, and all weather harms:
Strange ministrant of undescribed sounds,
That come a swooning over hollow grounds,
And wither drearily on barren moors:
Dread opener of the mysterious doors
Leading to universal knowledge—see,
Great son of Dryope,
The many that are come to pay their vows
With leaves about their brows!

Be still the unimaginable lodge
For solitary thinkings; such as dodge
Conception to the very bourne of heaven,
Then leave the naked brain: be still the leaven,
That spreading in this dull and clodded earth
Gives it a touch ethereal—a new birth:
Be still a symbol of immensity;
A firmament reflected in a sea;
An element filling the space between;
An unknown—but no more: we humbly screen
With uplift hands our foreheads, lowly bending,
And giving out a shout most heaven rending,
Conjure thee to receive our humble Paean,
Upon thy Mount Lycean!

FROM "PAN"

Oscar Wilde (1854–1900)

Oscar Wilde, the great Irish playwright and wit, was specifically calling Pan to return to England in this poem, but there is no reason those of us on the other side of the ocean can't ask him to add us to his itinerary.

O goat-foot God of Arcady!
This modern world is grey and old,
And what remains to us of thee?

———

Nor through the laurels can one see
Thy soft brown limbs, thy beard of gold,
And what remains to us of thee?

Ah, leave the hills of Arcady,
Thy satyrs and their wanton play,
This modern world hath need of thee.

———

Then blow some trumpet loud and free,
And give thine oaten pipe away,
Ah, leave the hills of Arcady!
This modern world hath need of thee!

"O GREAT GOD PAN" FROM *MOON MAGIC*

Dion Fortune (1890–1946)

O Great God Pan, return to earth again.
O come at my call, and show thyself to men.
Shepherd of goats, upon the wilds hill's way
Lead thy lost flock from darkness unto day.
Forgotten are the ways of sleep and night;
Men seek for them whose eyes have lost the light.
Open the door, the door that hath no key—
The door of dreams, whereby men come to thee.
The shepherd of goats, oh answer unto me!

"INVOCATION TO PAN" FROM *THE GREAT GOD PAN*

Helen Bantock (1868–1961)

The choral ballet The Great God Pan *opens with this lovely invocation of the god.*

Pan, god of the unfettered wild!
    Come from thy secret dwelling,
Where mighty mountains sleep, and, undefiled,
    The waters sweet are welling.
O, fearless, swift! O fierce and free!
God of the forests! God of liberty!
Pan, sing we a paean! Pan, we call on thee!
Pan, god of the unfettered mind,
Of faith and will unshaken,
Come, piping loud and wild upon the wind
Till sluggard worlds awaken.
Healer divine! Heart of the free!
Spirit of music! Soul of ecstasy!
Priest of delight! Thou laugher gay—all hail!
Twy-horned, goat-footed, lord of revelry!
The sweet singer, the light dancer, the wild piper—clear and shrill!
The keen hunter, the swift pursuer, the lord of fear—and deathless will!
Pan, to thee we raise our voices, Pan, great Pan, all hail!

FROM *SAPPHO*

Bliss Carman (1861–1929)

O Pan of the evergreen forest,
Protector of herds in the meadows,
Helper of men at their toiling,—
Tillage and harvest and herding. ...

Now even I come before thee
With oil and honey and wheat-bread,
Praying for strength and fulfilment
Of human longing, with purpose
Ever to keep thy great worship
Pure and undarkened.

FROM "ODE TO PAN"

John Warren, Lord de Tabley (1835–1895)

Darnel *is ryegrass, and* kex *refers to the dried, hollow stems of various plants.*

…Pan the bud-expander; who awakes
Nature, and is a god in nature's core
Seated, and one with nature evermore.
Pan is no cloudy ruler in dim haze,
No king of air-belts delicate afar.
But in the ripening slips and tangled ways
Of the blue cork-woods where the goat-herds are.
And we may find him by the bulrush pits.
Where the hot oxen chin-deep soaking lie;
Or in the mulberry orchard grass he sits
With milky kex and marrowy hemlocks nigh;
Where silken floating under-darnels tie
And mat the herbage of the summer-floor.
A god he is, this Pan, content to dwell
Among us, nor disdains the damp and hot wood-smell.
He is a god and more.

He loves the flaky boles of peeling pines
Brown as the sand; he loves the languid vines,
As the fruit darkens in their drooping leaves;
The crumpled poppies garnered among sheaves
Soften his eyes with color as of dreams.
The first few crisping leaf-falls on his ear
Herald the wasting year.
He feels the ivies push their stem-feet up
Against the beech-bole all in seams between,
And broaden downwards many a rounded cup
In orbed tops of mealy buds white-green.
Pan too will watch in open glare unseen
The quiet locust seething in the blaze
Upon the vine-leaves of the quarry ways.

MID-DECEMBER: THE COUNTRY DIONYSIA

The Country Dionysia is the second, smaller annual holiday in honor of Dionysus or Bacchus. It is a moveable feast day, being celebrated on different days in different districts. A much simpler affair than the City Dionysia (see page 64), it was celebrated with a procession through the village during which wine, loaves of bread, and images were carried. There were also often performances and competitions of short poems and songs rather than the full-length plays in competition at the City Dionysia. It would be easy to re-create a small Dionysia with some of the prayers and poems that follow.

FROM "PRAYERS AND FANTASIES"

Richard Aldington (1892–1962)

Richard Aldington was the husband of the poet HD, and a poet in his own right. He seems to have shared her love of Paganism as well.

Dionysios, lord of life and laughter, from whom come twin gifts of ecstasy, hear me.

I pray the noble Iacchos of reverent mien and wide tolerant eyes, to look mildly upon me and to show me the mystery of beauty, the mystery of vineyards, the mystery of death.

And I pray the young Dionysios, the bearer of the fawnskin, the charioteer of leopards, the lover of white breasts, to show me the mystery of love.

And grant that nothing ignoble may render me base to myself; let desire be always fresh and keen; let me never love or be loved through ennui, through pity or through lassitude.

HOMERIC HYMN TO DIONYSUS

Anonymous (ca. 700–500 BCE), translated by Hugh G. Evelyn-White

In this wonderful hymn, Dionysus shows himself to be the god who cannot be bound, though his vines can wrap themselves around anything. As is common in Dionysiac literature, those who refuse to acknowledge the divinity of the god are in for a nasty surprise. "Tyrsenian" means "Thracian" or, roughly, Balkan, while "withies" are flexible willow stems.

I will tell of Dionysus, the son of glorious Semele, how he appeared on a jutting headland by the shore of the fruitless sea, seeming like a stripling in the first flush of manhood: his rich, dark hair was waving about him, and on his strong shoulders he wore a purple robe.

Presently there came swiftly over the sparkling sea Tyrsenian pirates on a well-decked ship—a miserable doom led them on. When they saw him they made signs to one another and sprang out quickly, and seizing him straightway put him on board their ship exultingly; for they thought him the son of heaven-nurtured kings. They sought to bind him with rude bonds, but the bonds would not hold him, and the withies fell far away from his hands and feet: and he sat with a smile in his dark eyes. Then the helmsman understood all and cried out at once to his fellows and said:

"Madmen! what god is this whom you have taken and bind, strong that he is? Not even the well-built ship can carry him. Surely this is either Zeus or Apollo who has the silver bow, or Poseidon, for he looks not like mortal men but like the gods who dwell on Olympus. Come, then, let us set him free upon the dark shore at once: do not lay hands on him, lest he grow angry and stir up dangerous winds and heavy squalls."

So said he: but the master chid him with taunting words: "Madman, mark the wind and help hoist sail on the ship: catch all the sheets. As for this fellow we men will see to him. ... But in the end he will speak out and tell us his friends and all his wealth and his brothers, now that providence has thrown him in our way."

When he had said this, he had mast and sail hoisted on the ship, and the wind filled the sail and the crew hauled taut the sheets on either side. But soon strange things were seen among them. First of all sweet, fragrant wine ran streaming throughout all the black ship and a heavenly smell arose, so that all the seamen were seized with amazement when they saw it. And all at once a vine spread out both ways along the top of the sail with many clusters hanging down from it, and a dark ivy-plant twined about the mast, blossoming with flowers, and with rich berries growing on it; and all the thole-pins were covered with garlands. When the pirates saw all this, then at last they bade the helmsman to put the ship to land. But the god changed into a dreadful lion there on the ship, in the bows, and roared loudly: amidships also he showed his wonders and created a shaggy bear which stood up ravening, while on the forepeak was the lion glaring fiercely with scowling brows. And so the sailors fled into the stern and crowded bemused about the right-minded helmsman, until suddenly the lion sprang upon the master and seized him; and when the sailors saw it they leapt out overboard one and all into the bright sea, escaping from a miserable fate, and were changed into dolphins. But on the helmsman Dionysus had mercy and held him back and made him altogether happy, saying to him:

"Take courage … you have found favor with my heart. I am loud-crying Dionysus whom Cadmus' daughter Semele bare of union with Zeus."

Hail, child of fair-faced Semele! He who forgets you can in no wise order sweet song.

FROM "DEMETER"

HD (1886–1961)

Here Demeter, a goddess closely associated with Dionysus in antiquity, speaks and identifies the separation of Dionysus (Bromios) from his mother Semele (who was struck by Zeus's lightning while she was still pregnant with Dionysus) with her own separation from her daughter.

Many the children of gods
but first I take
Bromios, fostering prince,
lift from the ivy brake, a king.

Enough of the lightning,
enough of the tales that speak
of the death of the mother:
strange tales of a shelter
brought to the unborn,
enough of tale, myth, mystery, precedent—
a child lay on the earth asleep.

Soft are the hands of Love,
but what soft hands
clutched at the thorny ground,
scratched like a small white ferret
or foraging whippet or hound,
sought nourishment and found
only the crackling of ivy,
dead ivy leaf and the white
berry, food for a bird,
no food for this who sought,
bending small head in a fever,
whining with little breath.

Ah, small black head,
ah, the purple ivy bush,
ah, berries that shook and spilt
on the form beneath,
who begot you and left?

Though I begot no man child
all my days,
the child of my heart and spirit,
is the child the gods desert
alike and the mother in death—
the unclaimed Dionysios.

FROM "OLD AND NEW"

Sir Edmund Gosse (1849–1928)

In this excerpt from a poem celebrating the dual virtues of Paganism and Christianity comes this paean to Iacchus or Dionysus. A volute is a seashell that looks rather like a conch. Here "Orion" refers to the constellation and corybantic *means "frenzied." A* tabret *is a tambourine, and a* car, *here, is a chariot.*

… And now Iacchus, beautiful and glowing,
    Adown the hill-side comes,
With tabrets shaken high, and trumpets blowing,
    And resonance of drums.

The leopard-skin is round his smooth bright shoulders,
    The vine-branch round his hair;
The eyes that rouse delight in maid-beholders,
    Are glittering, glowworm-fair;
The king of all the provinces of pleasure,
    Lord of a wide domain,
He comes and brings delight that knows no measure,
    A full Saturnian reign.

O take me, Mænads, to your foxskin-chorus,
    Pink-lipped like volute-shells,

For I must follow where your chant sonorous
    Roars down the forest-dells;
The sacred frenzy rends my throat and bosom,
    I shout, and whirl where He,
Our vine-god, tosses like some pale blood-blossom,
    Borne on a windy sea.

Around the car, with streaming hair and frantic,
    The Mænads and wild gods,
And shaggy fauns and wood-girls corybantic
    Toss high the ivy-rods;
Brown limbs with white limbs hotly intertwining
    Whirl in a maddening dance,
Till, when at last Orion is declining,
    We slip into a trance.

KING EIRAPHIOTES

The Greek Anthology (ca. 100 BCE), translated by W. R. Paton

An ancient chant in honor of the god, where he is given a multitude of epithets: Eiraphiotes, or "Insewn," after his premature incubation while sewn into the thigh of Zeus; Boeotian, because Boeotia is the home of his family; Bromius, meaning "roarer," which perhaps refers to his periodic appearance in the form of a bull; and on and on. One has been left out here—"Indian-Slayer." This originally referred to a mythical war Dionysus and the maenads were said to have fought against various regions of India, a myth that is sometimes interpreted as referring to the introduction of wine-making into the area, but the legend is no longer much remembered.

    Evhoe! is an ecstatic cry associated with the worship of Dionysus.

Let us chant the king who loves the call of Evhoe, the King Eiraphiotes,
Tender-haired, rustic, much besung, fair of form,
Boeotian, Bromius, reveller, with vine-leaves in his hair,
Merry, productive, slayer of giants, the laugher,
Son of Zeus, twice-born, son of the Dithyramb, Dionysus,
Euius, with lovely locks, rich in vines, awaker of revels,
Jealous, very wrathful, envious, bestower of envy,
Gentle, sweet drinker, sweet-voiced, cozener,

Thracian, thyrsus-bearing, boon-companion, lion-hearted,

Desirable, twiner of violets, hierophant,

Reveller, horned, ivy-crowned, noisy,

Lydian, lord of the wine-press, dispeller of care,

Healer of sorrow, mystic, frenzied, giver of wine, thousand-shaped,

God of the night, shepherd-god, fawn-like, clothed in fawn-skin,

Spear-thrower, common to all, giver of guests, yellow-haired,

Prone to anger, stout of heart, lover of the mountain shade, wanderer on the mountains,

Deep drinker, wanderer, wearer of many garlands, constant reveller,

Mind-breaker, slender, wrinkled, clad in sheep-skin,

Leaper, satyr, son of Semele,

Jovial, bull-faced, slayer of Tyrrhenians, swift to wrath,

Chaser of sleep, liquid, hymeneal, dweller in the woods,

Mad for wild beasts, terrible, laughter-loving, wanderer,

Golden-horned, graceful, relaxer of the mind, golden-filleted,

Disturber of the soul, liar, bent on noise, tearer of the soul,

Seasonable, eater of raw flesh, nurtured on the mountains, making clamour on the mountains.

Let us chant the King who loves the call of Euhoe, the King Eiraphiotes.

FROM "CADMEIAN SEMELE WAS WITH CHILD BY THE THUNDERER"

Abraham Fraunce (1560?–1593?); modernized by B. Nolan

Iacchus is another name for Dionysus.

This same twice-born babe at length was called Iacchus,
Sweet boy, pleasant imp, fair lad, brave [fellow] Iacchus,
Never sad, free-tongued, free-heart, free-handed Iacchus,
And, when he wants his horns, as mild as a maiden, Iacchus,
But, when he has on his horns, as fierce as a tiger, Iacchus.

BACCHUS

Ralph Waldo Emerson (1803–1882)

Here Emerson calls for the true wine of Dionysus or Bacchus, that which "never grew in the belly of the grape" but instead "among the silver hills of heaven"—that indefinable ecstasy that Bacchus brings to the world.

The Styx is one of the rivers of Hades, and Erebus is the god of the first darkness. The Pleiads,
or Pleiades, are the cluster of stars known as the Seven Sisters.

Bring me wine, but wine which never grew
In the belly of the grape,
Or grew on vine whose taproots reaching through
Under the Andes to the Cape,
Suffered no savor of the world to 'scape.
Let its grapes the morn salute
From a nocturnal root
Which feels the acrid juice
Of Styx and Erebus,
And turns the woe of night,
By its own craft, to a more rich delight.

We buy ashes for bread,
We buy diluted wine;
Give me of the true,
Whose ample leaves and tendrils curled
Among the silver hills of heaven,
Draw everlasting dew;
Wine of wine,
Blood of the world,
Form of forms and mould of statures,
That I; intoxicated,
And by the draught assimilated,
May float at pleasure through all natures,
The bird-language rightly spell,
And that which roses say so well.

Wine that is shed
Like the torrents of the sun
Up the horizon walls;
Or like the Atlantic streams which run
When the South Sea calls.

Water and bread;
Food which needs no transmuting,
Rainbow-flowering, wisdom-fruiting;
Wine which is already man,
Food which teach and reason can.

Wine which music is;
Music and wine are one;
That I, drinking this,
Shall hear far chaos talk with me,
Kings unborn shall walk with me,
And the poor grass shall plot and plan
What it will do when it is man:
Quickened so, will I unlock
Every crypt of every rock.

I thank the joyful juice
For all I know;
Winds of remembering
Of the ancient being blow,
And seeming-solid walls of use
Open and flow.

Pour, Bacchus, the remembering wine;
Retrieve the loss of me and mine;
Vine for vine be antidote,
And the grape requite the lot.
Haste to cure the old despair,
Reason in nature's lotus drenched,
The memory of ages quenched;—
Give them again to shine.
Let wine repair what this undid,
And where the infection slid,
And dazzling memory revive.

Refresh the faded tints,
Recut the aged prints,
And write my old adventures, with the pen
Which, on the first day, drew
Upon the tablets blue
The dancing Pleiads, and the eternal men.

FROM ANOTHER HOMERIC HYMN TO DIONYSUS
Anonymous (ca. 700–500 BCE), translated by Hugh G. Evelyn-White

The Homeric hymn to Dionysus from which this excerpt is drawn is badly fragmented, but a few of the lines are reproduced below. It recounts how his mother Semele never gave birth to him at all: a mortal woman, she was consumed by the fire of lightning when she caught a glimpse of Zeus, the god who had impregnated her. Zeus, unable to save her, nevertheless rescued their child and, because he was premature, sewed the infant Dionysus into his own thigh, where he could finish out his gestation (this is why Dionysus is called the "Insewn"). Thus Dionysus is the god of two births: one male, one female.

Be favorable, O Insewn, Inspirer of frenzied women! We singers sing of you as we begin and as we end a strain, and none forgetting you may call holy song to mind. And so, farewell, Dionysus, Insewn, with your mother Semele whom men call Thyone.

FROM "ARIADNE"
Anonymous, 1866

A cithern or cittern is a guitar-like instrument.

Dionysus, Dionysus, ever laughing, ever free,
Leads the Fauns and sprightly Satyrs o 'er the smiling summer sea;
Mænads with your hair dishevelled, and your bosom glancing, sing
Glory to young Dionysus, glory to the fair Wine-King!

Dionysus, Dionysus, lead along the triumph brave!
Maenads, crown his head with flowers; he will conquer, he will save!
Fauns and satyrs, chant in your deftest, in great Diononysus' train!
Now from conch-shell, now from cithern, swelling raise the choral strain!

FROM "ODE TO DIONYSUS"

R. C. Trevelyan (1872–1951)

… Know, then, that I am Bacchus, born in a cradle of lightning:
The tendrilled vine, and every fruit and flower
Which Earth in spendthrift bounty of love brings forth,
The murmurs of the moon-watched mountain,
Dawn, and the heart of the waking Centaur
All these are mine. …

I am the hope of earth, the darling child of heaven.
None may withstand me, none.
But those that serve me well,
Large destinies are theirs, immortal recompense.
Thus also will I deal with thee,
If faithful as thou hast begun,
Thou shalt perform unto the end
The toil I set thy virtue. Lift thine eyes!

FROM "EVOE!"

Edith M. Thomas (1854–1925)

The "wand-bearers" here are the followers of Dionysus, who carry his sacred staff, the thyrsus. Evoe! is an exclamation of Dionysian revelling. The opening line is a reference to Plato, who wrote "Many are the thyrsus-bearers, but few are the mystics."

Iacchus is another name for Dionysus.

Many are the wand-bearers.
And who (ye ask) am I?
One who was born in madness,
"Evoe!" my first cry—
Who dares, before your spear-points,
To challenge and defy;

And the god, the true Iacchus,
So keep me till I die!

Many are the wand-bearers.
I bear with me no sign;
Yet, I was mad, was drunken,
Ere yet I tasted wine;
Nor bleeding grape can slacken
The thirst wherewith I pine;
And the god, the true Iacchus
Hears now this song of mine.

FROM A THIRD HOMERIC HYMN TO DIONYSUS

Anonymous (ca. 700–500 BCE), translated by Hugh G. Evelyn-White

A coombe is a small hillside valley. The location of the mythical Nysa is not clear.

I begin to sing of ivy-crowned Dionysus, the loud-crying god, splendid son of Zeus and glorious Semele. The rich-haired Nymphs received him in their bosoms from the lord his father and fostered and nurtured him carefully in the dells of Nysa, where by the will of his father he grew up in a sweet-smelling cave, being reckoned among the immortals. But when the goddesses had brought him up, a god oft hymned, then began he to wander continually through the woody coombes, thickly wreathed with ivy and laurel. And the Nymphs followed in his train with him for their leader; and the boundless forest was filled with their outcry.

And so hail to you, Dionysus, god of abundant clusters! Grant that we may come again rejoicing to this season, and from that season onwards for many a year.

MID-LATE DECEMBER: YULETIDE AND THE WINTER SOLSTICE

There's a lot going on during the Yuletide season. This includes, for Pagans, various festivities centered around the Winter Solstice, as well as the Saturnalia (the Roman festival of the god Saturn), and the birthday of the god Mithras or Mithra, which famously occurs on December 25 and is the direct ancestor of Christmas. All these different celebrations, however, have one thing in common: they all acknowledge the changing of the year and the rebirth of the light.

The following pieces are in keeping with the spirit of the solstice and the general Yuletide season; specific prayers to Saturn or Mithras appear under the heading of those holidays.

"DECEMBER" FROM *THE POET'S CALENDAR*
Henry Wadsworth Longfellow (1807–1882)

A little ode to the spirit of December, who is depicted here riding on Capricorn the Goat, carrying the thyrsus of Dionysus. Here the spirit of universal peace is ascribed to the season, rather than any particular faith.

Riding upon the Goat, with snow-white hair,
    I come, the last of all. This crown of mine
Is of the holly; in my hand I bear
    The thyrsus, tipped with fragrant cones of pine.
I celebrate the birth of the Divine,
    And the return of the Saturnian reign;—
My songs are carols sung at every shrine.
    Proclaiming "Peace on earth, good will to men."

FROM "THE MASQUE OF THE TWELVE MONTHS"
George Chapman (1559?–1634)

A winter hymn to the sun. Age—perhaps a reference to the hoary close of the old year—has "three knees" (or legs) because of the use of a cane.

Shine out, fair Sun, with all your heat,
    Show all your thousand-colored light!
Black Winter freezes to his seat;
    The grey wolf howls, he does so bite;
Crook'd Age on three knees creeps the street;
    The boneless fish close quaking lies
And eats for cold his aching feet;
    The stars in icicles arise:

Shine out, and make this winter night
Our beauty's Spring, our Prince of Light!

FROM "ON THE WINTER SOLSTICE, 1740"
Mark Akenside (1721–1770)

From the eighteenth century comes this reminder that spring is coming, even now.

But thou, my lyre, awake, arise,
And hail the sun's returning force:
Even now he climbs the northern skies,
And health and hope attend his course.
Then louder howl the aërial waste,
Be earth with keener cold embraced,
Yet gentle hours advance their wing;
And fancy, mocking winter's might,
With flowers and dews and streaming light
Already decks the newborn spring.

HERRICK'S CAROL
Robert Herrick (1591–1674)

Once again we have one of Herrick's wonderfully ambiguous poems, this time written to honor a "heavenly king" who "sees December turned to May." Take it to refer to whatever solar god you will.

This poem was later set to music and, for those interested in singing, can be found in the Oxford Book of Carols.

What sweeter music can we bring,
Than a carol, for to sing
The birth of this our heavenly King?
Awake the voice! Awake the string!
Heart, ear, and eye, and everything,
Awake! the while the active finger
Runs divisions with the singer.

Dark and dull night, fly hence away,
And give the honor to this day,
That sees December turn'd to May.
If we may ask the reason, say
The why and wherefore all things here
Seem like the springtime of the year?

Why does the chilling winter's morn
Smile like a field beset with corn?
Or smell like to a mead new-shorn,
Thus on the sudden? Come and see
The cause why things thus fragrant be:
'Tis He is born whose quickening birth
Gives life and luster public mirth
To heaven and the under-earth.

We see Him come, and know Him ours,
Who with His sunshine and His showers
Turns all the patient ground to flowers.
The Darling of the world is come,
And fit it is we find a room
To welcome Him. The nobler part
Of all the house here, is the heart.
Which we will give him; and bequeath
This holly and this ivy wreath,
To do him honor who's our King,
The Lord of all this revelling.

From "For the Vanadís"

Gudrun of Mimirsbrunnr (ca. 2015)

A final call to Freya to bring healing to her devotee. Asgard is one of the homes of the Norse gods; Vanaheim is another, specific to the Vanir, the divine family to which Freya belongs. Frith means, loosely, "security" or "peace."

Hail to the ambassador to Asgard
on the solstice morning
a ray of light in a cold white world,

bringing the green of Vanaheim's fields

and the gold of Vanaheim's courage.

Hail Freya Frithmaker, Bridge-Builder,

help me to hold out my hands with a smile

for I am dull and closed-in with years of mistrust

and I have forgotten the mystery of the open arms.

APPLE TREE WASSAIL

Traditional British

An excellent old British tradition! The "Apple Tree Wassail" is traditionally recited or sung to celebrate the dormant trees, thank them for their service, and encourage them to produce a good harvest. (Wassail comes from Anglo-Saxon and means "be hale," and it is also the name of a hot cider drink.) Trees are decorated with wool dipped in the previous year's cider, and, if there are enough participants, they hold hands in a circle around the trunk.

I have made one small change to this traditional version from Somerset, and that was to substitute "gods" for the singular form.

Old apple tree we wassail thee

And hope that thou shalt bear

For the gods do know

Where we shall be

To be merry another year.

For to bloom well

And to bear well, so merry let us be

Let every one drink up his cup

Here's health to the old apple tree

Capfuls! Hatfuls! Baskets full!

And a little heap under the stairs!

THE CUTTY WREN

Traditional Welsh

This is one of thousands of variants of folk songs, found throughout Britain and Ireland as well as in parts of the United States, that are part of a very old tradition which holds that the wren, the "King of All Birds," is the embodiment of winter, and must be hunted and killed near the Solstice in order to allow the light to return (the traditional date of the hunt is December 26). After his death the wren was crowned as a king and enshrined in a box, and then taken from door to door in the village, when songs like this would be sung. The tradition is still practiced, but need give animal lovers no alarm: an artificial wren has been used in all locales for many years now.

It is worth mentioning that some wren songs clearly refer to the death of something or someone substantially larger than a wren, a fact which has led some folklorists to suspect that the origin of these songs is very ancient indeed, and that they dimly recall a time when the Year King (or an effigy of the King) would have been sacrificed to ensure the survival of his people. But as with so many traditions, no one really knows the roots of it. The message is clear, however: it's time for the winter king's reign to end.

"The Solstice" could easily be substituted for "Old Christmas."

Joy, health, love, and peace be all here in this place
By your leave, we will sing concerning our king

Our king is well dressed, in the silks of the best
In ribbons so rare, no king can compare.

We have travelled many miles, over hedges and stiles
In search of our king, unto you we bring.

Old Christmas is past, Twelfth Night is the last,
And we bid you adieu, great joy to the new

HAIL TO SUNNA

Heidi Shewchuk (twenty-first century)

Sunna is the Norse and Germanic sun goddess. "Wassail" means "be in good health!"

Sunna's burning arrows
Pierce the gloom of midwinter
Her glory resounds triumphant
Across the dreaming land
And the first buds of spring will awake to her call.
Hail to Her who is the Queen of Heaven!
Burning Wheel of Creation!
Creatrix! Destroyer! Queen!
Her face of white hot gold
Shines upon me and I rejoice in Her glory.

The hawk circles high

delighting in the cloudless sky, while below the snow glitters like stars.

The little song birds sing proudly from the highest tree,

Rejoice! Rejoice! Sunna has returned!

Her face of bright favor smiles upon us all!

Hail to you Sunna, Queen of Heaven!

Wassail!

FROM "WASSAIL POEM"

Robert Herrick (1591–1674)

A blessing upon a household for a prosperous year. A manchet is a fine loaf of bread. Vegetarians may take "meat" in its archaic sense: solid food (that does not need to be derived from animals).

Give way, give way, ye gates, and win
An easy blessing to your bin
And basket, by our entering in.

May both with manchet stand replete;
Your larders, too, so hung with meat,
That though a thousand, thousand eat,

Yet, ere twelve moons shall whirl about
Their silv'ry spheres, there's none may doubt
But more's sent in than was served out.

Next, may your dairies prosper so,
As that your pans no ebb may know;
But if they do, the more to flow,

Like to a solemn sober stream,
Bank'd all with lilies, and the cream
Of sweetest cowslips filling them.

Then may your plants be press'd with fruit,
Nor bee or hive you have be mute,
But sweetly sounding like a lute.

PRAYER TO FRIGGA

Laurel Mendes

A prayer to remind us that we have a special duty to help those less fortunate in the darkest time of the year. Frigga is the great Mother of the Gods, and wife of Odin.

Frigga fair Goddess, who knows and says not,
Watch, ward and endow the humblest of hearths.

In this season of cold, fierce and biting,
faint warmth is found to bring cheer to any.

No splendor is there to grace pale grey walls.
No spruce twigs nor holly wait to be hung

Fear waits in corners and under the floors
Bare are the larders, vacant the cellars

Hunger and cold, the ancient companions,
Stand on the steps and knock at the doors

Hope now fares far away from such dwellings.
Forgotten is mercy, justice and peace.

Thoughtless, unseeing their "betters" pass by.
Smug in the wealth won at other's expense.

Frigga fair Goddess, who knows and says not
Teach humankind to remember our kin.

FROM "THE LADY HERTHA"

John Oxenford (1854)

This poem, from Charles Dickens's magazine Household Worlds, *reminds us gods may appear at any time to test the kindness and hospitality of mortals.*
    Hertha is a Germanic goddess of the earth.

Throw open, throw open the windows wide,
For now is the season of glad Yule-tide.
The Lady will pass through the frosty air,
In snow-white garb, and with flowing hair.

Hear you her voice as she floats along,
Through the wintry blast sounds her liquid song;
Twelve days will she wander—that Lady fair—
In snow-white garb, and with flowing hair.

A heavy mischief will fall, no doubt,
On him who shuts the Wand'rer out.
So open the windows wide. Take care
To welcome the lady with flowing hair.

FROM "BALLAD OF THE MARI LWYD"
Vernon Watkins (1906–1967)

The turning of the year is a time of birth, but also of death—of the old year, of the darkness, of the past. In Wales the custom of the Mari Lwyd, or Grey Mare, highlights this. The Mari Lwyd is a mare's skull carried on a pole from house to house in a village or town, whose inhabitants often try to refuse her entry before surrendering and allowing her in. In each house she chases and snaps at those present, while drinks are offered to the mummers who carry her. No one knows where the tradition comes from, or how old it is (it was first documented in 1800), but, modern doubters notwithstanding, it seems likely that it is a survival of a pre-Christian tradition.

This excerpt from Welsh poet Vernon Watkins's extraordinary poem would make an excellent part of a Mari Lwyd procession.

Mari Lwyd, Horse of Frost, Star-horse, and White Horse of the Sea, is
carried to us.
The Dead return.
Those Exiles carry her, they who seem holy and have put on corruption,
they who seem corrupt and have put on holiness.
They strain against the door.
They strain towards the fire which fosters and warms the Living.
The Living, who have cast them out, from their own fear, from their own
fear of themselves, into the outer loneliness of death, rejected them, and cast
them out for ever:
The Living cringe and warm themselves at the fire, shrinking from that
loneliness, that singleness of heart.

The Living are defended by the rich warmth of the flames which keeps
that loneliness out.
Terrified, they hear the Dead tapping at the panes; then they rise up,
armed with the warmth of firelight, and the condition of scorn.
It is New Year's Night.
Midnight is burning like a taper. In an hour, in less than an hour, it
will be blown out.
It is the moment of conscience.
The living moment.
The dead moment.
Listen.

DECEMBER 17–23: THE SATURNALIA

The week of Saturnalia celebrates the god Saturn (known to the Greeks as Cronos or Kronos), father of Jupiter, Juno, Ceres, Vesta, Neptune, and Pluto, among others. The nature of Saturn is full of contradictions: he is the father of the gods, but he ate his own children; he is the ruler of lead, but his reign was considered by the Romans to have been a glorious Golden Age, when the earth offered up fruits willingly to humankind and the labor of agriculture was not necessary. In keeping with Saturn's nature, the Saturnalia was always a topsy-turvy time, when normal rules of conduct were suspended, at least to a degree—a tradition which has influenced the modern holiday season. In ancient Rome slaves would be served at banquets by their masters and the poor were fed in a communal feast in the Forum; nowadays we carry on the tradition of granting license and feeding the hungry. During the Saturnalia, small gifts of money, candles, or honey were widely distributed, the ancestors of modern Christmas gifts.

ORPHIC HYMN TO KRONOS

Anonymous (ca. 200 CE?), translated by B. Nolan

Rhea, the mother of the gods, is the sister and wife of Kronos; it was her milk that created the Milky Way.

Venerable one, father of the blessed gods and of mortals, cunning, stainless, strong and courageous Titan, you destroy all and you create all. You are bound with unknowable chains to the ever-expanding Cosmos. Eternal Kronos, universal life-giver; Kronos, of numberless deceits, child of the earth and the starry sky, first of all, renowned Titan, who inhabit all parts of the universe, husband of Rhea, hear my prayer. Grant my life a happy and irreproachable ending.

FROM "SATURNALIA"

John Dos Passos (1896–1970)

Rhadamanthus is a son of Zeus and judge of the dead. He lives in the Isles of the Blessed. "Rime" is an old word for frost, while an orison *is a prayer. A slug-horn is a trumpet.*

In earth's womb the old gods stir,
Fierce chthonian deities of old time.
With cymbals and rattle of castanets,
And shriek of slug-horns, the North Wind
Bows the oak and the moaning fir,
On russet hills and by roadsides stiff with rime.

In nature, dead, the life gods stir,
From Rhadamanthus and the Isles,
Where Saturn rules the Age of Gold,
Come old, old ghosts of bygone gods;
While dim mists earth's outlines blur,
And drip all night from lichen-greened roof-tiles.

In men's hearts the mad gods rise
And fill the streets with revelling,
With torchlight that glances on frozen pools,
With tapers starring the thick-fogged night,
A-dance, like strayed fireflies,
'Mid dim mad throngs who Saturn's orisons sing.

FROM THE *ORPHIC ARGONAUTICA*

Anonymous (ca. fifth cen. CE), translated by Isaac Preston Cory

An account of how Cronos began the process of creation that ended in the birth of humankind.
Phanes is a deity peculiar to the Orphic tradition, here identified with Eros.

First (I have sung) the vast necessity of ancient Chaos,
And Cronus, who in the boundless tracts brought forth
The Ether, and the splendid and glorious Eros of a two-fold nature,
The illustrious father of night, existing from eternity,
Whom men call Phanes, for he first appeared.
I have sung the birth of powerful Brimo (Hecate), and the unhallowed deeds
Of the earth-born (giants), who showered down from heaven
Their blood, the lamentable seed of generation, from whence sprung
The race of mortals, who inhabit the boundless earth for ever.

KRONOS

Richard Hovey (1864–1900)

An ode to the lasting influence of Kronos, even after his defeat by his son Zeus; he is compared to a
plummeting meteor.

As one of those huge monsters of the sky,
    Fierce with the flame of fiery floating hair,
    Falls from the zenith through the upper air,
Threatening the planets from their paths on high,
Jarring creation from its harmony,
    Spreading on earth destruction and despair,
    Affrighting men to temples and vain prayer,
So from the summit of his majesty
He falls, and heaven is shaken as flame. Zeus reigns,
    Usurping; and no matter what is left—
How smooth or tangled grows his god-life's weft—
    With how swift footing or how slow the years
Speed on, for him forever there remains
    A thunder and a chaos in the spheres.

DECEMBER 25: MITHRAS'S DAY

Despite what you may have heard, Mithras (also known as Mithra or Mitra) is the reason for the Christmas season—according to the best Biblical scholarship, Jesus was born in the spring (few shepherds are sleeping out of doors with their sheep in December, even in the Middle East). But so popular was the cult of Mithras in antiquity that Christianity needed to absorb it along with a number of others in order to cut it out … and cut it out it eventually did. While we have a great many references to Mithras and numerous archeological relics, we have very little idea of what the Mithraic Mysteries actually entailed, and not one original Mithraic text has survived. It is a major loss to the Western world.

However, Mithras is a very ancient god, dating to a time long before "the glory that was Greece and the grandeur that was Rome," to a time when the peoples who would make up many of the modern nations of the East and West still lived all together. So if we have lost Mithras here in the West, we can find him again in India, in the pages of the *Rig Veda*, a collection of Sanskrit hymns likely composed between 1500 and 1200 BCE. And we can also find him in Zoroastrianism, the ancient Persian faith still practiced by adherents in modern Iran and in the worldwide Zoroastrian diaspora. Of course neither the Mithra of the Zoroastrians or the Mitra of the Hindus is identical with the Mithra of the West, but until we can recover our own, his near cousins can serve to light our path toward him. And, fortunately, Mithras has fired the imagination of some later Western poets, whose work is also included here.

FROM "MITHRA"

Charles L. Hildreth (1885)

… Resistless, deathless
Father of worlds and lord of storms and calms,
Thou at whose will the seasons bloom and fail,
Dispenser and destroyer, hail, all hail!

FROM THE "HYMN TO MITHRA" FROM THE *AVESTAS*

Anonymous (ca. 200 CE), translated by James Darmesteter

The Persian Mithras is a god of light and oaths, the one who sees to it that justice is done. In this very small excerpt from the "Hymn to Mithra" in the Avestas, *a sacred text of Zoroastrianism, Mithra himself is depicted as praying the Ahura Mazda, the creator god. Then Mithra receives the prayers of his followers, imploring his protection.*

The nature of the traditional sacrifice and libations are not clear, but the Zoroastrians were and are a strongly vegetarian faith.

We sacrifice unto Mithra, the lord of wide pastures … sleepless, and ever awake;
Who, with hands lifted up, rejoicing, cries out, speaking thus:

"O Ahura Mazda, most beneficent spirit! Maker of the material world, thou Holy One!

"If men would worship me with a sacrifice in which I were invoked by my own name, as they worship the other gods with sacrifices in which they are invoked by their own names, then I should come to the faithful at the appointed time; I should come in the appointed time of my beautiful, immortal life."

[So we pray:]

May we keep our field; may we never be exiles from our field, exiles from our house, exiles from our borough, exiles from our town, exiles from our country.

Thou dashest in pieces the malice of the malicious, the malice of the men of malice: dash thou in pieces the killers of faithful men!

Thou hast good horses, thou hast a good chariot: thou art bringing help at every appeal, and art powerful.

I will pray unto thee for help, with many consecrations, with good consecrations of libations; with many offerings, with good offerings of libations, that we, abiding in thee, may long inhabit a good abode, full of all the riches that can be wished for.

Thou keepest those nations that tender a good worship to Mithra, the lord of wide pastures; thou dashest in pieces those that delight in havoc. Unto thee will I pray for help: may he come to us for help, the awful, most powerful Mithra, the worshipful and praiseworthy, the glorious lord of nations.

For his brightness and glory, I will offer him a sacrifice worth being heard. …

HYMN OF THE GHEBERS

Helen Bantock (1868–1961)

Here the poet and lyricist Helen Bantock imagines a Mithraic rite complete with offerings of fire and incense. A Gheber *is an old term for a Zoroastrian.*

Dawn's dim, shadows are dying
Into the day;
And ever onward and upward,
We wend our way.
Mithra the mighty is shaking

His wings unfurled,
As he looks in gleaming splendor
Over the world.
On the peak of the Ghebers' mountain
Flashes his light.
Swiftly we kindle the altar,
High on the height.
Gifts to the Sun-god bringing
Fragrance and Flame.
Mithra the cloud-compeller,
Mighty his name!

FROM THE *RIG VEDA*

Anonymous (ca. 1500–1200 BCE), translated by Ralph T. H. Griffith

In the Rig Veda, *the ancient religious texts of Hinduism, the Adityas are seven high deities. Mitra is one; thus he is addressed as Aditya.* Mitra *means "friend" in Sanskrit.*

Mitra, when speaking, stirreth men to labour: Mitra sustaineth both the earth and heaven.
Mitra beholdeth men with eyes that close not. To Mitra bring, with holy oil, oblation.
Foremost be he who brings thee food, O Mitra, who strives to keep thy sacred Law, Āditya.
He whom thou helpest ne'er is slain or conquered, on him, from near or far, falls no
    affliction.
Joying in sacred food and free from sickness, with knees bent lowly on the earth's broad
    surface,
Following closely the Āditya's statute, may we remain in Mitra's gracious favor.
Auspicious and adorable, this Mitra was born with fair dominion, King, Disposer.
May we enjoy the grace of him the Holy, yea, rest in his propitious loving-kindness.
The great Āditya, to be served with worship, who stirreth men, is gracious to the singer.
To Mitra, him most highly to be lauded, offer in fire oblation that he loveth.
The gainful grace of Mitra, God, supporter of the race of man,
Gives splendor of most glorious fame.
Mitra whose glory spreads afar, he who in might surpasses heaven,
Surpasses earth in his renown. ...
Mitra to Gods, to living men, to him who strews the holy grass,
Gives food fulfilling sacred Law.

FROM THE *THEBAID*

Publius Papinius Statius (ca. 45–ca. 96 CE), translated by B. Nolan

In this Latin text, Mithras is equated with Phoebus Apollo, Osiris, and Hyerpion, the Titan sun god. He is described as struggling with a bull in a cave, a pose in which he was repeatedly depicted in antiquity. As scholar David Ulansey has suggested, this iconography may represent the Precession of Equinoxes—that is, the shifting of Earth's axis, which becomes noticeable every 2,150 years or so. This shift alters the visibility of different constellations at different times of the year. About 2,000 BCE the spring equinox, which had hitherto occurred in the sign of Taurus, began to take place in Aries: thus, the Bull was "slain" by the power of the god. "Persean" comes from Perseus, the Greek hero.

Lord Phoebus! Come to us and help us, remembering our past hospitality, and grant your blessings to Juno's fields, whether you are called the rose-tinged Titan Hyperion, as among the Persians, or Osiris the granter of the harvest, or Mithras, who beneath the rocky Persean cave wrestles with the reluctant horns.

FROM "ODE TO MITHRA"

Thomas Maurice (1792)

Mithra is again associated with the sun in this excerpt from an eighteenth-century English poem.

Mithra, we hail thee our immortal fire!
And, as we gaze on thy diffusive beam,
Drink from thy fountain life, and catch rekindling fire!

LUNAR PRAYERS

Every month brings opportunities to worship the lunar goddesses: at the new moon, the full moon, or any time when we look up in wonder at the night sky. In keeping with the moon's variable nature, there are many names for the goddess she represents: Artemis, Diana, Cynthia, Selene, Luna, Latonia, and many others. She has been celebrated by poets from antiquity to the present day, and there is no indication that even in an age of nascent space travel and exploration, the wonder she inspires in humankind will ever diminish.

QUEEN AND HUNTRESS

Ben Jonson (1572–1637)

This musical poem was written by one of William Shakespeare's friends and fellow playwrights. "Cynthia" is an epithet of the goddess Artemis, so called because she was believed to have been born on Mount Cynthus on the island of Delos. Hesperus is the Evening Star.

Queen and huntress, chaste and fair,
Now the sun is laid to sleep,
Seated in thy silver chair
State in wonted manner keep:
Hesperus entreats thy light,
Goddess excellently bright.

Earth, let not thy envious shade
Dare itself to interpose;
Cynthia's shining orb was made

Heaven to clear when day did close:
Bless us then with wished sight,
Goddess excellently bright.

Lay thy bow of pearl apart
And thy crystal-shining quiver;
Give unto the flying hart
Space to breathe, how short soever:
Thou that mak'st a day of night,
Goddess excellently bright.

FROM THE HOMERIC HYMN TO ARTEMIS

Anonymous (ca. 700–500 BCE), translated by Hugh G. Evelyn-White

I sing of Artemis, whose shafts are of gold, who cheers on the hounds, the pure maiden, shooter of stags, who delights in archery, own sister to Apollo with the golden sword. Over the shadowy hills and windy peaks she draws her golden bow, rejoicing in the chase, and sends out grievous shafts. The tops of the high mountains tremble and the tangled wood echoes awesomely with the outcry of beasts: earth quakes and the sea also where fishes shoal. But the goddess with a bold heart turns every way … when she is satisfied and has cheered her heart, this huntress who delights in arrows slackens her supple bow and goes to the great house of her dear brother Phoebus Apollo, to the rich land of Delphi, there to order the lovely dance of the Muses and Graces. There she hangs up her curved bow and her arrows, and heads and leads the dances, gracefully arrayed, while all they utter their heavenly voice, singing how neat-ankled Leto bare children supreme among the immortals both in thought and in deed.

Hail to you, children of Zeus and rich-haired Leto!

"COME WITH BOWS BENT" FROM *ATALANTA IN CALYDON*

Algernon Charles Swinburne (1837–1909)

These beautiful choruses in honor of Artemis are from Atalanta in Calydon, *Swinburne's epic poem about the virgin huntress Atalanta, devotee of the goddess.*

Come with bows bent and with emptying of quivers,
    Maiden most perfect, lady of light,
With a noise of winds and many rivers,
    With a clamor of waters, and with might;
Bind on thy sandals, O thou most fleet,
Over the splendor and speed of thy feet;
For the faint east quickens, the wan west shivers,
    Round the feet of the day and the feet of the night.

Where shall we find her, how shall we sing to her,
    Fold our hands round her knees, and cling?
O that man's heart were as fire and could spring to her,
    Fire, or the strength of the streams that spring!
For the stars and the winds are unto her
As raiment, as songs of the harp-player;
For the risen stars and the fallen cling to her,
    And the southwest-wind and the west-wind sing.

FROM "SELENE"

Anna Hempstead Branch (1875–1937)

Anna Hempstead Branch was an American poet who, like her subject, never married. Here she writes in the voice of the goddess, warning misogynists and abusers of women of the consequences of failing to acknowledge the goddess.

For in this world
I say there dwells a spirit and she lives
Hidden even from the gods, and of her face
Zeus has not dreamed. She is consuming, fierce,
Beautiful and withheld. She layeth waste
The gardens of men's flesh—and I am She.

I am the fearful Huntress. With my hounds
I all men must pursue until they seek
My silent altar in an ancient place
No man has thought on and no eye has seen.
I am the Runner. I am the goddess chaste.
If with thy fleshly eye thou shouldst perceive
Mine angry whiteness, swiftly would I slay.
For I am set apart and spiritual,
And me in spiritual ways thou must discern. ...

So all seen things
Shall drive thee to my bosom, mine—that men
Flee from in terror, hating me, the strong,
The ancient, the eternal, the wide spread,
The many-breasted mother, the Unseen!
Dreadful am I to them; yes, feared the most
Of all the gods—whom Zeus from the beginning
Made separate and supreme, relentless, fierce,
The great avenger, scourger of men's souls,
Flesh-eater! Aye! Me do they hate indeed.
And they would slay me in my secret lair
And smite me with sharp whips and bleed with swords
And drive me to the market branded 'slave,'
Me, the fierce Woman, mistress of living men!
This would they do and nudge each other and cry
'Well done' to one another.
But I am set
Beyond the reach of hate. Not any sword,
No, not the sharpest, can search out my breast
Here in my silence where I sit and watch
With my eternal laughter and disdain
And scorn unspeakable. Justly they fear,
For I am goddess of the bow and strike
With my bright arrows all who know me not.
Yes, with my darts pursue them till they pluck

From out their breasts the bleeding barbs of sense
And cast them underneath their feet and fall
With faces in the dust crying, 'Pity us,
Oh, Vanquisher of all things! Ease in us
Our sharp affliction, heal our wounds and take
Thine anguish from us.' Them do I heal indeed.
But those who see, yet heed not, being unwise,
How this earth trembles and brightness ails and time
Blows all things from us like a mist disturbed
By silent air; all those that having perceived
My dangerous presence have not sought with gifts
My altar, and from consecrated urns
Pour no libations of rich tears, I scourge
With my sharp rods and I unleash my hounds
And set them on them, dividing their frantic flesh,
And drive them into Hell. For I am queen
Of earth and of the shades, and of the gods
The dark mysterious mother, and the dead
Worship me in deep places.

CARMINA 34

Gaius Valerius Catullus (ca. 84–ca. 54)

This hymn to Diana by the great Roman poet Catullus seems at first glance to have been written for recital by a group of children, though it may never have been intended for performance. Diana is also called Latonia, ("daughter of Leto)," Juno Lucina (in her role as helper of laboring women), Trivia or "Three-fold," and Luna.

We belong to Diana,
Unmarried boys and girls;
We who belong to Diana
Sing to her.

O Daughter of Leto, O great
Child of Greatest Jove,
Whom your mother bore on Delos
Hard by the olive tree,

So that you might become queen
Of the mountains, queen of the thickets,
And of the unknown wilds,
And the wandering rivers;

Women in labor call
You Juno Light-bringer,
Powerful Trivia you are
Called, and Luna of the baleful light.

You sail, goddess, through your
Monthly course, measuring out the year,
Filling the country houses
Of farmers with good foods.

By whatever holy name
Is pleasing to you, be blessed,
And help, with your good aid,
As you always have, our people.

From the Homeric Hymn to Selene

Anonymous (ca. 700–500 BCE), translated by Hugh G. Evelyn-White

Unlike Artemis or Diana, the moon goddess Selene was not a virgin. She had a daughter with Zeus, son of Cronos, who was named Pandia ("All-Bright").

And next, sweet voiced Muses, daughters of Zeus, well-skilled in song, tell of the long-winged Moon. From her immortal head a radiance is shown from heaven and embraces earth; and great is the beauty that ariseth from her shining light. The air, unlit before, glows with the light of her golden crown, and her rays beam clear, whensoever bright Selene having bathed her lovely body in the waters of Ocean, and donned her far-gleaming raiment, and yoked her strong-necked, shining team, drives on her long-maned horses at full speed, at eventime in the mid-month: then her great orbit is full and then her beams shine brightest as she increases. So she is a sure token and a sign to mortal men.

Once the Son of Cronos was joined with her in love; and she conceived and bare a daughter Pandia, exceeding lovely amongst the deathless gods.

Hail, white-armed goddess, bright Selene, mild, bright-tressed queen!

THE NEW MOON

Traditional Scottish, translated by Alexander Carmichael

Once again, the vague "Three-in-One" may be interpreted however the worshipper would like. Laving here means "bathing."

By grace of the Three-in-One.
If to-night, O moon, thou hast found us
    In peaceful, happy rest,
May thy laving lustre leave us
    Seven times still more blest.

    O moon so fair,
    May it be so,
    As seasons come,
    And seasons go.

"CHORUS OF HUNTERS (TO ARTEMIS)" FROM *THE GREAT GOD PAN*

Helen Bantock (1868–1961)

O awake! O awake! Dian's wings are unfurled,
Maiden swift, Maiden sweet as the rose of the world!
Hark, afar! hark, away! comes the call of the horn,
for the huntress divine strings the bow of the morn.
Come, away!
Let us rise, let us climb to the heart of the wild!
O awake! Hear the song of the maid undefiled!

"DAEMON, INITIATE, SPIRIT" FROM *THE HIPPOLYTUS OF EURIPIDES*

HD (1886–1961)

A daemon is not, of course, a demon, but rather a generic name for a spirit. This beautiful invocation may be accompanied by an offering of pale flowers, as the second verse describes.

Daemon, initiate, spirit
Of the god-race, Artemis,

Latona's daughter,
Child of Zeus,
Of all maids loveliest,
We greet you, mistress:
You dwell in you father's house,
The gold-wrought porches of Zeus,
Apart in the depth of space.

Of all maids, loveliest,
I greet you, Artemis,
loveliest upon Olympus:
dearest, to you this gift,
flower set by flower and leaf,
broken by uncut grass,
where neither scythe has dipped
nor does the shepherd yet
venture to lead his sheep;
there it is white and fragrant,
the wild-bee swirls across;
as a slow rivulet,
mystic peace broods and drifts:
Ah! but my own, my dearest,
take for your gold-wrought locks
from my hands these flowers,
as from a spirit.

FROM "A HYMN TO ARTEMIS"

Maurice Hewlett (1861–1923)

English novelist and poet Maurice Hewlett here refers to Artemis as "Amarynthinian" because she had a famous shrine in Amarynthia, Euboea, an island off the coast of Greece. The Caryatides are the maidens of Karyai, an ancient Greek town. "Stygian" means "underworld." "Soothest" here means "truest," and "hest" is "behest."

Queen of the upper air, crown'd Artemis!
Quick-girdled huntress and moon-diadem'd,

O patroness of all our keen endeavor,
Lady that life from life dost sever,
Hear thou from haunt Eubœan!
Life out of life, seed unto seed thou givest,
Thou potent in the Stygian shades infernal
As in the blue supernal;
Potent thou too in the green habitations
Of teeming Earth, whose nations
Adore in thee their holiest aspirations,
See their wholesome, see their pure
Stroke and striving imaged sure
In thine implacable, chaste, thy virgin meditations.

Thou to be sought in dewy Arcadian haunts,
Soothest, chastest and cleanest!
Where broodeth the dove, where the wood pecker chants
His mocking refrain.
Sacred to thee are birds of the air, and all cattle,
The mountain track, the glade where in battle,
Clashing their antler'd heads, stags beat amain
Earth for the herd's dominion:
Thee glorify the hawks, each strain of the pinion
Is as a hymn of thy praise, swifter than sight!
For in thee the gladness of strength, and beauty of strength,
In thee the clearness of light and throbbing of light,
Have all their crown, O deathless Queen of the night,
Amarynthinian!

ORPHIC HYMN TO SELENE

Anonymous (ca. 200 CE), translated by Thomas Taylor

Hear, Goddess queen, diffusing silver light,
bull-horned and wandering through the gloom of Night.
With stars surrounded, and with circuit wide
Night's torch extending, through the heavens you ride:

Female and Male with borrowed rays you shine,
and now full-orbed, now tending to decline.
Mother of ages, fruit-producing Moon,
whose amber orb makes Night's reflected noon:
Lover of horses, splendid, queen of Night,
all-seeing power bedecked with starry light.
Lover of vigilance, the foe of strife,
in peace rejoicing, and a prudent life:
Fair lamp of Night, its ornament and friend,
who gives to Nature's works their destined end.
Queen of the stars, all-wife Diana hail!
Decked with a graceful robe and shining veil;
Come, blessed Goddess, prudent, starry, bright,
come moony-lamp with chaste and splendid light,
Shine on these sacred rites with prosperous rays,
and pleased accept your suppliant's mystic praise.

"LOVELY GODDESS OF THE BOW" FROM *ARADIA,* OR *THE GOSPEL OF WITCHES*

Author unknown (ninteenth century)

Debate rages about the origin of Aradia, *or* The Gospel of the Witches: *is it a genuine survival of Italian Paganism, a hoax perpetrated by folklorist Charles Godfrey Leland, or a mishmash collection of folklore and superstition put together and embellished by a mysterious Italian fortune-teller? As far as this prayer goes, however, it hardly matters: it is a beautiful hymn to Diana.*

Lovely Goddess of the bow!
Lovely Goddess of the arrows!
Of all hounds and of all hunting
Thou who wakest in starry heaven
When the sun is sunk in slumber
Thou with moon upon they forehead,
Who the chase by night preferrest
Unto hunting in the daylight,
With thy nymphs unto the music

Of the horn—thyself the huntress,
And most powerful: I pray thee
Think, although but for an instant,
Upon us who pray unto thee!

Fair goddess of the rainbow,
Of the stars and of the moon!
The queen most powerful
Of hunters and the night!
   We beg of thee thy aid,
   That thou mayst give to us
The best of fortune ever!

FROM THE SECOND HOMERIC HYMN TO ARTEMIS

Anonymous (ca. 700–500 BCE), translated by Hugh G. Evelyn-White

Meles is the river that flows through Smyrna, in Turkey, where a statue to Artemis once stood in the public square.

Muse, sing of Artemis, sister of the Far-shooter, the virgin who delights in arrows, who was fostered with Apollo. She waters her horses from Meles deep in reeds, and swiftly drives her all-golden chariot through Smyrna to vine-clad Claros where Apollo, god of the silver bow, sits waiting for the far-shooting goddess who delights in arrows. And so hail to you, Artemis, in my song and to all goddesses as well. Of you first I sing and with you I begin. ...

FROM THE *DIONYSIACA*

Nonnus (fifth century CE), translated by B. Nolan

Mene is the goddess who presides over the months, and so is equated here with the moon.

O daughter of the Sun, Mene of many turnings, mother of all! O Selene, driver of the silver chariot! O many-named Hecate, who in the night shakes your magical torch in your hand, o come, wanderer in the night. ...

PRAISED BE DIANA'S FAIR AND HARMLESS LIGHT

Sir Walter Raleigh (1552–1618)

Sir Walter Raleigh, who founded the doomed Roanoke Colony in Virginia, wrote this hymn to Diana before his execution for treason. Circe is, of course, the nymph in the Odyssey *who enslaves men and changes them into animals when she is tired of them.*

Praised be Diana's fair and harmless light;
Praised be the dews wherewith she moists the ground;
Praised be her beams, the glory of the night;
Praised be her power by which all powers abound.

Praised be her nymphs with whom she decks the woods,
Praised be her knights in whom true honor lives;
Praised be that force by which she moves the floods;
Let that Diana shine which all these gives.

In heaven queen she is among the spheres;
In aye she mistress-like makes all things pure;
Eternity in her oft change she bears;
She beauty is; by her the fair endure.

Time wears her not: she doth his chariot guide;
Mortality below her orb is placed;
By her the virtue of the stars down slide;
In her is virtue's perfect image cast.

    A knowledge pure it is her worth to know:
    With Circes let them dwell that think not so.

FROM *ENDYMION*

John Keats (1795–1821)

Endymion was a shepherd who fell passionately in love with Selene. In his long poem celebrating the myth, Keats included this hymn to the moon. For the record, "spooming" means "rushing" or "surging before the wind." (And no, you shouldn't have known that; even two hundred years ago Keats was criticized for his use of obscure vocabulary.) Tellus here is Tellumo, the Roman god of the earth, spouse of the earth goddess.

O Moon! the oldest shades 'mong oldest trees
Feel palpitations when thou lookest in:
O Moon! old boughs lisp forth a holier din
The while they feel thine airy fellowship.
Thou dost bless every where, with silver lip
Kissing dead things to life. The sleeping kine,
Couched in thy brightness, dream of fields divine:
Innumerable mountains rise, and rise,
Ambitious for the hallowing of thine eyes;
And yet thy benediction passeth not
One obscure hiding-place, one little spot
Where pleasure may be sent: the nested wren
Has thy fair face within its tranquil ken,
And from beneath a sheltering ivy leaf
Takes glimpses of thee; thou art a relief
To the poor patient oyster, where it sleeps
Within its pearly house.—The mighty deeps,
The monstrous sea is thine—the myriad sea!
O Moon! far-spooming Ocean bows to thee,
And Tellus feels his forehead's cumbrous load.

From "On the Evening and the Morning"

George Moses Horton (1789–1867?)

George Horton was an enslaved American poet who was liberated by the Union Army during the Civil War. While still enslaved, he taught himself to read and received help and encouragement from students at the University of North Carolina. He published two books of poetry before the Civil War, making him the first African-American poet to have a book published in the United States. In this poem, he describes the rising of the moon and makes Diana the bringer of morning as she chases the night away.

> At length the silver queen begins to rise,
> And spread her glowing mantle in the skies,
> And from the smiling chambers of the east,
> Invites the eye to her resplendent feast. . . .
>
> The night-hawk's din deserts the shepherd's ear.
> Succeeded by the huntsman's trumpet clear,
> O come Diana, start the morning chase
> Thou ancient goddess of the hunting race.

From "To Artemis"

Callimachus (ca. 310/305–ca. 240 BCE),
adapted from the translation by Alexander William Mair

Tityus was a giant who assaulted Artemis's mother Leto, and was killed by Artemis before he could rape her. Haemus of Thrace was the son of Boreas, god of the north wind. Mysian Olympus is a mountain in modern Turkey, not to be confused with Mount Olympus, home of the Olympians, which is in Greece. Artemis is the lady of Munychia because there was a festival to her there; there was also a temple to her at Pherae. Oeneus was a king who forgot to honor Artemis at harvest time; the goddess laid waste to his fields as a punishment.

Artemis, Lady of Maidenhood, Slayer of Tityus, golden were your arms and golden your belt, and a golden car did you yoke, and golden bridles, goddess, did you put on your deer. And where first did your horned team begin to carry you? To Thracian Haemus, whence comes the hurricane of Boreas bringing evil breath of frost to cloakless men. And where did you cut the pine and from what flame did you kindle it? It was on Mysian Olympus, and you did put in it the breath of flame unquenchable, which your Father's bolts distil.

And how often goddess, did you make trial of your silver bow? First at an elm, and next at an oak did you shoot, and third again at a wild beast. But the fourth time—not long was it before you did shoot at the city of unjust men, those who to one another and those who towards strangers wrought many deeds of sin, forward men, on whom you will impress your grievous wrath. On their cattle plague feeds, on their tilth feeds frost, and the old men cut their hair in mourning over their sons, and their wives either are smitten or die in childbirth, or, if they escape, bear birds whereof none stands on upright ankle. But on whomsoever you lookest smiling and gracious, for them the tilth bears the corn-ear abundantly, and abundantly prospers the four-footed breed, and abundant waxes their prosperity: neither do they go to the tomb, save when they carry there the aged. Nor does faction wound their race—faction which ravages even the well-established houses: but brother's wife and husband's sister set their chairs around one board.

O Lady of Munychia, Watcher of Harbors, hail, Lady of Pherae! Let none disparage Artemis. For Oeneus dishonoured her altar and no pleasant struggles came upon his city. Nor let any contend with her in shooting of stags or in archery.... Neither let any woo the Maiden.... Nor let any shun the yearly dance.... Hail, great queen, and graciously greet my song.

HYMN TO DIANA

Fausto Salvatori (1870–1929), translated by B. Nolan

This hymn (in the original Italian) was set to music by Puccini.

Glory to you, when in the silent nights,
You offer, O Cynthia, the shining rays of love.
Glory to you, when in the burning afternoons,
You strengthen, O Diana, the courage of the brave.
Your divine eye watches always over
Your faithful, fearless followers,
You lead them to the most daring feats,
You support them through the difficult ways.
From the snowy Alpine peaks to the
Sounding shores of Sicily, through
Open fields and shaded woods
Where you love to meet the wild ones,

Over the lakes, where the waves kiss
The white-petalled flowers,
May this reach you, like a joyful echo,
This fervent song of love!

"LADY MOST REVERED" FROM *HIPPOLYTUS*

Euripides (480–406 BCE), translated by E. P. Coleridge

Lady, most revered lady, daughter of Zeus, welcome, Artemis, welcome, daughter of Leto and Zeus, you who are the most beautiful by far among the virgins, and in mighty heaven you dwell in the richly-gilded palace of Zeus. Welcome most beautiful, most beautiful throughout Olympus!

"CHASTE GODDESS" FROM *NORMA*

Felice Romani (1788–1865), translated by B. Nolan

This is the opening of one of the most famous arias in the history of opera, in which Norma, a Druid priestess, calls upon the moon goddess in the sacred grove. If you're interested in hearing it in the original Italian, the Maria Callas recording is very good.

Chaste goddess, bathing in silver light
These ancient, sacred trees,
Turn your beautiful face toward us
Without your veil of clouds.

Calm, O goddess, calm,
All burning hearts, and
Over-zealous emotion,
Spread on earth the sweet peace
Which you make reign in heaven.

"MAIDEN AND MISTRESS" FROM *ATALANTA IN CALYDON*

Algernon Charles Swinburne (1837–1909)

A prayer to Artemis the Maiden.

Maiden, and mistress of the months and stars
Now folded in the flowerless fields of heaven,
Goddess whom all gods love with threefold heart,

Being treble in thy divided deity,

A light for dead men and dark hours, a foot

Swift on the hills as morning, and a hand

To all things fierce and fleet that roar and range

Mortal, with gentler shafts than snow or sleep;

Hear now and help and lift no violent hand. …

"O ARTEMIS QUEEN OF THE GROVES" FROM *PHAEDRA*

Seneca (ca. 4 BCE–65 CE), adapted from the translation by Frank Justus Miller

A prayer to ward off a curse, magical or otherwise. Here Artemis is once again conjoined with Hecate, goddess of magic.

O Artemis, queen of the groves, who in solitude love your mountain-haunts, and who upon the solitary mountains are alone held holy, change for the better these dark, ill-omened threats.

O great goddess of the woods and groves, bright orb of heaven, glory of the night, by whose changing beams the universe shines clear, O three-formed Hecate, lo, you are at hand, favoring our undertaking. … To this end direct your powers; so may you wear a shining face and, the clouds all scattered, fare on with undimmed horns. … Be near, goddess, in answer to our call; hear now our prayers.

FROM "THE PRAISE OF ARTEMIS"

Sir Edmund Gosse (1849–1928)

"Cephissus" is the name of two different rivers, both in Greece.

By Cephissus'
    Silver stream,
White narcissus
    Blossoms gleam,
And the chilly
Waterlily
Opens stilly
    Cups of cream.

The soft night
   Scarce forgets
Scent of white
   Violets,
Ere there blows
Rose on rose,
And their snows
   The wind frets.

Through the shadows
   And perfume,
By the meadows
   Deep in bloom,
Who comes singing
Blithe, and bringing
Light upspringing
   Through the gloom?

At her feet
   Breaks the dawn,
Fond and fleet
   As a fawn
Up the skies
See! it flies,
And night dies
   On the lawn.

By her fingers
   Hangs a bow,
While there lingers
   Round her so
A god's glory
Dim and hoary,
Wreathed in story
   Long ago.

Round her mild
    Brows and fair
Clings a wild
    Huntress air,
At her side,
Girdled, hide
Arrows tried,
    And a spear.

With elation
    Half divine,
Pour libation,
    Oil and wine;
While it blazes,
Chant her praises,
Crowned with daisies,
    Wreathed with pine.

And narcissus
    Blossoming,
From Cephissus
    Duly bring,
At her altar
Praise, exalt her,
Never falter,
    Ever sing.

TO ARTEMIS

Andrew Lang (1844–1912)

For thee soft crowns in thine untrampled mead
    I wove, my lady, and to thee I bear;
Thither no shepherd drives his flocks to feed,
    Nor scythe of steel has ever labored there;
    Nay, through the spring among the blossoms fair

The brown bee comes and goes, and with good heed
Thy maiden, Reverence, sweet streams doth lead
    About the grassy close that is her care!

Souls only that are gracious and serene
    By gift of god, in human lore unread,
May pluck these holy blooms and grasses green
    That now I wreathe for thine immortal head—
I that may walk with thee, thyself unseen,
And by thy whispered voice am comforted.

WEDDING PRAYERS

There are many prayers throughout this volume that would be appropriate for a wedding ceremony—hymns for the Feast of Juno, the Veneralia, and the Aphrodisia would be good places to start—but here are some additional pieces especially for use in Pagan nuptials.

BRIDE (TWO TRANSLATIONS)
Sappho (ca. 630–ca. 570 BC)

The "goddess of Paphos" is Aphrodite, who is also the "Cyprian." Hesperus is the Evening Star.

Prose translation by Anne Bunner:

Bride, teeming with rosy loves, bride, fairest image of the goddess of Paphos, go to the couch, go to the bed, softly sporting, sweet to the bridegroom. May Hesperus lead thee rejoicing, honoring Hera of the silver throne, goddess of marriage.

Verse translation by Henry de Vere Stacpoole:

Bride, around whom the rosy leaves are flying,
Sweet image of the Cyprian undying,
The bed awaits thee; go, and with him lying,
Give to the groom thy sweetness, softly sighing.
May Hesperus in gladness pass before thee,
And Hera of the silver throne bend o'er thee.

FROM *ORFEO*

Alessandro Striggio the Younger (ca. 1573–1630)

This is an excerpt from one of the earliest operas, the L'Orfeo *of Claudio Monteverdi. Hymen is the god of marriage. He traditionally carries a torch.*

Come, Hymen, do come
With your burning torch
Like the rising sun
Bringing peaceful days to these lovers:
Banish forever the shadows
And horrors of pain and grief.

FROM "ODE TO PSYCHE"

John Keats (1795–1821)

The story of Cupid and Psyche, as originally told in the ancient Roman novel The Golden Ass, *is one of the great love stories of the world: the mortal Psyche's trials and triumphs in search of love won her the gift of immortality. Here the poet Keats pledges his devotion to her, and promises to build her a dedicated temple—at least in his mind.*

Yes, I will be thy priest, and build a fane
    In some untrodden region of my mind,
Where branched thoughts, new grown with pleasant pain,
    Instead of pines shall murmur in the wind:
Far, far around shall those dark-cluster'd trees
    Fledge the wild-ridged mountains steep by steep;
And there by zephyrs, streams, and birds, and bees,
    The moss-lain Dryads shall be lull'd to sleep;
And in the midst of this wide quietness
A rosy sanctuary will I dress
    With the wreath'd trellis of a working brain,
        With buds, and bells, and stars without a name,

With all the gardener Fancy e'er could feign,
    Who breeding flowers, will never breed the same:
And there shall be for thee all soft delight
    That shadowy thought can win,
A bright torch, and a casement ope at night,
    To let the warm Love in!

SONG FROM *AS YOU LIKE IT*

William Shakespeare (1564–1616)

Hymen, the son of Apollo, is the god of the wedding feast and marriage more generally.

Wedding is great Juno's crown;
O blessed bond of board and bed!
'Tis Hymen peoples every town;
High wedlock then be honored.
Honor, high honor, and renown,
To Hymen, god of every town!

FROM THE THIRD ELEGY

Albius Tibullus (55–19 BCE), translated by Theodore C. Willliams

Pactolian means "golden," so the early Imperial poet Tibullus here asks the goddesses Juno and Venus to give him a wife rather than that river of gold. Juno is "Saturnian" because she is the daughter of Saturn.

No! not dominion, nor Pactolian stream,
    Nor all the riches the wide world can give!
    These other men may ask. My fondest dream
    Is, poor but free, with my true wife to live.

Saturnian Juno, to all nuptials kind,
    Receive with grace my ever-anxious vow!
    Come, Venus, wafted by the Cyprian wind,
    And from thy car of shell smile on me now!

FROM "EPITHALAMIUM"

A. E. Housman (1859–1936)

An epithalamium is a wedding song sung to the bride on her way to the bridal chamber. Here, though, Housman is writing for the groom from the perspective of his male friends, who have given the groom a golden cup with which to pour a libation to the god of marriage. "Hesper" is Hesperus, the god of the evening star. Urania is the muse of astronomy, and Hymen, god of weddings, is her son. Helicon is a mountain in Greece.

He is here, Urania's son,
Hymen come from Helicon;
God that glads the lover's heart,
He is here to join and part.
So the groomsman quits your side
And the bridegroom seeks the bride:
Friend and comrade yield you o'er
To her that hardly loves you more.

———

Happy bridegroom, Hesper brings
All desired and timely things.
All whom morning sends to roam,
Hesper loves to lead them home.
Home return who him behold,
Child to mother, sheep to fold,
Bird to nest from wandering wide:
Happy bridegroom, seek your bride.

Pour it out, the golden cup
Given and guarded, brimming up,
Safe through jostling markets borne
And the thicket of the thorn;
Folly spurned and danger past,
Pour it to the god at last.

FROM "EPITHALAMION"

Edmund Spenser (1552/1553–1599)

An excerpt from a more traditional epithalamion, by the author of The Faerie Queene. *"Eke" here means "also," and "smart" means "distress."*

And thou great Juno, which with awful might
the laws of wedlock still dost patronize,
And the religion of the faith first plight
With sacred rites hast taught to solemnize:
And eke for comfort often called art
Of women in their smart,
Eternally bind thou this lovely band,
And all thy blessings unto us impart.

FROM "EPITHALAMION OF PHILIBERT DE SAVOIE"

Marc-Claude de Buttet (1530–1586), translated by B. Nolan

Come away, come away, happy lovers!
Bashful Venus, who has moved two hearts,
And holy Juno take you by the hand,
The joyful Hymen, whose triumph this is,
Will embrace you forever with a perfect, holy desire.
A kindly peace, a mutual love, will be with you forever,
May your pleasures always be so, without fail.

ANGUS THE LOVER

Ethna Carbery (1864–1902)

Angus or Aengus is the youthful Irish god of love.

I follow the silver spears flung from the hands of dawn.
Through silence, through singing of stars, I journey on and on:
The scattered fires of the sun, blown wide ere the day be done,
Scorch me hurrying after the swift white feet of my fawn.

I am Angus the Lover, I who haste in the track of the wind,
The tameless tempest before, the dusk of quiet behind,
From the heart of a blue gulf hurled, I rise on the waves of the world,
Seeking the love that allures, woeful until I find.

The blossom of beauty is she, glad, bright as a shaft of flame,
A burning arrow of life winging me joy and shame,
The hollow deeps of the sky are dumb to my searching cry,
Rending the peace of the gods with the melody of her name.

My quest is by lonely ways–in the cairns of the mighty dead,
On the high-lorn peaks of snow–panting to hear her tread,
At the edge of the rainbow well whose whispering waters tell
Of a face bent over the rim, rose-pale, and as roses red.

Thus she ever escapes me–a wisp of cloud in the air,
A streak of delicate moonshine; a glory from otherwhere;
Yet out in the vibrant space I shall kiss the rose in her face,
I shall bind her fast to my side with a strand of her flying hair.

FROM "TO THE GODS"

Adam Oehlenschläger (1779–1850), translated by Rune Bjørnsen

Freya is the Norse goddess of love, beauty, and fertility.

Come down to us then
Lovely Freya! Joy of the North!
Bring my bride to my hall,
Embrace us with your golden chain.
Surround us in your hair so bold,
That no hero's might can withstand.

FROM *OEDIPUS AT COLONUS*

Nicolas-François Guillard (1752–1814), translated by B. Nolan

We implore the blessings
of our guardian goddesses,
let us tie, under their auspices,
The sacred knots of Hymen and of Peace.

BRIDAL SONG

Helen Bantock (1868–1961)

Helen Bantock was the wife of the British composer Granville Bantock, and she wrote the librettos for many of his compositions. This is from their song cycle called Songs of Egypt, *in which the bride on her wedding day is equated with Hathor.*

Fling wide, oh dawn, thy golden portals
To greet the fairest bride.
Sweetly sound thy lutes, O maidens,
Singing hymns of praise.
Sing of her eyes where shadows sleeping,
Are still as watersprings at eve,
Where sweet as some pale water blossom,
Broodeth the soul of love.

Oh! sing her praises, scent her tresses
With dropping odours from the South,
Till all her garments smell of myrrh,
Sandal and frankincense.
Come, celebrate with joy the festal day,
Let music and let song be made,
For beautiful as goddess of the morning,
Beautiful as Hathor is the bride.

FUNERAL PRAYERS

For those times when we gather together to celebrate those who have gone before us, here's a selection of works on death, the afterlife, and the journey between them. Other appropriate pieces may be found in the section dedicated to Samhain.

FROM "HYMN TO PROSERPINE"

Algernon Charles Swinburne (1837–1909)

Victorian poet Algernon Charles Swinburne wrote several poems for Proserpine in her aspect as goddess of the Underworld. For Swinburne she was the greatest of the gods because she rules over the greater portion of our existence—the time after we die. And he argues here that human death, often seen as something that separates mortal nature from the divine nature, is the very thing that makes us akin to the great goddess who descends to the Underworld: "I am also … thy brother; I go as I came unto earth."

But I turn to her still, having seen she shall surely abide in the end;
Goddess and maiden and queen, be near me now and befriend.
O daughter of earth, of my mother, her crown and blossom of birth,
I am also, I also, thy brother; I go as I came unto earth.
In the night where thine eyes are as moons are in heaven, the night where thou art,
Where the silence is more than all tunes, where sleep overflows from the heart,
Where the poppies are sweet as the rose in our world, and the red rose is white,
And the wind falls faint as it blows with the fume of the flowers of the night,
And the murmur of spirits that sleep in the shadow of Gods from afar
Grows dim in thine ears and deep as the deep dim soul of a star,

In the sweet low light of thy face, under heavens untrod by the sun,

Let my soul with their souls find place, and forget what is done and undone.

Thou art more than the Gods who number the days of our temporal breath;

Let these give labor and slumber; but thou, Proserpina, death.

Therefore now at thy feet I abide for a season in silence. I know

I shall die as my fathers died, and sleep as they sleep; even so.

For the glass of the years is brittle wherein we gaze for a span;

A little soul for a little bears up this corpse which is man.

So long I endure, no longer; and laugh not again, neither weep.

For there is no God found stronger than death; and death is a sleep.

ORPHIC TABLET

Anonymous (ca. 300–200 BCE),

translated by Radcliffe G. Edmonds

This is a translation of the famous Petalia tablet, which was found at an archeological site in southern Italy in the nineteenth century. The tablet, a thin leaf of incised gold, dates from about the third century BCE and was designed to be put in the grave of an initiate in the Orphic Mysteries as a totenpass *(death passport)—a document meant to guide the soul of the deceased in the next world, and allow it to enter into paradise.*

Although little is known of the Orphic Mysteries, we do know that they emphasized the reality of life after death, and they also seemed to have insisted on the divine origin of humans: "I am the child of Earth ... but my race is heavenly." This was a distinct departure from more traditional Greek thought but, judging from the hundreds of similar tablets unearthed at archeological sites in Europe and the Middle East, it was a popular one.

You will find in the halls of Hades a spring on the left,

and standing by it, a glowing white cypress tree;

Do not approach this spring at all.

You will find another, from the lake of Memory,

refreshing water flowing forth. But guardians are nearby.

Say: "I am the child of Earth and starry Heaven;

But my race is heavenly; and this you know yourselves.

I am parched with thirst and I perish; but give me quickly

refreshing water flowing forth from the lake of Memory."

And then they will give you to drink from the divine spring,
And then you will celebrate? [rites? with the other] heroes. ...

FROM "RESPONSE TO COURTIERS"

Nicolas Vauquelin, Sieur des Yveteaux (1567–1649), translated by B. Nolan

Here Mercury, in his role as the guide of souls, brings the dead to be judged by Rhadamanthus, son of Zeus and Underworld judge.

And Mercury one day—
Determined by our destiny—
Will convey us in a boat
To the place where, it's said,
Dark and awe-full Pluto reigns,
The mighty monarch of the shadows.
In that place all are made equal,
After so much labor and work,
The numbers there are ever increasing,
And kings and their courtiers,
As well as commoners,
Will have Rhadamanthus as their judge.

FROM "THE GARDEN OF PROSERPINE"

Algernon Charles Swinburne (1837–1909)

Swinburne not only praises the goddess in this poem but the existence of death itself, which he regarded as a place of refuge from the sorrows of living: "We thank with brief thanksgiving/Whatever gods may be/That no life lives for ever;/That dead men rise up never;/That even the weariest river/Winds somewhere safe to sea."

Pale, beyond porch and portal,
    Crowned with calm leaves, she stands
Who gathers all things mortal
    With cold immortal hands;
Her languid lips are sweeter
Than love's who fears to greet her

To men that mix and meet her
    From many times and lands.

She waits for each and other,
    She waits for all men born;
Forgets the earth her mother,
    The life of fruits and corn;
And spring and seed and swallow
Take wing for her and follow
Where summer song rings hollow
    And flowers are put to scorn.

There go the loves that wither,
    The old loves with wearier wings;
And all dead years draw thither,
    And all disastrous things;
Dead dreams of days forsaken,
Blind buds that snows have shaken,
Wild leaves that winds have taken,
    Red strays of ruined springs.

We are not sure of sorrow,
    And joy was never sure;
To-day will die to-morrow;
    Time stoops to no man's lure;
And love, grown faint and fretful,
With lips but half regretful
Sighs, and with eyes forgetful
    Weeps that no loves endure.

From too much love of living,
    From hope and fear set free,
We thank with brief thanksgiving
    Whatever gods may be
That no life lives for ever;
That dead men rise up never;
That even the weariest river
    Winds somewhere safe to sea.

PRAYER OF THE SOUL AFTER DEATH

Anonymous (ca. 350 BCE), translated by Radcliffe Guest Edmonds

This plea to Persephone (Phersephoneia) comes from another Orphic death-pass found in a grave in southern Italy. Eukles ("The Glorious One") and Eubouleus ("The One of Good Counsel") are epithets of Hades.

Pure I come from the pure, Queen of those below the earth,
And Eukles and Eubouleus and the other gods and daimons;
For I also claim that I am of your blessed race.
Recompense I have paid on account of deeds not just;
Either Fate mastered me or the lightning bolt thrown by the thunderer.
Now I come, a suppliant, to holy Phersephoneia,
That she, gracious, may send me to the seats of the blessed.

ORPHIC HYMN TO CHTHONIC HERMES

Anonymous (ca. 200 CE?), translated by B. Nolan

In this hymn, Hermes appears in his role as the guide of souls from this world to the next and is considered to be the (metaphorical?) child of Dionysus and Aphrodite. Kokytos is one of the rivers of the Underworld, while Tartarus is the lowest depth of Hades.

You wander the road everyone must travel, the road by the river Kokytos from which none return; you lead into the vastness of the earth the souls of humankind. Hermes, child of Dionysus and Paphian Aphrodite of the fluttering eyelashes, you haunt the halls of the palace of Persephone, you lead the fearful souls to their haven when the deadly hour is upon them. Your wand grants sleep or wakefulness, as you will. The Queen gave you this sacred task, to lead through wide Tartarus the ever-living souls of women and of men. O holy one, give a good end to the lives of we who worship you.

THE ISLES OF THE BLESSED

Andrew Lang (1844–1912)

Now the light of the sun, in the night of the earth, on the souls of the true
    Shines, and their city is girt with the meadow where reigneth the rose;
And deep is the shade of the woods, and the wind that flits o'er them and through,
    Sings of the sea, and is sweet from the isles where the frankincense blows.

Green is their garden and orchard, with rare fruits golden it glows,
    And the souls of the Blessed are glad in the pleasures on earth that they knew,
And in chariots these have delight, and in dice and in minstrelsy those;
    And the savor of sacrifice clings to the altars and rises anew.
But the souls that Persephone cleanses from ancient pollution and stain,
    These at the end of the age—be they prince, be they singer, or seer—
These to the world shall be born as of old, shall be sages again;
    These of their hands shall be hardy, shall live, and shall die, and shall hear
Thanks of the people, and songs of the minstrels that praise them amain,
    And their glory shall dwell in the land where they dwelt, while year calls unto year!

FROM "ELYSIUM"

Friedrich von Schiller (1759–1805), translated by B. Nolan

German poet and philosopher Schiller here imagines the blessed fields of Elysium, where the honored dead may go.

The days of sorrowful lamenting are over!
The joyful feast of paradise silences every complaint.
Eternal happiness, eternal bliss,
A babbling brook running through laughing meadows.

Neverending May,
youthful and gentle,
Blesses the fields,
The hours pass by in golden dreams,
The soul swells to fill infinite space,
Truth tears the veil in two here.

The heart overflows
With infinite joy,
Here there is no name for painful suffering,
Gentle delight is the closest thing to pain.

Here faithful spouses embrace,
Kissing on the green velvet grass,
Gently caressed by the scented west wind.

Love finds its triumph here,
Celebrating an endless wedding feast
Safe from death's cruel blow.

MONOLOGUE III

Friedrich Hölderlin (1770–1843), translated by B. Nolan

Here death is seen as a source of joy as well as regret. The "bow of Iris" is the rainbow.

Ha! Jupiter, liberator! Nearer and nearer
Comes my hour, and from the highlands
Comes the well-known messenger of the night,
The evening wind—to me, love's messenger.
It's here! The time has come! Oh, beat now, heart,
And stir the blood.
I am coming. Dying? It's only a step
In the dark. But, my eyes, you want to see!
I'm satisfied, I long for nothing any longer
Except my sacrifice. It is well with me.
O bow of Iris! When your arc is revealed
Through silver clouds, over churning waters,
As you are then, so is my joy.

FROM "PROSERPINE"

Richard Watson Dixon (1833–1900)

Richard Watson Dixon was the son of a Protestant minister, but that did not stop him from writing this plea to Proserpine.

Daughter of earth, be merciful
In Hades to our hopes and fears;
Art thou not orphaned on thy throne,
Far from the happy light that shone,
Far from thy ravished maiden zone,
Far from thy mother's tears!

ORPHIC HYMN TO PLUTO

Anonymous (ca. 200 CE?),
translated by Frederick C. Grant, modernized by B. Nolan

Pluto is the equivalent of Hades, but mingled with some of the aspects of Ploutos, the Greek god of wealth. While it might seem strange to blend death and wealth together, to the ancients they were joined by their close association with the earth.

The mystes *were initiates in the Orphic Mysteries.*

O you who dwell in the underearthly house, mighty of soul
Amid the deep-shadowed, never-lighted fields of Tartarus,
You scepter-bearing Zeus of the underworld,
Accept favorably this offering, O Pluto:
You who hold the keys of the whole world,
Who vouchsafe all wealth to the generations year by year,
You who alone hold all sway over the world's third part—
The world, dwelling place of the immortals, solid ground where mankind dwells—
You who have set your throne in the gloomy realm below,
In far-flung Hades, dismal, measureless, all-embracing, torn by tempestuous winds,
Where dark Acheron winds about the deep roots of earth
You who rule mortals by the power of death, and receive all;
Great God, Wise Counselor;
You who once did marry the daughter of holy Demeter,
Snatching her away from the pleasant meadows
And carrying her through the sea in thy swift chariot
To the cave in Attica, in Eleusis' vale
Where stand the gates of Hades.
You alone are ruler of all things visible and invisible,
Inspired God, All-ruler, most holy, most highly praised,
Who rejoice over the worthy mystes and his sacred ministrations.
I invoke you and implore you,
Graciously come, and show yourself favorable to your initiates!

FROM *FRIDTHJOF'S SAGA*

Esaias Tegnér (1782–1846), translated by Thomas and Martha Holcomb

Esaias Tegnér was a Swedish bishop and Romantic poet. The Allfather is, of course, Odin.

And now, farewell, ye children, our work is done;
Unto the Allfather gladly we hasten on,
Like weary rivers longing for sea's caressing;
On you be Thor's and Odin's and Frey's rich blessing.

FROM "TO THE GODS"

Adam Oehlenschläger (1779–1850), translated by Rune Bjørnsen

Mímir is a wise being in Norse mythology, and so his well is a symbol of wisdom.

Odin Allfather!
let your Light
Shine strong in my heart!
Fear of death
You alone have might to heal.
Teach me to find Mimir's well
Between the dark forest trees,
Teach me to cool my flames
In the cool well of wisdom.

Appendix 1
Prayers for
Gods and Goddesses

Chorus from *Hippolytus*
From "The Return of Aphrodite"
From a Homeric Hymn to Aphrodite (II)
From "Epithalamion" (cummings)

ARES

"Ares" from *The Suppliant Maidens* ⋆
Homeric Hymn to Ares
Orphic Hymn to Ares
From "Ares, God of War"

ARTEMIS/CYNTHIA

Homeric Hymn to Artemis ⋆
From the Second Homeric Hymn to Artemis
From "To Artemis" (Callimachus)
Queen and Huntress
Come with Bows Bent
"Chorus of Hunters (To Artemis)" from *The Great God Pan*
"Daemon, Initiate, Spirit" from *The Hippolytus of Euripides*
From "A Hymn to Artemis"
From "To Artemis" (Callimachus)
"Lady Most Revered" from *Hippolytus*
"Maiden and Mistress" from *Atalanta in Calydon*
"O Artemis Queen of the Groves" from *Phaedra*
From "The Praise of Artemis"
To Artemis (Lang)

ASCLEPIUS

Homeric Hymn to Asclepius
Orphic Hymn to Asclepius
From "Erythraean Paean to Asclepius"

ATHENA

Hymn to Athena
Pallas Athena

From "The Bath of Pallas"
From the Orphic Hymn to Athena
From "Pallas-Athena" (Dodge)
From *The Eumenides*
Excerpts from Proclus' Hymn to Athena (August)
From "Athena" (Clay)
"Stern Goddess" from the *Thebaid*
From "Apollo" (August)
From *The Knights*
From "Athena" (Tramana)
From *The Women at the Thesmophoria*
Stanzas from "Athene"

CASTOR AND POLLUX (THE DIOSCURI)

Fragment of a Hymn to the Dioscuri
From "Boatman's Song to the Dioscuri"
From the Homeric Hymn to Castor and Pollux (January)
Castor and Pollux (January)
From "Idyll XXII"
From "Homer's Hymn to Castor and Pollux"
Fragment 2

CRONOS

Orphic Hymn to Kronos
From the *Orphic Argonautica*
Kronos

DEMETER

From the Homeric Hymn to Demeter
From "The Road Mender"
At Eleusis
From "The Story of Eleusis"
From "Demeter" (Hill)
Demeter (Coatsworth)

From "Apollo" (September)
From "An Eleusinian Chant"
From "The Appeasement of Demeter"
From "Demeter" (H.D.)
To the Demeter of Cnidos
From "Demeter" (Callimachus)
From "Demeter" (September)
From *Demeter, A Mask*

DIONYSUS

Dionysus, the Giver of the Grape
From "The Praise of Dionysus"
"O you of many names" from *Antigone*
From "The Bride of Dionysus" (March)
"Now Call the God" from *The Frogs*
Orphic Hymn to Dionysus Licnitus
From "Hymn to Dionysus"
Chorus from *The Frogs*
Chorus from *The Bacchae*
From "Paean to Dionysus"
From *Oedipus Rex*
From "Prayers and Fantasies"
Homeric Hymn to Dionysus
From "Demeter" (December)
From "Old and New"
King Eiraphiotes
From "Cadmeian Semele was with Child…" (December)
From Another Homeric Hymn to Dionysus
From "Ariadne"
From *The Bride of Dionysus*
From "Evoe!"
From A Third Homeric Hymn to Dionysus

EIRENE (PEACE)

From "Pythian Ode 8"

EROS/CUPID AND PSYCHE

Orphic Hymn to Eros

Eternal Eros

From "Ode to Psyche"

From "A Hymn to Aphrodite" (Proclus)

From "The Hippolytus of Euripides"

EUNOMIA

Prayer to Eunomia

GAIA, EARTH, NATURE

Homeric Hymn to Earth, Mother of Us All

Orphic Hymn to Gaia

From "Hymn to Nature"

Orphic Hymn to Nature

HARMONIA

From "A Hymn to Harmony"

HECATE

From the *Dionysciaca*

Hymn to Hecate and Janus

"O Artemis Queen of the Groves" from *Phaedra*

HELIOS

From the Homeric Hymn to Helios (June)

Orphic Hymn to Helios

Hymn to Helios

Hymn to the Sun (Mesomedes)

From "The Last Oracle"

HEPHAESTOS

Homeric Hymn to Hephaestos

Orphic Hymn to Hephaestos

Hephaestus

HERA

Homeric Hymn to Hera
Psyche's Prayer to Hera
Orphic Hymn to Hera
Lady Hera
From "Hera Parthenia"

HERMES

Hermes (Anonymous)
From the Homeric Hymn to Hermes
Hermes (Thompson)
To Hermes (Alcaeus of Mytilene)
Orphic Hymn to Hermes
From "The Advent of Hermes"
The Emerald Tablet
Hermes of the Ways
From "Hermes" (Tramana)
An Invocation of Hermes as the Good Mind
From "Response to courtiers"
Orphic Hymn to Chthonic Hermes

HESTIA

Homeric Hymn to Hestia
Orphic Hymn to Hestia
From a Homeric Hymn to Aphrodite
Hymn to Hestia
From *The Fasti*
Second Homeric Hymn to Hestia

HORAI (SEASONS)

Orphic Hymn to the Horai

HYGEIA

Prayer to Hygeia (January)
From "Ode to Hygeia"

Orphic Hymn to Hygeia
From "To Hygeia"

KOURETES/CORYBANTES
From the Orphic Hymn to the Kouretes

MAIA
From "A Poet's Calendar"
Fragment of an Ode to Maia, Written on May-Day 1818
From the Homeric Hymn to Hermes

MUSES
Orphic Hymn to the Muses
To the Muses
Hymn to the Muse
From "A Hymn to the Muses"
From "A Hymn to the Muses" (2) (*n.b.* both are in January)
From "Ode to Apollo"
Second Delphic Hymn to Apollo
Hymn to Calliope and Apollo
From "The Homeric Hymn to the Muses and Apollo"

NEREUS AND NEREIDS
Orphic Hymn to Nereus
From the Orphic Hymn to Nereids

NIKE
From "Ode 11" (Bacchylides)
Orphic Hymn to Victory

NYMPHS
Orphic Hymn to the Nymphs

OCEANUS
Orphic Hymn to Oceanus

PAN

"Of Pan We Sing" from *Pan's Anniversary*
An Invocation to Pan
Strophe from *Ajax*
From "Sun and Flesh (Credo in Unam)"
A Note from the Pipes
Prologue of the Unborn
"Beloved Pan" from *Phaedrus*
From "Villanelle of the Living Pan"
From "Nymphs"
Homeric Hymn to Pan
Pan (Ledwidge)
From "The Eternal Pan"
We Worship Pan
From "Apollo" (February)
Epidaurian Hymn
From "Holy Satyr"
From "Nympholept"
A Hymn to Pan
From "The Shepherd's Holiday"
Orphic Hymn to Pan
From "Pan-Worship"
Pan (Emerson)
Hymn to Pan
"Hymn to Pan" from *Endymion*
From "Pan" (Wilde)
From *Moon Magic* (December)
"Invocation to Pan" from *The Great God Pan*
From "Sappho" (December)
From "Ode to Pan"

PERSEPHONE/KORE

From "The Return of Persephone"
From "Spring"
Greek Fragments

Orphic Hymn to Persephone
From "Persephone" (Masters)
Persephone (Manning)
Prayer of the Soul After Death

PHOEBUS APOLLO

Second Delphic Hymn to Apollo
From "Ode to Apollo"
From "To Apollo" (Horace)
Hymn to Calliope and Apollo
From "Apollo" (Carpenter)
From the Homeric Hymn to Apollo
From "Chant of Apollo's Priestess"
From "The Last Oracle"
From the Homeric Hymn to the Muses and Apollo
From "Apollo" (Callimachus)
From *Apollo et Hyacinthus*
"Father Phoebus" from the *Thebaid*
To Apollo (Epigram from Book 9)
Song to Apollo
From First Delphic Hymn to Apollo
Apollo (Aristonos)
Lord Phoebus
From "Apollo"

POSEIDON

From the Homeric Hymn to Poseidon
Orphic Hymn to Poseidon
"Poseidon" from *The Knights*
"Poseidon" from *On Animals*

PROTEUS

Orphic Hymn to Proteus

RHEA

Orphic Hymn to Rhea

SELENE

From "Selene"
From the Homeric Hymn to Selene
Orphic Hymn to Selene
From the *Dionysiaca*

TETHYS

Orphic Hymn to Tethys

THANATOS

Orphic Hymn to Thanatos

THEIA

Theia

THEMIS

Orphic Hymn to Themis

THETIS

"Thetis" from Aethiopica

TYCHE

Orphic Hymn to Tyche
Fortune
Fortune (Nonnus)
From Olympian Ode 12

ZEUS

Homeric Hymn to Zeus
"Zeus Fills the Heavens" from *Phaenomena*
Orphic Hymn to Zeus of the Lightning

The Palaikastro Kouretes Hymn
Zeus Is the First
Zeus and Destiny
To Jove the Beneficent
From *Alcibiades II*
Evensong
Father Zeus
Orphic Hymn to Zeus
From "Isis" (November)
Orphic Hymn to Daemon
From "Hymn to Zeus" (November)
From *Mnemosyne*

ROMAN GODS AND GODDESSES

ASCLEPIUS AND HYGEIA
(*SEE UNDER* GREEK GODS AND GODDESSES)

BACCHUS
Bacchus (Chénier)
Bacchus (Emerson)

BELLONA
From *Anelida and Arcite*

CERES
"O Ceres and Libera" from *Against Verres*
The Oak of Ceres
From *The Fasti*
To Ceres
From "Three Prayers to Ceres"
"Ceres' Blessing" from *The Tempest*
From "The Complaint of Ceres"
From "Invocation to Ceres"
Ceres (Thurston)

CONCORDIA

"Hymn to Peace" from *The Fasti*

"Prayer to Concordia" from *Pharsalia*

Chorus from *Peace*

CYBELE

From "Cybele"

From *Hymn to the Mother of the Gods*

From "Sun and Flesh (Credo in Unam)"

Orphic Hymn to the Mother of the Gods

From *De Rerum Natura*

From "Apollo" (April)

Chorus from *Philoctetes*

DIANA (LUCINA, LATONA)

Carmina 34

"Lovely Goddess of the Bow" from *Aradia*

Praised Be Diana's Fair and Harmless Light

From *Endymion*

From "On Morning and Evening" (Lunar Prayers)

Hymn to Diana

"Chaste Goddess" from *Norma*

FAUNUS

From "To Faunus"

FLORA

From "Arcadian Hymn to Flora"

FORTUNA

From "O Fortuna"

From "Ode to Fortune"

JANUS

Roman Medley

Offering to Janus

Come Janus, Come New Year

Hymn to Hecate and Janus

JUNO

From "But What at Sacred Juno's Feet"

From "The Nuptials of Juno"

Juno's Song from *The Tempest*

From "On Juno"

From "Epithalamion" (Spenser)

JUPITER/JOVE

To Jove the Beneficent

Evensong

From "Isis" (November)

Monologue III

LARES

From "A Hymn, to the Lares"

From Elegy 1.10 (Tibullus)

A Short Hymn, to the Lares

From "To the Lares"

LIBERA

"O Ceres and Libera" from *Against Verres*

MARS

Carmen Arvale (Song of the Arvals)

"Father Mars" from *De Agri Cultura*

Hymn to Mars

From *Anelida and Arcite*

From "The Light of Stars"

MERCURY

Ode to Mercury

From *The Fasti* (Mercury)

From "Valerie's Rhyming Invocations to the Four Quarters"

From "Hymn to Mercury"

MINERVA (*SEE* ATHENA)

MITHRAS

From "Mithra"

From the "Hymn to Mithra" from the *Avestas*

Hymn of the Ghebers

From the *Rig Veda*

From the *Thebaid*

From "Ode to Mithra"

MOTHER EARTH

"O Gentle Createress" from the *Thebaid*

From "A Litany to Earth"

NEPTUNE

A Hymn in Praise of Neptune

From "Isis" (July)

Hymn to Neptune

PHOEBUS APOLLO
(*SEE UNDER* GREEK GODS AND GODDESSES)

PLUTO

Orphic Hymn to Pluto

POMONA

Pomona (Anonymous)

Pomona (Scollard)

From "Pomona" (Griffith)

PROSERPINE/PROSERPINA

From "Proserpine Gathering Violets"
Song of Proserpina
Departure of Proserpine
Strophe from "The Search After Proserpina"
From "Hymn to Proserpine"
From "Garden of Proserpine"
From "Proserpine" (Dixon)

SATURN

Saturnalia (December)

VENUS

From *The Vigil of Venus*
From "Venus de Milo"
From *De Rerum Natura*
To Venus (Beaumont and Fletcher)
Hymn to Venus

VESTA

From *The Vestal*
From *The Fasti*

VULCAN

From "On Vulcan"

CELTIC GODS AND GODDESSES

ANGUS/AENGUS

Angus the Lover

BLODEUWEDD

The Wife of Llew
From "The Song of Blodeuwedd on May Morning"

BRIGIT

Brigit of the Judgements

Smooring the Fire

Imbolc Chant

From *Where the Forest Murmurs*

CERNUNNOS

An Invocation to Pan

DANU/DANA

Dana

From "The Love-Song of Drostan"

GREEN MAN

Green Man

GWYDION

From "The Spoils of Annwn"

LUGH/LLEW LLAW GYFFES

The Birth and Naming of Llew

From "The Coming of Lugh"

From "The Second Battle of Moytura" (August)

Fate

Lughnasadh Dance

From "The Shadow House of Lugh"

MANANNÁN MAC LIR

From *The Voyage of Bran*

MORRÍGAN

The Washer of the Ford

TARANIS/TIRANES

From *Bonduca*

NORSE/GERMANIC GODS AND GODDESSES

BALDUR

Choruses from "The Sun-God's Return"
From "Balder Dead"

FREY

From "To the Gods" (Lúnasa)

FREYA

Prayer to Freya
Hymns to Freyja (May)
From "To the Vanadís" (May)
From "To the Gods" (May)

FRIGGA

Prayer to Frigga

HERTHA

From "Hertha"
Hertha (Chesson)
From "The Lady Hertha"

ODIN

From "Odin's Rune Song" from the *Hávamál* (November)
From "Odin's Ravens' Song"
From "Fridthjof's Saga" (Funeral Prayers)

SUNNA

Sun Hail
Hail to Sunna

THOR

From "The Gods of the North" (January)
From "The Challenge of Thor"
From "To the Gods" (January)
Hammersong
From "The Descent of Frea" (January)

MIDDLE EASTERN GODS AND GODDESSES

ASTARTE

Stanzas from "A Hymn to Astarte"
Hymn to Astarte

HATHOR

Sirius
Bridal Song

INANA/INANNA

From a Hymn to Inana
From "Inanna and the King"
From "Hymn to Inana as Ninegala"

ISHTAR

Incantation to Ishtar
From "Ishtar" (April)
From "A Royal Hymn to Ishtar"

ISIS

Invocation of Isis
From "Tannhauser"
From *Commentaries on Plato's "Timaeus"*
Isis (Mace)
"I am the star," from *Moon Magic*
Hymn to Isis from Her Temple at Philae III
From "Forces of Things" (August)

Hymn to Isis II (August)
From "The Golden Ass"
Prayer to Isis (Walshe)
Fellowship of Isis Prayer
The Cyme Inscription
"Prayer to Isis" from *The Golden Ass*
Tears of Isis
Lament for Osiris from *Cleopatra*
Lament of Isis
"Isis Speaks" from *The Golden Ass* (August)
At the Feet of Isis
From "Hymn to Isis from Her Temple at Philae VI"
From *The Golden Ass* II (November)
From "Isis"
From "Hymn to Isis III" (November)

MITHRA (*SEE* MITHRAS, UNDER ROME)

APPENDIX 2
PRAYERS FOR NATURE

While there are many works in this book which refer to the creations and workings of nature, this is a brief list of poems that refer to certain natural places or natural phenomena in a significant way.

MOUNTAINS AND CAVES
To Hygeia
Prologue of the Unborn
From "Nymphs"
Homeric Hymn to Pan
Epidaurian Hymn
Chorus from *Philoctetes*
To Hermes (Alcaeus of Mytilene)
Second Delphic Hymn to Apollo
Apollo (Aristonoos from Corinth)
From *Mnemosyne*
"O Artemis Queen of the Groves" from *Phaedra*

SPRINGS, STREAMS, RIVERS, AND RAIN

Hermes of the Ways
From the First Delphic Hymn to Apollo
Orphic Hymn to Oceanus
Hymn to Isis from Her Temple at Philae III
From "The Bath of Pallas"
From "The Praise of Artemis"
We Worship Pan

STORMS

From "Descent of Frea" (January)
From "Homeric Hymn to Castor and Pollux"
From "Idyll XXII" (Theocritus)
From the Orphic Hymn to the Kouretes
Orphic Hymn to Zeus of the Lightning
From "Mithra" (Hildreth)

STARS AND PLANETS

From "Boatman's Song to the Dioscuri"
Castor and Pollux (Croly)
From "A Hymn to Harmony"
Chorus from *The Frogs*
To Venus (Beaumont and Fletcher)
From "Hymn to Inana as Ninegala"
"I am the star," from *Moon Magic*
Orphic Hymn to Hephaestos
From "The Light of Stars"
Sirius

DAWN

Imbolc Chant
From *Where the Forest Murmurs*
From *"Persephone"* (Masters)
Hymn to the Sun (Delavigne)

To the Sun (Tiedge)
Song from *Demeter, A Mask*
Choruses from "The Sun-God's Return"
"O Fair-Faced Sun" from *Atalanta in Calydon*
Hymn at Sunrise
Hymn to the Sun (Holmès)

FIRE

From *Where the Forest Murmurs*
From *The Vestal*
Orphic Hymn to Hestia
From *The Fasti* (Vesta)

FORESTS, THICKETS, AND TREES

An Invocation to Pan
From "Villanelle of the Living Pan"
A Hymn to Pan
From "Apollo" (February)
The Oak of Ceres
From "Demeter" (Callimachus)
"Odin's Rune Song" from the *Hávamál*
"Hymn to Pan" from *Endymion*
"Invocation to Pan" from *The Great God Pan*
From "Ode to Pan" (Warren)
Apple Tree Wassail
"Chaste Goddess" from *Norma*
From "Sappho" (December)

FIELDS, GLENS, MEADOWS

Chorus from *Peace*
From "Sun and Flesh (Credo in Unam)"
Pan (Ledwidge)
From "The Homeric Hymn to Demeter"
From "Proserpine Gathering Violets"

From "The Homeric Hymn to Demeter"

From "The Road Mender"

From "Spring"

Orphic Hymn to the Horai

From "For the Vanadís" (March)

On Lady Day

John Barleycorn

From "An Eleusinian Chant"

From "Apollo" (Demeter)

Ceres (Thurston)

Demeter (Coatsworth)

Strophe from "The Search After Proserpina"

From the "Hymn to Mithra" (from the *Avestas*)

From "Elysium"

To Artemis (Lang)

Oceans, Seas

From "The Vigil of Venus" (April)

A Hymn in Praise of Neptune

Orphic Hymn to Poseidon

Orphic Hymn to Tethys

From *Isis* (Neptune)

From *The Voyage of Bran*

Orphic Hymn to Nereus

From the Orphic Hymn to Nereids

"Poseidon" from *On Animals*

Hymn to Neptune

From "The Return of Aphrodite"

Homeric Hymn to Dionysus

From "Ariadne"

Earth

From *De Rerum Natura*

Homeric Hymn to Earth, Mother of Us All

Orphic Hymn to Gaia
"O Gentle Creatress" from the *Thebaid*
From "A Litany to Earth"
From "Hertha"
Hertha (Chesson)
Ceres
From "Apollo" (Demeter)
From *Demeter, A Mask*

AIR

From "Valerie's Rhyming Invocations to the Four Quarters"
Orphic Hymn to Hera

APPENDIX 3
PRAYERS FOR MAGICAL PURPOSES

PRAYERS FOR HEALING

Orphic Hymn to Asclepius

Prayer to Hygieia (January)

Orphic Hymn to Hygieia (January)

From "To Hygeia"

Orphic Hymn to Hestia

From "To Apollo" (Horace)

Orphic Hymn to Poseidon

Orphic Hymn to Zeus

PRAYERS FOR A PARTNER

From "Sappho" (Lewis, July)

Hymn to Venus (Holmès)

From "Hymn to Aphrodite" (Sappho)

From *The Third Elegy* (Tibullus)

PRAYERS FOR GROWING

Chorus from *Peace*

"Of Pan We Sing" from *Pan's Anniversary*

Carmen Arvale (Song of the Arvals)

"Father Mars" from *De Agri Cultura*

From "The Story of Eleusis"

Orphic Hymn to the Nymphs

"Ceres' Blessing" from *The Tempest*

From "The Complaint of Ceres"

Orphic Hymn to Adonis

From *The Fasti* (Ceres and Earth)

From "Invocation to Ceres"

From *A May-Day Interlude*

From "Inanna and the King"

"Zeus Fills the Heavens" from *Phaenomena*

Orphic Hymn to Gaia

From "Pomona" (Griffith)

From "Demeter" (Hill)

From "Demeter" (Callimachus)

Apple Tree Wassail

From the *Thebaid* (Mithras)

From "To Faunus"

PRAYERS FOR SALVATION

Fragment of a Hymn to the Dioscuri

From "Idyll XXII"

Lady Hera (Sappho)

Fortune (Nonnus)

From *The Eumenides*

Orphic Hymn to Zeus

PRAYERS FOR PROTECTION

From Elegy 1.10 (Tibullus)

Smooring the Fire

"Father Mars" from *De Agri Cultura*

Greek Fragments

From "Paean to Dionysus"

To Ceres (Pye)

Beltane Blessing

From "Olympian Ode 12"

From "Homeric Hymn to Poseidon"

PRAYERS FOR PROSPERITY

Incantation to Ishtar

From "Invocation to Ceres"

Orphic Hymn to Hestia

Hymn to Hestia

Orphic Hymn to Tyche

Orphic Hymn to Poseidon

Orphic Hymn to Zeus

Orphic Hymn to Rhea

"Lovely Goddess of the Bow" from *Aradia*

BIBLIOGRAPHY

Aeschylus. *Aeschylus: With an English Translation*. London: W. Heinemann, 1922–1926.

———. *The House of Atreus: Being the Agamemnon, Libation-Bearers, and Furies*. London: Macmillan, 1920.

Akenside, Mark. *In the Poems of Mark Akenside*. London, 1772.

Alcaeus, and James Stanislaus Easby-Smith. *The Songs of Alcæus: Memoir and Text, with Literal and Verse Translations and Notes*. Washington, D.C.: W. H. Lowdermilk, 1901.

Aldington, Richard. *The Complete Poems of Richard Aldington*. London: A. Wingate, 1948.

Allen, Grant. *The Return of Aphrodite*. S.l.: s.n., 18–?.

All the Year Round (London) 4, no. 90 (August 20, 1870): 277.

American Poetry, 1922: A Miscellany. New York: Harcourt, Brace, 1922.

Anderson, William, and Clive Hicks. *Green Man: The Archetype of Our Oneness with the Earth*. London: HarperCollins, 1990.

Annis, William S. *Mesomedes 1: Hymn to the Muses*. http://www.aoidoi.org/poets/mesomedes/meso-1.pdf.

Anonymous. "Ariadne." *Sharpe's London Magazine of Entertainment and Instruction for General Reading* (November 1866): 262.

Apuleius. *Metamorphoses*. Turnhout: Brepols Publishers, 2010.

———. *The Metamorphoses: Or Golden Ass of Apuleius of Madaura*. Trans. Harold Edgeworth Butler. Oxford: Clarendon Press, 1910.

Aristophanes. *The Frogs of Aristophanes: Acted at Athens in the Year B.C. 405*. Trans. Benjamin Bickley Rogers. London: Bell, 1902.

———. *Aristophanes: Eleven Comedies*. London: Athenian Society, 1912.

Arnold, Matthew. *Poetical Works of Matthew Arnold*. London: Macmillan, 1890.

Asquith, Herbert. *The Volunteer: And Other Poems*. London: Sidgwick & Jackson, 1915.

Ausonius, Decimus Magnus. *Ausonius: With an English Translation*. Ed. and trans. Hugh G. (Hugh Gerard) Evelyn-White. With a contribution by Paulinus of Pella. London: W. Heinemann, 1919–1921.

Bacchylides, and R. C. Jebb. *The Poems and Fragments*. Cambridge: University Press, 1905.

Bantock, Granville, and Helen F. Bantock. *The Great God Pan: A Choral Ballet in Two Scenes with a Prologue: Part I [Vocal Score]*. London: Novello & Company, 1913.

———. *Sappho: Nine Fragments for Contralto / Neun Fragmente Für Eine Altstimme*. Leipzig, Germany: Breitkopf & Härtel, 1906.

———. *Songs of Egypt / Egyptische Gesänge: A Cycle of Six Songs*. Leipzig: Breitkopf & Härtel, 1898.

———. *Songs of Persia / Persische Gesänge: A Cycle of Six Songs*. Leipzig: Breitkopf & Härtel, 1898.

Barber, Margaret Fairless, and Mary Emily Dowson. *The Complete Works of Michael Fairless [pseud.]: With a Biographical Note*. New York: E. P. Dutton, 1932.

Beament, W. O. *The Apple Tree Wassail—A Survival of a Tree Cult*. Dorchester: Dorset Natural History & Archaeological Society, 1929.

Beard, M. "The Cult of the 'Great Mother' in Imperial Rome: The Roman and the 'Foreign.'" *Greek and Roman Festivals: Content, Meaning, and Practice*. Oxford: Oxford University Press, 2012.

Beaumont, Francis. *Comedies and Tragedies Written by Francis Beaumont and Iohn Fletcher*. London: Printed for Humphrey Robinson and for Humphrey Moseley, 1647.

Behn, Aphra. *A Pindarick Poem on the Happy Coronation of His Most Sacred Majesty James II and His Illustrious Consort Queen Mary by Mrs. Behn*. University of Michigan. https://quod.lib.umich.edu/e/eebo/A27308.0001.001/1:2?rgn=div1;view=fulltext.

Bellini, Vincenzo, and Felice Romani. *Norma: Tragedia lirica in due atti*. Turin: Teatro Regio, 2001.

Bellows, Henry Adams. *The Poetic Edda*. New York: American-Scandinavian Foundation, 1923.

Berg, R. M. van den. *Proclus' Hymns: Essays, Translations, Commentary*. Leiden, NL: Brill, 2001.

Bernstein, Frances. *Classical Living: A Month to Month Guide to Ancient Rituals for Heart and Home*. New York: HarperCollins, 2000.

Billingsley, Nicholas. *Kosmobrephia*. London, 1658.

Bishop, Gerald. *A May-Day Interlude*. Campden, UK: Essex House Press, 1904.

Boughton, Rutland, and William Sharp. *The Immortal Hour: Music-Drama*. London: Stainer & Bell, 1920.

Boulanger, Lili. *Hymne au soleil*. Paris: Société anonyme des éditions Ricordi, 1918.

Braithwaite, William Stanley, ed. *The Book of Elizabethan Verse*. 1907.

Branch, Anna Hempstead. *Rose of the Wind: And Other Poems*. Boston: Houghton Mifflin, 1910.

Brians, Paul. *Reading About the World*. Vol. 1. New York: Harcourt College, 1999.

Bridges, Robert. *Demeter: A Mask*. Oxford: Clarendon Press, 1905.

Brown, Robert. *A Trilogy of the Life-to-Come: And Other Poems*. London: David Nutt, 1887.

Browning, Elizabeth Barrett, and H. W Preston. *The Complete Poetical Works of Elizabeth Barrett Browning*. Cambridge ed. Boston: Houghton, Mifflin, 1900.

Burns, Robert. *Songs and Poems*. Mount Vernon, NY: Peter Pauper Press, 1945.

Buttet, Marc-Claude de. *Épithalame ou nosses de très illustre et Magnanime Prince Emmanuel Philibert de Savoye et de très vertueuses Princesse Marguerite de France, Duchesse de Berry, sœur unique du Roy*. Œuvre en vers publiée à Paris, de l'imprimerie de Robert Estienne.avec privilège, 1559.

Callimachus. *Hymns and Epigrams. Lycophron. Aratus*. Trans. A. W. and G. R. Mair. Loeb Classical Library vol. 129. London: William Heinemann, 1921.

Campbell, David A. *Greek Lyric*. Cambridge, MA.: Harvard University Press, 1982–1988.

Campbell, Lewis. *Sophocles*. New York: Appleton, 1880.

Carbery, Ethna, and Seumas MacManus. *The Four Winds of Eirinn: Poems*. New ed. Dublin: M. H. Gill, 1918.

Carman, Bliss. *Sappho*. London: Chatto and Windus, 1907.

Carmichael, Alexander. *Carmina Gadelica: Hymns and Incantations with Illustrative Notes on Words, Rites, and Customs, Dying and Obsolete*. Edinburgh, UK: Oliver and Boyd, 1928.

Carpenter, Henry Bernard, and James Jeffrey Roche. *A Poet's Last Songs*. Boston: J. G. Cupples, 1891.

Cato, Marcus Porcius, and Marcus Terentius Varro. *On Agriculture*. Trans. William Davis Hooper and Harrison Boyd Ash. Cambridge, MA: Harvard University Press, 1934.

Centlivre, Susanna. *Ode to Hygeia by Mrs. Centlivre*. London, 1716.

Chadwick, Nora K. *The Celts*. Harmondsworth, UK: Penguin Books, 1970.

Chapman, George. *The Masque of the Twelve Months*. London, 1848.

Chaucer, Geoffrey. *A One-Text Print of Chaucer's Minor Poems: Being the Best Text of Each Poem in the Parallel-Text Edition, Etc., for Handy Use by Editors and Readers*. Ed. Frederick James Furnivall. London: Pub. for the Chaucer Society by N. Trubner, 1868.

Chénier, André. *Poesies choisies de André Chénier*. Ed. Jules Derocquigny. Oxford: Clarendon Press, 1907.

Chesson, Nora Hopper, and W. H. (Wilfrid Hugh) Chesson. *Selected Poems*. London: A. Rivers, 1906.

Cicero, Marcus Tullius, and Charles Duke Yonge. *The Orations of Marcus Tullius Cicero*. London: G. Bohn, 1851.

Clay, Henry E. *Poems by Henry E. Clay*. London: Elkin Mathews, 1910.

Coatsworth, Elizabeth J. "Demeter." *Poetry* 23, no. 5 (1924): 258–259.

Congreve, William. *A Hymn to Harmony: Written In Honour of St. Cecilia's Day, M DCC I. By Mr. Congreve. Set to Musick by Mr. John Eccles, Master of Her Majesties Musick*. London: printed for Jacob Tonson within Grays-Inn Gate next Grays-Inn Lane, 1703.

Cory, Isaac Preston, and Edward Richmond Hodges. *Cory's Ancient Fragments of the Phoenician, Carthaginian, Babylonian, Egyptian and Other Authors*. A new and enl. ed. London: Reeves & Turner, 1876.

Croly, George. *Castor and Pollux*. London, 1830.

Crowley, Aleister. *The Holy Books of Thelema*. Boston: Samuel Weiser, 1983.

———. *The Works of Aleister Crowley*. Des Plaines, IL: Yogi Publication Society, 1974.

cummings, e e. *Tulips and Chimneys*. New York: Thomas Seltzer, 1923.

———, et al. *Eight Harvard Poets*. New York: Laurence J. Gomme, 1917.

Daharja Veitch, Leanne. *The Wheel of the Year: A Pagan Song Cycle*. 2004.

Darmesteter, James. *The Zend-avesta*. 2nd ed. Oxford: Clarendon Press, 1895.

De Tabley, John Byrne Leicester Warren, baron. *The Collected Poems of Lord De Tabley*. London: Chapman & Hall, 1903.

De Vere, Aubrey. *The Poetical Works of Aubrey De Vere*. New ed. London: Kegan Paul, Trench, 1884.

Dittenberger, Wilhelm. *Sylloge Inscriptionum Graecarum*. Leipzig: S. Hirzel, 1898.

Dixon, Richard Watson, Shirley M. C. Johnson, and Todd K. Bender. *The Collected Poems of Canon Richard Watson Dixon, 1833–1900*. New York: P. Lang, 1989.

Dodge, Arlita. "Pallas Athena." *The Bookman; a Review of Books and Life* (New York) 44, no. 4 (December 1916): 381.

Duff, J. Wright, and Arnold M. Duff, trans. *Minor Latin Poets*. Vol. 1. Loeb Classical Library. Cambridge, MA: Harvard University Press, 1934; rev. 1935.

Dunn, Patrick. *The Orphic Hymns: A New Translation for the Occult Practitioner*. Woodbury, MN: Llewellyn Worldwide, 2018.

Edelstein, Emma Jeannette Levy, and Ludwig Edelstein. *Asclepius: A Collection and Interpretation of the Testimonies*. Baltimore: Johns Hopkins University Press, 1945.

Edmonds, Radcliffe G. *The "Orphic" Gold Tablets and Greek Religion: Further Along the Path*. Cambridge: Cambridge University Press, 2011.

Electronic Corpus Text of Sumerian Literature.

Elizabeth, Vandiver. "Sappho's Hymn to Aphrodite." Diotma. diotima-doctafemina.org /translations/greek/sapphos-hymn-to-aphrodite/.

Emerson, Ralph Waldo. *Emerson's Complete Works*. Ed. James Elliot Cabot. Riverside ed. Boston: Houghton, Mifflin, 1893.

Euripides. *Choruses from Iphigeneia in Aulis and the Hippolytus of Euripides*. Trans. H. D. London: Egoist, 1919.

———. *Hippolytus*. Trans. Gilbert Murray. London: G. Allen & Unwin, 1902.

———. *The Plays of Euripides*. Trans. into English prose from the text of Paley by Edward P. Coleridge, 2 vols. London: George Bell and Sons, 1891.

———. *The Tragedies of Euripides*. Trans. T. A. Buckley. Bacchae. London: Henry G. Bohn, 1850.

Evans, Herbert Arthur. *English Masques*. Freeport, NY: Books for Libraries Press, 1971.

Farjeon, Eleanor. *Pan-Worship: And Other Poems*. London: E. Mathews, 1908.

Faulkner, Andrew, and Owen Hodkinson. *Hymnic Narrative and the Narratology of Greek Hymns*. Leiden: Brill, 2015.

Finch, Annie. *Calendars*. Dorset, VT: Tupelo Press, 2003.

Fitz-Hugh, Thomas. *Carmen Arvale, Seu Martis Verber: Or, The Tonic Laws of Latin Speech and Rhythm; Supplement to the Prolegomena to the History of Italico-Romanic Rhythm*. Charlottesville: Anderson Brothers, University of Virginia, 1908.

Fletcher, John. *Bonduca*. London: Malone Society, 1951.

Fortune, Dion. *Moon Magic*. Boston: Weiser Books, 2003.

Foster, John L., and Susan T. Hollis. *Hymns, Prayers, and Songs: An Anthology of Ancient Egyptian Lyric Poetry*. Atlanta, GA: Scholars Press, 1995.

Fraunce, Abraham. *In the Third Part of the Countesse of Pembrokes Yuychurch. Entituled, Amintas Dale. Wherein Are the Most Conceited Tales of the Pagan Gods in English Hexameters Together with Their Auncient Descriptions and Philosophicall Explications*. London, 1592.

Furley, William D., and Jan Maarten Bremer. *Greek Hymns: Selected Cult Songs from the Archaic to the Hellenistic Period*. Studien und Texte zu Antike und Christentum, 9, 10. Tübingen, Germany: Mohr Siebeck, 2001.

Gagliano, Marco da, Ottavio Rinuccini, and James Erber. *La Dafne*. London: Cathedral Music, 1978.

Geo Bancroft Griffith. *Dollar Monthly Magazine* (Boston) 22, no. 2 (August 1865): 150.

Gosse, Edmund. *New Poems*. London: C. Kegan Paul, 1879.

Grant, Frederick C. *Hellenistic Religions: The Age of Syncretism*. New York: Liberal Arts Press, 1953.

Griffith, R. T. H. (Ralph Thomas Hotchkin). *The Hymns of the Rigveda*. Benares, India: E. J. Lazarus.

Gudrun of Mimirsbrunnr. "For the Vanadis." http://www.northernpaganism.org /shrines/freya/praising-freya/for-the-vanadis.html.

HD (Hilda Doolittle). *Hymen*. New York: H. Holt and Company, 1921.

Heliodorus of Emesa. *The Aethiopica*. Athens: Privately printed for the Athenian Society, 1897.

Hermes. *Thrice-Greatest Hermes: Studies In Hellenistic Theosophy and Gnosis*. Trans. G. R. S. Mead. London: Theosophical Publishing Society, 1906.

Herrick, Robert. *The Complete Poems*. Vol. 2. London: Chatto and Windus, 1876.

Hesiod, and Homer. *The Hesiod, the Homeric Hymns and Homerica*. Trans. Hugh G. Evelyn-White. New and rev. ed. Cambridge, MA: Harvard University Press, 1936.

Hewlett, Maurice Henry. *Songs and Meditations*. Westminster: Archibald Constable, 1896.

Hill, Eleanor Deane. *Demeter*. Oxford: B. H. Blackwell, 1918.

Hölderlin, Friedrich. *Der Tod des Empedokles. Neue Ausgabe im 150 Jahr seit der Geburt Hölderlins*. Ed. Wilhelm von Scholz. Leipzig: Insel-Verlag, 1920.

Holmès, Augusta Mary Anne. *Hymne à Vénus: Pour ténor ou soprano*. Paris: Henri Tellier, 1894.

Hope, A. D. *Collected Poems, 1930–1965*. New York: Viking Press, 1966.

Hopper, Nora. *Dirge for Aoine and Other Poems*. London, 1906.

Horace. *Horace: Satires*. Paris: Librairie Hachette, 1873.

Horton, George Moses. *Poems by a Slave*. Philadelphia: s.n., 1837.

Housman, A. E. *Last Poems*. London: Richards Press, 1930.

Hovey, Richard. *To the End of the Trail*. New York, 1908.

https://archive.org/stream/in.ernet.dli.2015.88800/2015.88800.The-Le-Gallienne-Book-Of-American-Verse_djvu.txt.

https://artflsrv03-uchicago-edu.proxy.library.upenn.edu/philologic4/frantext0917/navigate/2061/102/?byte=369611.

https://artflsrv03-uchicago-edu.proxy.library.upenn.edu/philologic4/frantext0917/navigate/255/30/?byte=145624.

https://diotima-doctafemina.org/translations/coptic/the-thunder-perfect-mind/.

https://el.wikisource.org/wiki/%CE%95%CE%BB%CE%B5%CE%B3%CE%B5%CE%AF%CE%B1%CE%B9_%CE%98%CE%B5%CF%8C%CE%B3%CE%BD%CE%B9%CE%B4%CE%BF%CF%82.

http://www.fellowshipofisis.com/prayers.html.

https://www.lieder.net/lieder/get_text.html?TextId=6894.

https://www.lieder.net/lieder/get_text.html?TextId=352367.

https://www.lieder.net/lieder/get_text.html?TextId=44505&Transliterate=LIEDERNET.

http://www.odins-gift.com/pclass/tothegods.htm.

http://www.odins-gift.com/poth/H/hailtosunna.htm.

http://www.odins-gift.com/poth/H/hammersong.htm.

http://www.odins-gift.com/poth/H/hymntofreya1.htm.

http://www.odins-gift.com/poth/P/prayertofreya.htm.

http://www.odins-gift.com/poth/P/prayertofrigga.htm.

http://www.odins-gift.com/poth/S/sunhail.htm.

http://www.perseus.tufts.edu/hopper/text?doc=Ael.+NA+1.

http://www.perseus.tufts.edu/hopper/text?doc=Perseus%3Atext%3A1999.01.0064%3Ab
ook%3DEp%3Apoem%3D11.

http://www.perseus.tufts.edu/hopper/text?doc=Perseus%3Atext%3A1999.01.0161%3Ab
ook%3DI.%3Apoem%3D5.

http://www.perseus.tufts.edu/hopper/text?doc=Perseus%3Atext%3A1999.01.0161%3Ab
ook%3DO.%3Apoem%3D12.

http://www.perseus.tufts.edu/hopper/text?doc=Perseus%3Atext%3A1999.01.0175%3At
ext%3DAlc.+2%3Asection%3D138b.

http://www.perseus.tufts.edu/hopper/text?doc=Perseus%3Atext%3A2008.01.0472%3Ab
ook%3D1%3Achapter%3D1.

http://www.perseus.tufts.edu/hopper/text?doc=Perseus%3Atext%3A2008.01.0485.

http://www.perseus.tufts.edu/hopper/text?doc=Perseus:text:2008.01.0485.

https://search-proquest-com.proxy.library.upenn.edu/docview/135747151?pq-
origsite=summon&http://hdl.library.upenn.edu/1017/8291.

https://www.thelatinlibrary.com/catullus.shtml.

https://www.thelatinlibrary.com/statius/theb1.shtml.

Hudson-Williams, T. (Thomas). *Early Greek Elegy: The Elegiac Fragments of Callinus, Archilochus, Mimnermus, Tyrtaeus, Solon, Xenophanes, and Others.* New York: Garland, 1987.

*The Independent. ... Devoted to the Consideration of Politics, Social and Economic Tendencies,
History, Literature, and the Arts* (New York) 77, no. 3403 (February 23, 1914): 265.

Irwin, Thomas. "To Faunus." *Dublin University Magazine* 58, no. 344 (August 1861): 170.

Jonson, Ben. *Ben Jonson: Selected Masques.* New Haven, CT: Yale University Press, 1970.

"'Joy, Health, Love, and Peace.' Roud No. 19109." Vaughan Williams Memorial Library.
www.vwml.org/vwml-help-2/.

Julian. *The Works of the Emperor Julian.* Cambridge, MA.: Harvard University Press, 1913.

Keats, John, and John Barnard. *John Keats, the Complete Poems*. 3rd ed. Harmondsworth, Middlesex, England: Penguin Books, 1988.

Klautzsch, Oberlehrer. *Schiller's Gedichte: Klage der Ceres und das Eleusische Fest, Verglichen Mit den Mythen des Alterthums*. Brandenburg, Germany: 1857.

Kramer, Samuel Noah. *Inanna and the King: Ancient Near Eastern Texts Relating to the Old Testament with Supplement*. Ed. James B. Pritchard. Princeton, NJ: Princeton University Press, 1969.

The Ladies Garland (Harpers Ferry) 4, no. 12. (September 1, 1827): 48.

Lampman, Archibald. "Sirius: Californian Illustrated." *Current Literature* 14, no. 10 (1893): 206.

Landels, John G. *Music in Ancient Greece and Rome*. London: Routledge, 1999.

Lang, Andrew. *The Poetical Works of Andrew Lang*. London, 1923.

———. *Rhymes à la Mode*. London: Kegan Paul, Trench, Trübner, 1890.

Leconte de Lisle. *Poésies complètes de Leconte de Lisle: Poèmes antiques—poèmes et poésies (ouvrages couronnés par L'académie Française)—poésies nouvelles*. Paris, 1858.

Ledwidge, Francis. *The Complete Poems of Francis Ledwidge*. New York: Brentano's, 1919.

Lee-Hamilton, Eugene. *Apollo and Marsyas: And Other Poems*. London: E. Stock, 1884.

Leland, Charles Godfrey. *Aradia: Or the Gospel of the Witches*. Oxon, UK: Mandrake Press, 2000.

Lenzi, Alan. *Reading Akkadian Prayers and Hymns: An Introduction*. Atlanta: Society of Biblical Literature, 2011.

Lewis, Estelle Anna Blanche Robinson. *Sappho: A Tragedy*. London: Trübner, 1875.

Llewellyn-Williams, Hilary. *Hummadruz*. Bridgend, UK: Seren, 2001.

Long, Asphodel P. *In a Chariot Drawn by Lions: The Search for the Female in Deity*. Freedom, CA: Crossing Press, 1993.

Longfellow, Henry Wadsworth. *In the Harbor: Ultima Thule*. Boston: Houghton, Mifflin, 1882.

———. *The Poems of Henry Wadsworth Longfellow*. New York: Heritage Press, 1943.

Louÿs, Pierre, and André Dignimont. *Les Chansons de Bilitis*. Lausanne: Aux Editions du Livre (H. Kaeser, 1947).

Lubbock, John. *The Pleasures of Life*. Chicago: Henneberry, 1887.

Lucan. *The Civil War (Pharsalia)*. Trans. J. D. Duff. Cambridge, MA: Harvard University Press, 2014.

Lucretius Carus, Titus. *Lucretius on the Nature of Things*. London: G. Bell and Sons, 1901.

Lully, Jean-Baptiste, and Phillipe Quinault. *Isis: Tragedie lyrique en 5 actes et un prologue*. Paris: T. Michaelis.

Mace, Frances L. (Frances Laughton). *Legends, Lyrics and Sonnets*. Boston: Cupples, Upham, 1883.

Macleod, Fiona. *The Hour of Beauty: Songs and Poems*. Portland, ME: Thomas B. Mosher, 1907.

Manning, Frederic. "Persephone." *English Review* (December 1909): 6.

Marcus, N. Tod. "Greek Inscriptions, VI. A Hymn to Pan." *Greece and Rome* 3, no.7 (October 1933): 49–52.

Martial. *Martial: Epigrams*. Trans. Walter C. A. Ker. *Martial: Epigrams*. Vol. 2. London: Heinemann, 1919–1920.

Mascagni, Pietro. *Iris: Opera complete per canto e pianoforte*. Milan: Ricordi, 1954.

Masters, Edgar Lee. *Invisible Landscapes*. New York: Macmillan, 1935.

McConnell, J. B. "The Advent of Hermes." *Lakeside Monthly*, August 1, 1871: 154.

Mercadante, Saverio, and Salvatore Cammarano. *La Vestale: Opéra Complet*. Paroles Italiennes. Édition De Luxe. Paris: Mme. Ve. Launer, 184–?

Meredith, G. "The Appeasement of Demeter." *Macmillan's Magazine*, 56, no. 335 (1887): 374–377.

Merivale, Herman Charles. *Florien*. London: Remington, 1884.

Meyer, Kuno, Scél Túan maic Cairill, and Dindsenchas. *The Voyage of Bran, Son of Febal, to the Land of the Living: An Old Irish Saga*. London: D. Nutt, 1895.

Monteverdi, Claudio, Alessandro Striggio, Giovanni Salviucci, Ottorino Respighi, and Claudio Guastalla. *L'orfeo: Favola Pastorale*. Milan: A. & G. Carisch, 1935.

Moréas, Jean. *Poèmes et Sylves: 1886–1896*. 1996. https://artfl-project.uchicago.edu/content/artfl-frantext.

Mozart, Wolfgang Amadeus. *Apollo et Hyacinthus*. Leipzig: Breitkopf and Härtel, 1907.

Murray, Gilbert. *The Frogs of Aristophanes*. London: G. Allen & Sons, 1908.

———. "The Hymn of the Kouretes." *Annual of the British School at Athens* 15 (1908): 357–365.

Newton, Isaac. "Keynes MS. 28." The Chymistry of Isaac Newton. Ed. William R. Newman. June 2010.

Nicholson, D. H. S. and A. H. E. Lee, eds. *The Oxford Book of English Mystical Verse*. Oxford: Clarendon Press, 1917.

"Ode to Mithra, Sung by the Persian Army After Engagement." *New Annual Register, Or, General Repository of History, Politics, and Literature* (January 1793): 181–83.

Oehlenschläger, Adam Gottlob. *The Gods of the North: An Epic Poem*. London: W. Pickering [etc.], 1845.

———. "To the Gods." Odin's Gift. Trans. Rune Bjørnsen. http://www.odins-gift.com/pclass/tothegods.htm.

Œuvre en vers publiée à Paris, de l'imprimerie de Robert Estienne. avec privilège, 1559.

Orff, Carl. *Carmina Burana: Cantiones profanae: Cantoribus et choris cantandae comitantibus instrumentis atque imaginibus magicis: For 3 Solo Voices, Chorus and Orchestra/Für 3 Solostimmen, Chor und Orchester*. London: E. Eulenburg, 1981.

Ovid. *Ovid's Fasti*. Ed. Thomas Keightley. 2nd ed. London: Whittaker, 1848.

Oxenford, John. "The Lady Hertha." *Household Words* 8, no. 201 (January 28, 1854): 516–17.

Parke, H. W. *Festivals of the Athenians*. Ithaca, N.Y.: Cornell University Press, 1977.

Parnell, Thomas, Richard Hole, and Henry James Pye. *The Batrachomuomachia, Or, The Battle of the Frogs and Mice, with the Hymns and Epigrams of Homer*. London: Wittingham and Rowland, 1810.

Paton, W. R. (William Roger). *The Greek Anthology in 5 Volumes with an English Translation*. London: W. Heinemann, 1916–1918.

Pendderwen, Gwydion. *Wheel of the Year*. San Francisco: Nemeton, 1979.

Piatt, John James. *To The Lares*. New York, 1872.

Plato. *Plato: With an English Translation by Harold North Fowler and an Introduction by W. R. M. Lamb*. London: W. Heinemann, 1917.

The Plays of Euripides. Trans. into English prose from the text of Paley by Edward P. Coleridge. 2 vols. London: George Bell and Sons, 1891.

Poetry: A Magazine of Verse 13, no. 2 (November 1918).

Powell. Coll. *Alex*. S.l., s.n. Print.

Puccini, Giacomo, Carlo Abeniacar, and Pietro Spada. *Inno a Diana: Per canto e pianoforte*. Rome: Boccaccini & Spada, 1987.

Putnam, Bertha Haven, and Madeline Vaughn Abbott. "Pallas Athena." Unpublished sheet music, 1993.

Quiller-Couch, Arthur, ed. *The Oxford Book of English Verse: 1250–1900*. Oxford: Clarendon Press, 1919.

Raleigh, Walter, and Agnes Mary Christabel Latham. *The Poems of Sir Walter Raleigh*. Cambridge, MA: Harvard University Press, 1951.

Redman, Harry Newton. *Isis*. [S.l.]: The composer, 1920.

Renberg, Gil H. "Public and Private Places of Worship in the Cult of Asclepius at Rome." *Memoirs of the American Academy in Rome* 51–52 (2006): 87–172.

Ricciardelli, Gabriella. *Inni Orfici*. [Rome]: Fondazione Lorenzo Valla, 2000.

Rimbaud, Arthur. *Reliquaire: Poésies*. [S.l.]: Ligaran, 2015.

———. *Œuvres de Arthur Rimbaud: Vers et proses*. Ed. Paterne Berrichon. Paris: Mercure de France, 1918.

Roberts, Walter Adolphe. *Pierrot Wounded: And Other Poems*. New York: Britton, 1919.

[Russell, George William]. *Collected Poems*. London: Macmillan, 1919.

Sacchini, Antonio, and Nicolas François Guillard. *Oedipe à Colone: [Opera Seria in Three Acts]*. S.l.: MRF Records, 1979.

Sackville, Margaret. *A Hymn to Dionysus and Other Poems*. London: E. Mathews, 1905.

Saggs, H. W. F. *The Greatness That Was Babylon: A Sketch of the Ancient Civilization of the Tigris-Euphrates Valley*. New York: New American Library, 1968.

Sappho. *The Poems of Sappho*. London: Williams and Norgate, 1924.

———. *Ta Poiēmata*. Ed. Sōtērēs Kakisēs. Second ed. Athens: Kedros, 1979.

———. *Sappho: Memoir, Text, Selected Renderings and a Literal Translation*. Trans. Henry Thornton Wharton with paraphrases in verse by Anne Bunner. New York: Brentano's, 1920.

Sayers, F. *Poems, Containing Dramatic Sketches of Northern Mythology, &c*. 4th ed. Norwich: Printed by Stevenson and Matchett for Messrs. Cadell and Davies, London, 1807.

Schiller, Friedrich. *Complete Works of Friedrich Schiller: In Eight Volumes*. New York: P. F. Collier, 1902.

Schreiber, Charlotte Elizabeth (Bartie) Guest, and Alfred Trübner Nutt. *The Mabinogion: Medieval Welsh Romances*. Long Acre, UK: David Nutt, 1902.

Schubert, Franz. *An Die Sonne, [D. 439]: Für 4 Singstimmen Mit Begleitung Des Pianoforte*. Wiesbaden: Breitkopf and Härtel, 1897.

———. *Elysium: Gedicht Von Fr. V. Schiller*. [S.l.]: Breitkopf and Härtel, 1897.

———. *Lied Eines Schiffers an Die Dioskuren. Von Joh. Mayrhofer, D360/Op. 65 No.1, A Flat Major*. Wiesbaden: Breitkopf and Härtel, 1895.

Scollard, Clinton. "Pomona." *Current Literature* (New York) 8, no. 2 (October 1891): 257.

Scullard, H. H. *Festivals and Ceremonies of the Roman Republic*. Ithaca, NY: Cornell University Press, 1981.

Seneca, Lucius Annaeus. *Seneca's Tragedies*. Trans. Frank Justus Miller. London: W. Heinemann, 1917.

Shakespeare, William. *As You Like It*. Ed. Alan Brissenden. Oxford, UK: Clarendon, 1994.

———. *Shakespeare's Tempest*. Ed. Albrecht Wagner. Berlin: E. Felber, 1900.

Sharp, William. *From the Hills of Dream*. Edinburgh, UK: P. Geddes & Colleagues, 1896.

———. *Where the Forest Murmurs: Nature Essays*. London: Pub. at the offices of *Country Life*, by G. Newnes, 1906.

Sharpe's London Magazine of Entertainment and Instruction for General Reading (November 1866): 262.

Shelley, Mary Wollstonecraft. André Henri Koszul. *Proserpine and Midas: Two Unpublished Mythological Dramas*. Ed. André Henri Koszul. London: Humphrey Milford, 1922.

Shelley, P. Bysshe. N. Fraistat, D. H. Reiman. *The Complete Poetry of Percy Bysshe Shelley*. Ed. N. Fraistat and D. H. Reiman. Baltimore: Johns Hopkins University Press, 2000.

Shelley, Percy Bysshe. *The Poetical Works of Percy Bysshe Shelley: Ed. by Mrs. Shelley, with a Memoir*. New York: Hurd and Houghton, 1878.

Sinclair, May. "Fragment of a Hymn to Apollo." *Literature* 6 (London) February 10, 1900: 122.

Smart, Christopher. *The Poetical Works of Christopher Smart* vol. 5, *The Works of Horace, Translated into Verse*. Oxford: Oxford University Press, 2014.

Sophocles. *The Ajax of Sophocles*. London: G. Allen & Unwin, 1919.

———. *Sophocles: The Plays and Fragments with Critical Notes, Commentary, and Translation in English Prose*. Trans. R. C. Jebb. Cambridge: The University Press, 1883.

Spenser, Edmund. *Epithalamion*. Ed. Cortlandt van Winkle. New York: F. S. Crofts, 1926.

Speyer, Leonora von Stosch. *A Canopic Jar*. New York: E. P. Dutton, 1921.

Spross, Charles Gilbert, and Alfred H. Hyatt. *Ishtar, an Assyrian Love Song*. Cincinnati, OH: John Church, 1911.

Stacpoole, H. De Vere. *Sappho: A New Rendering*. London: Hutchinson, 190–?.

Starhawk. *The Spiral Dance: A Rebirth of the Ancient Religion of the Great Goddess*. San Francisco: Harper & Row, 1979.

Statius, Papinus. *The Thebaid of Statius, Translated into English Verse, with Notes and Observations; and a Dissertation upon the Whole by Way of Preface*. Oxford: Clarendon Press, 1787.

Stedman, Edmund Clarence. *Apollo*. Boston: Houghton Mifflin, 1908.

Stephen, Leslie, and Sidney Lee. *Dictionary of National Biography, 1885–1900*. London: Smith, Elder, 1891.

Stobaeus, Joannes, Alfredo Adolfo Camús, and Karl Tauchnitz. *Ioannis Stobaei Florilegium: Ad Optimorum Librorum Fidem Editum*. Ed. stereotypa. Leipzig: Sumptibus et typis Caroli Tauchnitii, 1838.

Stoddard, Richard Henry. *The Poems of Richard Henry Stoddard*. Complete ed. New York: Charles Scribner's Sons, 1880.

Stokes, Whitley. *The Second Battle of Moytura*. *Revue Celtique* 12 (1891): 52.

Strauss, Richard, and Emanuel Bodman. *Vier Gesänge Für eine Singstimme Mit Begleitung des Orchesters*, Op. 33. Berlin: Ed. Bote & G. Bock, 1897.

Svarlien, Diane Arnson. *The Odes of Pindar in Perseus Project 1.0*. New Haven, CT: Yale University Press, 1991.

Swinburne, Algernon Charles. *The Complete Works of Algernon Charles Swinburne*. London: W. Heinemann, 1925.

———. *Swinburne's Atalanta in Calydon and Erechtheus*. Ann Arbor, MI: G. Wahr, 1922.

T. N. "To Hygeia." *Gentleman's Magazine: And Historical Chronicle* 3 (1822): 258.

Tailhade, Laurent. *Le Jardin Des Rêves, Poésies*. Paris: A. Lemerre, 1880.

Taylor, Thomas. *The Mystical Hymns of Orpheus: Translated from the Greek, and Demonstrated to Be the Invocations Which Were Used in the Eleusinian Mysteries*. 2nd ed., with considerable emendation, alterations, and additions. Chiswick: C. Whittingham, 1824.

Tegnér, Esaias. *Fridthjof's Saga: A Norse Romance*. Chicago: S. C. Griggs, 1877.

Theocritus, Bion, and Moschus. *Greek Bucolic Poets: Theocritus, Bion, Moschus*. Trans. J. M. Edmonds. Cambridge, MA: Harvard University Press, 2014.

———. *Theocritus, Bion and Moschus*. Rendered into English Prose by Andrew Lang. London: Macmillan, 1892.

Thomas, Edith M. "Evoe!" *Current Opinion* (New York) 55, no. 6 (December 1913): 438.

Thompson, Eloise Bibb. *Poems*. New York: Monthly Review, 1895.

Thompson, Francis. *Complete Poems of Francis Thompson*. New York: Modern Library, 1911.

Thompson, William. *An Hymn to May: By William Thompson, M. A. of Queen's College Oxon*. London: printed and sold by R. Dodsley in Pall-Mall, T. Waller in Fleetstreet, and M. Cooper at the Globe in Pater-Noster-Row, 1746.

Thorpe, Benjamin. *The Edda of Sæmund the Learned from the Old Norse or Icelandic with a Mythological Index*. London: Trübner, 1865.

Thurston, Charlotte W. "Ceres." *Youth's Companion* (Boston) 81, no. 48 (November 28, 1907): 606.

Tibullus. *Carmina*. Ed. Ernst Karl Christian Bach. Leipzig: Libraria Hahnia, 1819.

———. *The Elegies of Tibullus: Being the Consolations of a Roman Lover, Done in English Verse*. Trans. Theodore Chickering Williams. Boston: R. G. Badger, 1905.

Tramana, Juanita. "Athena." *Art and Archaeology* 4 (1916): 5.

———. "Hermes." *Art and Archaeology* 3 (1916): 249.

Trevelyan, R. C. *The Bride of Dionysus: A Music-Drama, and Other Poems*. London: Longmans, Green, 1912.

Turgenev, Ivan Sergeevich. *Poems in Prose*. Boston: Cupples, Upham, 1883.

Underwood, E. W. "To the Demeter of Cnidos" (poem). *Art and Archaeology* 9 (1920): 222.

Vanderlip, Vera Frederika. *The Four Greek Hymns of Isidorus and the Cult of Isis*. Toronto: A. M. Hakkert, 1972.

Wade, Thomas. *The Nuptials of Juno: A Descriptive Poem*. London, 1825.

Walshe, Christina. *Songs of Womanhood*. London: J. H. Larway, 1912.

Watkins, Vernon Phillips. *Ballad of the Mari Lwyd: And Other Poems*. [2nd ed.] London: Faber and Faber, 1947.

Watson, William. *The Collected Poems*. New York: John Lane, 1889.

Wilcox, Ella Wheeler. *Poetical Works of Ella Wheeler Wilcox: With Index of Titles and Index of First Lines*. Toronto: Musson, 1917.

Wilde, Oscar. *The Poems of Oscar Wilde*. Ed. Robert Baldwin Ross. Authorized ed. Boston: J. W. Luce, 1909.

Yale Review 94, no. 2 (April 2006): 124–130.

Young, Ella, and Maud Gonne. *Celtic Wonder-tales*. Dublin: Maunsel, 1910.

Žabkar, Louis V. *Hymns to Isis in Her Temple at Philae*. Hanover, N.H.: Published for Brandeis University Press by University Press of New England, 1988.

CREDITS

Grateful thanks are due to the following copyright holders for their permission to reprint the following works:

Alcaeus: "Come hither, leaving the island of Pelops" from GREEK LYRIC, VOL. I, edited and translated by David A. Campbell, Loeb Classical Library Volume 142, Cambridge, MA: Harvard University Press, Copyright 1982 by the President and Fellows of Harvard College. Loeb Classical Library is a registered trademark of the President and Fellows of Harvard College.

Alcman: "Fragment 2" from GREEK LYRIC, VOL. II, edited and translated by David A. Campbell, Loeb Classical Library Volume 143, Cambridge, MA: Harvard University Press, Copyright 1988 by the President and Fellows of Harvard College. Loeb Classical Library is a registered trademark of the President and Fellows of Harvard College.

Anderson, William: "Green Man" from *Green Man: The Archetype of Our Oneness with the Earth* by William Anderson and Clive Hicks. Reprinted by permission of Mrs. Jennifer Anderson. All rights reserved.

Anonymous: "For Poseidon," "For Pan," translated by Patrick Dunn, from *The Orphic Hymns: A New Translation for the Occult Practitioner.* Llewellyn Worldwide, Limited, 2018. Reprinted by permission of the publisher. All rights reserved.

Anonymous: Excerpt from "Hymn to Inana as Ninegala," translated by J. A. Black, G. Cunningham, J. Ebeling, E. Flückiger-Hawker, E. Robson, J. Taylor, and G. Zólyomi, from the

Electronic Text Corpus of Sumerian Literature. Reprinted by permission of the Faculty of Oriental Studies, University of Oxford. All rights reserved.

Anonymous: "Hymn at Sunrise," translated by John L. Foster, from *Hymns, Prayers, and Songs: An Anthology of Ancient Egyptian Lyric Poetry*. Atlanta, GA: Scholars Press, 1995. Reprinted by permission of the Society of Biblical Literature. All rights reserved.

Anonymous: Excerpt from "Inanna and the King," translated by Samuel Noah Kramer, from *Ancient Near Eastern Texts Relating to the Old Testament with Supplement*. Pritchard, James B. (Ed.). Princeton, N.J.: Princeton University Press, 1969. Reprinted by permission of the publisher. All rights reserved.

Anonymous: Excerpt from "A Royal Hymn to Ishtar," translated by Alan Lenzi, from *Reading Akkadian Prayers and Hymns: An Introduction*. Atlanta, GA: Society of Biblical Literature, 2011. Reprinted by permission of the Society of Biblical Literature. All rights reserved.

Anonymous: "Orphic Hymn to the Mother of the Gods," "Orphic Hymn to Nature," translated by Asphodel P. Long, from *In a Chariot Drawn by Lions: The Search for the Female In Deity*. Freedom, CA: Crossing Press, 1993. Reprinted by permission of Anthony Long. All rights reserved.

Anonymous: Excerpt from "The Thunder, Perfect Mind," translated by Anne McGuire, from *Diotima: Materials for the Study of Women and Gender in the Ancient World* (v. 2.0). Reprinted by permission of the translator. All rights reserved.

Anonymous: Excerpts from two Orphic gold tablets, translated by Radcliffe G. Edmonds III, from Edmonds, Radcliffe G., *The "Orphic" Gold Tablets and Greek Religion: Further Along the Path*. Cambridge, MA: Cambridge University Press, 2011. Copyright Cambridge University Press, 2011. Reproduced with permission of the licensor through PLSclear.

Anonymous: "Incantation to Ishtar," translated by H. W. F. Saggs, from *The Greatness That Was Babylon: A Sketch of the Ancient Civilization of the Tigris-Euphrates Valley*. New York: New American Library, 1968. Copyright 1962 and 1988. Reproduced with permission of the Licensor through PLSclear.

Anonymous: "Hymn to Isis from Her Temple at Philae III," translated by Louis V. Žabkar, from *Hymns to Isis from Her Temple at Philae*, by Louis V. Žabkar (Brandeis University Press). Copyright 1988 by the Trustees of Brandeis University. Used by permission.

Limēnios son of Thoinos: "Second Delphic Hymn to Apollo" by Limēnios son of Thoinos, translated by Richard Hooker, from *Reading About the World*. Vol. 1, by Paul Brians. Reprinted by permission of Paul Brians. All rights reserved.

Llewellyn-Williams, Hilary: "An Invocation to Pan," "The Song of Blodeuwedd on May Morning" by Hilary Llewellyn-Williams, from *Hummadruz*, Seren Books, 2001. Reprinted by permission of the publisher. All rights reserved.

Masters, Edgar Lee: Excerpts from "Hymn to Nature," "Persephone" from *Invisible Landscapes* by Edgar Lee Masters, 1935. Reprinted by permission of John D. C. Masters. All rights reserved.

Mendes, Laurel: "Prayer to Frigga" by Laurel Mendes. Reprinted by permission of the author. All rights reserved.

Pendderwen, Gwydion: "On Lady Day," "Lughnasadh Dance," from *Wheel of the Year*, 1979. Reprinted by permission of the Church of All Worlds. All rights reserved.

Pindar: Excerpt from "Pythian Ode 8" by Pindar, translated by Diane Arnson Svarlien, 1990. Reprinted by permission of the translator. All rights reserved.

Proclus: "To the Muses" by Proclus, translated by R. M. van den Berg. Berg, R. M. *Proclus' Hymns: Essays, Translations, Commentary*, Brill, 2001. Reprinted by permission of the publisher. All rights reserved.

Reimer-Møller, Lavrans: "Hammersong" by Lavrans Reimer-Møller. Reprinted by permission of Morgan Moler. All rights reserved.

Robertson, Olivia: Excerpt from a prayer to Isis ("Divine Isis, Goddess of Ten Thousand names…."). Reprinted by permission of the Fellowship of Isis. All rights reserved.

Sappho: "Sappho's Hymn to Aphrodite" by Sappho, translated by Elizabeth Vandiver. Published in *Diotíma: Materials for the Study of Women and Gender in the Ancient World* (v. 2.0). Reprinted by permission of the translator. All rights reserved.

Shewchuk, Heidi: "Hail to Sunna" by Heidi Shewchuk. Copyright Heidi Shewchuk. Reprinted by permission of the author. All rights reserved.

Starhawk: Excerpt from "Valerie's Rhyming Invocations to the Four Quarters" from *The Spiral Dance* by Starhawk. Copyright 1979, 1989, 1999 by Miriam Simos. Used by permission of HarperCollins Publishers.

Stormbringer, Hilla: "Sun Hail" by Hilla Stormbringer. Reprinted by permission of the author. All rights reserved.

Userkare-meramun: Excerpt from "Hymn to Isis from Her Temple at Philae VI" from *Hymns to Isis from Her Temple at Philae*, by Louis V. Žabkar (Brandeis University Press). Copyright 1988 by the Trustees of Brandeis University. Used by permission.

Veitch, Leanne Daharja: "Lammas," "Samhain" from *Wheel of the Year*, 2004. Reprinted by permission of the author. All rights reserved.

Watkins, Vernon: Excerpt from "The Ballad of the Mari Lwyd" from *Ballad of the Mari Lwyd and Other Poems.* Reprinted by permission of Gwen Watkins. All rights reserved.

INDEX